W0364687

Grammar in Profile

Grammatisches Übungsbuch für die Sekundarstufe II

3. aktualisierte Auflage

Grammar in Profile

Grammatisches Übungsbuch für die Sekundarstufe II

3. aktualisierte Auflage

Herausgegeben von
Rosemary Hellyer-Jones und Peter Lampater
sowie Paul Aston und Glenys Schindler

Ernst Klett Sprachen GmbH
Stuttgart

3. aktualisierte Ausgabe

Auflage 3 8 7 6 5 4 | 2014 13 12 11

Nachfolger von 978-3-12-506241-1
Alle Drucke dieser Auflage sind unverändert und können im Unterricht nebeneinander verwendet werden.
Die letzte Zahl bezeichnet das Jahr des Druckes. Das Werk und seine Teile sind urheberrechtlich geschützt. Jede Nutzung in anderen als den gesetzlich zugelassenen Fällen bedarf der vorherigen schriftlichen Einwilligung des Verlags. Hinweis zu § 52 a UrhG: Weder das Werk noch seine Teile dürfen ohne eine solche Einwilligung eingescannt und in ein Netzwerk eingestellt werden. Dies gilt auch für Intranets von Schulen und sonstigen Bildungseinrichtungen. Fotomechanische oder andere Wiedergabeverfahren nur mit Genehmigung des Verlags.

© Ernst Klett Sprachen GmbH, Rotebühlstraße 77, 70178 Stuttgart, 1996. Alle Rechte vorbehalten.
Internetadresse: www.klett.de / www.lektueren.com

Herausgegeben von Rosemary Hellyer-Jones M. A. und Peter Lampater, Ehingen (Donau)
sowie Paul Aston, York und Glenys Schindler, Würzburg

Redaktion: Inge Schäfer, Bettina Höfels

Layoutkonzeption: Sandra Vrabec
Gestaltung und Satz: Satz & mehr, Besigheim
Umschlaggestaltung: Sandra Vrabec
Druck und Bindung: Medienhaus Plump GmbH, Rolandsecker Weg 33, 53619 Rheinbreitbach

Printed in Germany

ISBN 978-3-12-506242-9

9 783125 062429

Contents

Vorwort

Konzeption

Grammar in Profile ist ein grammatisches Übungsbuch für die Sekundarstufe II.
Es ist in zwei Schwierigkeitsstufen gegliedert:
Die Abschnitte *Check-up* und *Basic Rules and Exercises* können ab Klasse 10 eingesetzt werden, in leistungsstarken Gruppen auch früher.
Die *Advanced Rules and Exercises* wenden sich vor allem an die letzten zwei Jahrgangsstufen, in leistungsstarken Gruppen können sie auch früher bearbeitet werden.

Das Übungsangebot hat die Förderung der mündlichen und schriftlichen Ausdrucksfähigkeit zum Ziel. Darüber hinaus wird die Kenntnis und der sichere Gebrauch der wichtigsten Strukturen der englischen Sprache gefestigt. Die Darstellung der strukturellen Phänomene und die entsprechenden Übungen zielen nicht auf eine vollständige Abdeckung aller grammatischen Gebiete ab, sondern konzentrieren sich auf besonders fehlerträchtige Bereiche der englischen Grammatik.

Die einzelnen Kapitel sind in sich abgeschlossen und brauchen daher nicht in der vorgegebenen Reihenfolge behandelt zu werden. Je nach den grammatischen Defiziten einer Lerngruppe können einzelne Kapitel oder Teile davon gezielt im Unterricht eingesetzt werden. Neben dem Einsatz im Klassenunterricht eignen sich die *Check-ups* in Verbindung mit den *Basic Rules* in besonderen Maße auch für das Selbststudium.

Aufbau

Die 22 Kapitel gliedern sich jeweils in die drei Teile *Check-up, Basic Rules and Exercises* und *Advanced Rules and Exercises.*

CHECK-UP

Jedes Kapitel wird durch eine Seite mit *Check-up*-Übungen eingeleitet. Hierbei handelt es sich um relativ einfache Übungen mit eindeutigen Lösungen. Sie dienen zur Beurteilung des Kenntnisstandes. Die Lösungen der *Check-up*-Übungen sind am Ende des Buches abgedruckt. Dadurch ist eine umgehende Selbstkontrolle möglich.

BASIC RULES AND EXERCISES

Die *Basic Rules* zu Beginn dieses Teils sind eine Zusammenfassung der wichtigsten Strukturen des Kapitels. Grammatische Regeln werden hier in leicht verständlichem Englisch gegeben, einprägsame Beispielsätze verdeutlichen das jeweilige grammatische Phänomen. Dadurch ermöglichen die *Basic Rules* eine schnelle Wiederbewusstmachung der Grammatikregeln. Gleichzeitig bieten sie Hilfestellung bei der Bearbeitung der auf sie folgenden *Basic Exercises.*
Die *Basic Exercises* werden meistens durch einen authentischen Belegtext eingeleitet, der zur Demonstration des strukturellen Phänomens dient und in Verbindung mit den *Basic Rules* zu einer kognitiven Analyse der Verwendungsweise der jeweiligen Strukturen auffordert. Außerdem werden auch inhaltliche Fragen zum Text gestellt, bei deren Beantwortung die betreffenden Strukturen verwendet und geübt werden.
Es folgt ein breites Angebot unterschiedlicher Übungstypen.
Sowohl die *Basic Exercises* als auch die *Advanced Exercises* enthalten *Mediation*- und Übersetzungsübungen. Diese sollen Unterschiede zwischen dem englischen und dem deutschen Sprachgebrauch bewusst machen.

Vom Prinzip der eindeutigen situativen Einbettung und der völligen Kontextualisierung wird nur in einigen wenigen Fällen abgewichen, um gezielt bestimmte wichtige Besonderheiten darzustellen und zu üben.

ADVANCED RULES AND EXERCISES

Die *Advanced Rules and Exercises* werden durch grammatische Regeln eingeleitet, die über die *Basic Rules* hinausgehen. Ihnen folgt ein Angebot anspruchsvollerer Übungen, die erhöhte sprachliche Anforderungen stellen. Bei den Kapiteln 14, 20 und 22 wurde auf eine Regelerweiterung verzichtet; hier unterscheiden sich die *Advanced Exercises* nur im Schwierigkeitsgrad von den *Basic Exercises*.

Tipps und Zusatzinformationen

Zu zahlreiche Regeln und Übungen finden sich nützliche Tipps (durch eine Glühbirne gekennzeichnet) sowie zusätzliche Regeln (in blauer Umrandung).
Folgendes Icon 👥 verweist auf die Möglichkeit zur Gruppenarbeit. Zusätzliche, weiterführende Übungen sind mit ☆ gekennzeichnet.

Textsorten

Grammar in Profile behandelt Grammatik nicht isoliert als Selbstzweck, sondern macht die enge Verbindung von Text und Struktur, von Stil und Grammatik und die Einheit von Grammatik und Sprache sichtbar. Die Übungstexte sind deshalb weitgehend authentisch und führen somit die reale Verwendung der englischen Sprache vor Augen. Über die rein sprachpraktische Übungsfunktion von *Grammar in Profile* hinaus versucht das Buch, zur Lektüre englischsprachiger Originaltexte anzuregen.

Sachtexte

Die authentischen Übungstexte umfassen landeskundlich informative Auszüge aus Sach- und Geschichtsbüchern sowie Zeitungsartikel zu einer Vielzahl aktueller Themen.

Cartoons

Neben Cartoons, die für bildgesteuerte Übungen verwendet werden, enthält das Buch eine große Anzahl von Cartoons, an die sich keine Übungen anschließen. Diese stellen auflockernde Elemente dar, dienen jedoch gleichzeitig als authentische Belege für die Verwendung bestimmter Strukturen. Alle Cartoons bieten vielfältige Sprachanlässe im Rahmen des zu behandelnden Grammatikpensums.

Literatur

Bei der Auswahl der vielfältigen literarischen Übungstexte wurden neben den strukturellen Gesichtspunkten vor allem auch motivationale Aspekte berücksichtigt.
Die Textauswahl umfasst Auszüge aus Romanen, Kurzgeschichten und Dramen sowie Gedichte. Neben bekannten britischen Autoren kommen auch zahlreiche Vertreter der amerikanischen Literatur zu Wort.

Die Textsortenvielfalt in *Grammar in Profile* soll die mannigfaltigen Verwendungsmöglichkeiten struktureller Elemente verdeutlichen. Die sorgfältig abgestuften Übungen haben zum Ziel, die Schülerinnen und Schüler zum sicheren, stilistisch richtigen Gebrauch der englischen Sprache hinzuführen.

1 Present Tense –

Simple and Progressive Aspects

CHECK-UP

1 The law of attraction?

Fill in the verbs in the present tense – simple or progressive form.

	It is 12.30 on a fine June day, and the sun ____ as Tom ____ out of his office,	shine · come
	____ down Queen's Street and ____ into the park. On a bench near the duck	walk · go
	pond he ____ someone he ____.	see · know
TOM	Hello, Amy! What ____ you ____ here?	do
AMY	Oh, hi, Tom! I ____ here for a while, enjoying the sun.	sit
	I ____ here during the lunch hour, usually with a book!	come/often
TOM	Well, I ____ I ____ you! What ____ you ____?	hope · not interrupt · read
AMY	An absolutely fascinating book! It ____ to Emily. I ____ to the	belong · get/just
	end of the first chapter. It's called 'The Strangest Thing', and it's	
	about the law of attraction. Emily ____ a lot of people ____	say · talk
	about that these days.	
TOM	The law of attraction? What ____ that ____?	mean
AMY	Well, as far as I ____ it, it ____ to mean that you ____ things into	understand · seem · attract
	your life through your thoughts and feelings. Like a magnet!	
	That's why people who ____ bad luck ____ it, but happy	expect · get/usually
	feelings ____ more happiness into your life!	bring
TOM	What? But that ____ absurd. You ____ that, surely?	sound · not believe
AMY	Well, I ____ to wonder! – Hey, look, Emily ____! How weird!	begin · come
	Normally I ____ her here.	see/never
TOM	Strange. Well, as my mother ____: Talk of the devil and the devil ____.	say/always · appear
AMY	Quiet, Tom! Hi, Emily! Come and join us. We ____ the ideas in	discuss/just
	that book you lent me.	

18 **weird** very strange

2 The new postman

Fill in the correct present tense forms.

One day, a new postman ____ to a house and ____ in through the gate.	come · walk
To his horror, a big, angry-looking dog ____ on the front doorstep.	bark
"Don't worry," ____ the lady of the house. "He ____ a noise. He ____ that	say · make/just · do/always
when anyone ____ to the door. And anyway, you ____ the old proverb:	come · know
'A barking dog ____.'"	bite/never
"Yes," ____ the postman. "I ____ the old proverb, and you ____ the old	say · know · know ·
proverb. The only trouble is: ____ the dog ____ the old proverb?"	know

BASIC RULES AND EXERCISES

Simple present	
It **rains** a lot in Ireland. Fresh air and sunshine **do** you good.	▸ to express **facts** and what is generally accepted as **true**
We usually **go** to Spain in the summer. Do you always **stay** at the same place?	▸ to describe **habits** (what *always*, *often*, *sometimes*, *never* happens)
It's the usual story: the girl **goes** on holiday, **meets** the boy of her dreams, and they **fall** in love at first sight …	▸ for a **series of happenings** (e.g. in a story or summary)
Frank **doesn't like** coach tours.	▸ to express **attitudes/feelings**, and **states** that do not change (see list of verbs below)
Present progressive	
I'**m writing** this card on the beach. Right now the sun **is shining**, and it'**s getting** really hot.	▸ to describe activities/happenings that **are going on at the moment**, and **gradual developments**
You'**re doing** a lot of swimming these holidays!	▸ for happenings going on **over a longer period of time** (not necessarily just now), but seen as **temporary**

Common verbs which are normally used only in the simple form, because they describe a **state** rather than an **action**:

know	*like*	*see*	*be*	*have (= own)*
think	*love*	*hear*	*sound*	*contain*
believe	*hate*	*feel*	*look (=aussehen)*	*belong to*
remember	*want*	*notice*	*seem*	*consist of*
forget	*wish*	*realize*	*mean*	*cost*

"You'd better make a decision soon. The continents are starting to drift apart."

1 What's the moral?

1.1 Describe each situation in detail.

Remember:
To describe the activities in pictures or illustrations you use the progressive form.

1.2 Complete the proverbs below with the correct verbs. (Which form do you need, and why?) Then decide which proverb fits which picture.

- **a** It's not work that ____, but worry.
- **b** Many hands ____ light work.
- **c** The early bird ____ the worm.
- **d** Great minds ____ alike *(= in the same way).*
- **e** The more you ____, the more you ____.
- **f** It's love that ____ the world go round.

make • get • think • catch • want • kill • make

1.3 Now look at the following proverbs, and explain what you think they mean. Try to think of situations that would fit them. (Do you know German equivalents for any of them?)

- **a** It takes two to make a quarrel.
- **b** A watched pot never boils.
- **c** Too many cooks spoil the broth *(= soup).*
- **d** When the going gets tough, the tough get going.
- **e** God helps them that help themselves.
- **f** When poverty comes in at the door, love flies out of the window.
- **g** The apple never falls far from the tree.
- **h** He who fights and runs away, lives to fight another day.

2 Fashion-conscious teenagers

2.1 Fill in the correct present tense forms.

Alex O'Connell, a reporter for The Times, is in a big London clothes shop – just a few days before Christmas.

a	"The fittest guy in your class ____ you a lot. He ____ great, and he's funny	like · look
	and kind. You ____ him, too, but he ____ badly. In fact, his clothes really	like · dress
	____ good. So, ____ you ____ to go on a date with him when he ____?"	not look · agree · ask
	The three teenage girls ____ at me in disbelief when they ____ this	stare · hear
	question. "No way!" they ____ at once.	answer
b	It is Saturday afternoon in Top Shop in Oxford Street, which ____ to be the	claim
	biggest clothes shop in the world. The girls I ____ to now ____ their	talk · do
	Christmas shopping. As a Christmas shopping trip it ____ rather	seem
	unconventional, however, as the only things the girls ____ for are clothes.	look
	And the clothes they ____ to get will be only for themselves. Most of the	want
	teenagers in the store today ____ with their mothers. And they ____ a great	shop · have
	time.	
c	"I ____ shopping," ____ Terri, 15. "When I ____ down town and ____	love · say · go · see
	something I really ____, I ____ over to where my mum ____ and she	like · go · work
	____ me the money." But now it ____ late, and Terri's mother – like all	give · get
	the other mothers who ____ around – ____ to get tired.	stand · begin
d	This Christmas, teenage shoppers ____ more than ever on fashion.	spend
	They ____ to have plenty of money and, more importantly, they ____	seem · know
	exactly what they ____ and where to get it. Although teenage boys ____	want · become
	more fashion-conscious, the female sector of the teenage market ____	remain
	the most important.	
e	A recent survey for a teen magazine ____ that their teenage readers	show
	– average age 14 – ____ between £10 and £20 a week, a lot of which	spend
	____ on fashion and beauty. But where ____ the money ____ from?	go · come
	Not just pocket money. Terri ____ a paper round and ____ £20 a week.	do · earn
	Serena, another 15-year-old, who – I ____ – ____ expensive trainers and	notice · wear
	a designer jacket, ____ at a hairdresser's on Saturdays, where she ____	work · get
	£20 for shampooing people's hair.	
f	I ____ Terri why she and her friends ____ clothes so important. "We	ask · find
	____ to be in fashion and have the right stuff," she ____. "When you	need · say
	____ different, people ____ to stare at you – or even ____ at you. Nobody	look · start · laugh
	____ that."	like

Based on an article in *The Times Magazine*

2.2 What do you find out from the text about teenage girls in Britain?

2.3 Where does your money come from? What do you spend it on?

2.4 The girls in the text are only 15. Does the 'right stuff' to wear become less important as you get a bit older?

3 Macon and Sarah

Anne Tyler's bestselling novel 'The Accidental Tourist' tells the story of how Macon Leary tries to adapt to life when his wife, Sarah, leaves him. In this scene, Macon and Sarah have met to discuss the situation.

"Sarah," he said. "It's been awful living apart. I think you ought to come home … Sarah?"
"It's not possible," she told him. Her eyes were very steady.
"I'm sorry," she said more gently. "But it would never work."
"All I'm saying is, I think we ought to start over."
"I am starting over," she said, "I'm doing everything I can to start over, but that doesn't mean I want to live the same life twice. I'm trying to branch off in new directions. I'm taking some courses. I'm even dating a little."
"Dating?"
"I've been going out with this physician."
There was a pause. Macon said, "Why not just call him a doctor."
Sarah briefly closed her eyes. "Look," she said, "I know this is hard for you. It's hard for both of us. But we really didn't have much left, don't you see? Look who you turned to when you broke your leg: your sister Rose! You didn't even let me know, and you do have my telephone number. But no, you called on your family. You're closer to them than you ever were to me."
"That's not true," Macon said. "Or rather it's not the point. I mean, in one sense of course we're closer; we're blood relations."
"Playing that ridiculous card game no one else can fathom," Sarah said. "Picking apart people's English. Quibbling over *method*. The kind of family that always fastens their seatbelts."
"For God's sake, Sarah, what's wrong with fastening your seatbelt?"
"They always go to one restaurant, the one their grandparents went to before them, and even there they have to rearrange the silver and set things up so they're sitting around the table the same way they sit at home. They have to have their six glasses of water every day. They don't believe in ballpoint pens. They don't believe in hello and goodbye."
"Hello? Goodbye?" Macon said.
"Just watch yourself some time. The best house in the world might come on the market, but you can't buy it because you've ordered these address labels for the old house, a thousand five hundred gummed labels, and you have to use them up before you move."
"That wasn't me, it was Charles," Macon said.
"Yes, but it could have been you. And his wife divorced him for it, and I don't blame her."

From *The Accidental Tourist* by Anne Tyler

5 **gentle** soft, kind • 7 **to start over** (AE) to start again • 9 **to branch off in new directions** to start doing new things • 12 **physician** [fɪˈzɪʃn] doctor (formal English) • 14 **briefly** for a short time • 18 **the point** *here:* the important thing • 20 **to fathom** [fæðəm] to understand (sth very difficult) • 21 **to quibble** to argue (about sth unimportant) • 30 **(gummed) label** small piece of paper for sticking (e.g. on envelopes) • 31 **Charles** Macon's elder brother

3.1 Describe how Sarah is living her new life without Macon. (See lines 8-12)

3.2 Macon and his family have some habits and characteristics that Sarah dislikes. What are they? (See lines 20-26)

3.3 Now explain the reason for the use of the different present tense forms in lines 7-10 and 21-26

3.4 What kind of people do you find fault with?
I can't stand/don't like/hate people who …

4 Better to be safe than sorry

Explain in a few sentences, in English, how pickpockets work and what the police advise. These words and expressions may be useful:

to be very busy (2) • check-in desk (3) • pickpocket (4) • trolley (6) • cash (12) • to pay special attention (15) • crowd (of people) (17) • to divert sb's attention (19) • valuables (20) • to take the loot (22) • suspicious (23) • to bump into (24) • to get at sth (30)

Es ist neun Uhr an einem regnerischen Tag am Anfang der Schulferien. Am Flughafen herrscht Hochbetrieb. Viele Menschen stehen vor den Abflugschaltern Schlange. Alle freuen sich auf ihren Urlaub und träumen schon von weißen Sandstränden. An Taschendiebe denkt niemand. Eine junge Frau reist mit ihren zwei kleinen Kindern. Sie schiebt einen Gepäcktrolley mit einem schweren Koffer und zwei Reisetaschen. Ihre Handtasche hängt über ihre Schulter. Als eins der Kinder zu weinen anfängt, legt sie die Handtasche in den Gepäcktrolley und bückt sich, um das Kind hochzuheben. Ein paar Sekunden später, als sie ihre Tasche wieder über die Schulter hängen will, merkt die junge Frau mit Entsetzen, dass sie weg ist – und mit ihr die Flugtickets, Pässe, und eine Menge Bargeld. Um sie herum sind viele Leute, aber niemand scheint etwas gesehen zu haben. Eine typische Szene.

Die Polizei warnt:

- Seien Sie besonders aufmerksam in Menschenansammlungen auf Flughäfen und Bahnhöfen. Taschendiebe lieben Menschenmengen. Sie arbeiten in der Regel im Team. Oft lenkt der eine den Passagier ab. Während er das tut, stiehlt der andere Geld oder Wertsachen aus Hosentasche oder Handtasche. Dann übernimmt ein dritter die Beute.
- Seien Sie misstrauisch, wenn jemand sie anrempelt, zum Beispiel während Sie in einen Zug einsteigen. Selbst wenn jemand Sie nur anspricht und um Auskunft bittet, kann es sein, dass diese Person versucht, Sie abzulenken, während ein anderer auf die Gelegenheit wartet an Ihre Wertsachen zu kommen.

VORSICHT IST BESSER ALS NACHSICHT.

Based on a leaflet from the Bundesgrenzschutz

ADVANCED RULES AND EXERCISES

Present simple	Present progressive
Fred **always borrows** my books. ▸ I don't mind.	Fred **is always borrowing** my books and **forgetting** to give them back. ▸ I'm sick of it.
for **neutral statements**	to express the speaker's **feelings**, usually of **annoyance**, about someone's habits (with *always, constantly*)

I **think** I've read this book before. ▸ *Ich glaube, …* This dictionary **has** over 1,000 pages. ▸ *… hat / umfasst …* The cartoons in this book **are** very funny. ▸ *… sind sehr lustig.*	I'**m thinking** of joining the library. ▸ *Ich überlege, ob …* I usually read the paper while I'**m having** breakfast. ▸ *… während ich frühstücke.* My uncle can't read or write. – **Are** you **being** funny? ▸ *Machst du Witze?*

Certain verbs which normally express a state (e.g. *have, be, think*) can be used in the progressive form, but with a different ('dynamic') meaning.

1 Caring about the environment

a Kim and Mike often talk about helping the environment. Kim tells Mike he isn't doing enough. "You're always talking about saving energy," says Kim. "But what do you do? You still drive to work every day! I'm always telling you to use your bike."

b "I'm thinking of starting next week," says Mike. "Anyway, I think you're being a bit unfair," he continues. "You're always using the car for short journeys yourself."
"Well, I always use it for shopping," Kim says. "That isn't so much, surely?"

c Anne and Bob eat a lot of organic food. "There's a farm shop near us where we get chickens and eggs," Anne explains, "and our supermarket has a good choice of organic fruit and vegetables." "We're eating less meat than we used to," she goes on. "And we try to avoid fast food altogether. At least I do. Bob isn't so strict about that. He's always getting hamburgers and stuff like that. But all in all, we're trying our best to be green."

d "We're always having arguments about holidays, though," says Bob. "Anne's always wanting to fly off to some exotic resort. But I just want a quiet week down in Cornwall. We always have a great time there anyway."

1.1 **Work in groups, and find examples of the same verb (e.g. *talk*) used in both the simple and the progressive form. Explain the difference in meaning.**

☆ **1.2** **How about you? What do you do (regularly) to help the environment? How are you trying to improve?**
What are you always intending to do (… but never manage to do)? And what about others you know?

2 Past Tense –
Simple and Progressive Aspects

CHECK-UP

1 The Hollerday Hill fire

Complete the text with past tense forms.
Use the past progressive wherever suitable.

About 18 months ago, I ____ a most unusual experience. At the time,	have
I ____ in a house on the cliffs between the two Devon villages of Lynton	live
and Lynmouth. I ____ the railway station at Taunton quite regularly to go	use
to London, and I always ____ the drive back across Exmoor and along	enjoy
the coast to Lynton.	
At about nine o'clock one winter evening, while I ____ from Taunton in	return
my car, I ____ round a bend in the road and suddenly ____ that the whole	drive · see
of the sky above the hill in front of me ____ bright orange and red with	be
flames. I ____ about five miles from Lynton, and I ____ that must be where	be · know
the flames ____ from. Wanting to get home as soon as possible, I ____ my	come · increase
speed and, while I ____ , I ____ to keep my eye on the flames. Sometimes	drive · try
I ____ sight of them when the road ____ and ____ . But even from several	lose · twist · turn
miles away, it ____ clear that a major fire ____ rapidly through the village.	seem · spread
Even though I ____ quickly now, it ____ me several minutes to cross the	drive · take
moors to the top of Countisbury Hill, where there is a good view down	
to the two villages. When I ____ the top of the hill, I ____ to see at least ten	reach · expect
or twenty houses on fire. Strangely, from this position I ____ nothing at all.	see
There ____ no fire to be seen, and none of the houses below ____ .	be · burn
Everything ____ just as quiet and peaceful as ever.	look
Next morning, when I ____ into the village to collect my newspaper,	go
I ____ the newsagent about it, and he ____ me there had been no fire in	ask · tell
the village at all the previous night.	
"Where ____ you ____ the flames?" he ____ .	see · ask
"They ____ to be coming from some houses on the hill behind the village."	seem
"Ah. Hollerday Hill," he ____ , and ____ wisely. "The big house on Hollerday	say · nod
Hill. It ____ right down to the ground."	burn
"But I ____ you ____ there hadn't been any fire last night!"	think · say
Suddenly I ____ that the old man ____ at me rather strangely. "You mis-	notice · look
understand me," he ____ . "The Hollerday Hill fire ____ over fifty years ago."	explain · happen

Adapted from *Mind Over Body* by Vernon Coleman

BASIC RULES AND EXERCISES

Simple past	
In 1434 the River Thames **froze** over, and the frost in London **lasted** from November till February. The London train **came** in two hours late yesterday because of the snow.	▸ for **completed activities, events or states** in the past, often with adverbials of past time (*yesterday, last January, 20 years ago, in 1434*, etc.)
It **snowed** all night. Next morning after breakfast Harry **ran** outside and **joined** his friends. He **picked** up a handful of snow and **began** to make it into a snowball …	▸ for a **series of actions or happenings** in the past (in stories, reports, etc.)
Past progressive	
It **was snowing** when I walked home last night. While I **was passing** the church, Mr Barker stopped and offered me a lift in his car.	▸ to describe the **'background' to past events,** or the **'accompanying circumstances'** (*what was happening at that time*)
Everyone was busy. Alice **was clearing** the snow in front of the garage, David **was sweeping** the path, and little Tommy **was helping** with his toy snow plough. It was just five o'clock, but it **was** already **beginning** to get dark.	▸ for **several activities or happenings** all going on **at the same time,** and for **gradual developments**

Verbs that describe a **state** rather than an **action** don't usually appear in the progressive form. For a list of verbs that are normally used in the simple form only, turn to page 17.

1 The Heffalump

A. A. Milne is world-famous for his children's books about Christopher Robin, the little boy whose teddy bear (Winnie-the-Pooh) and other toy animals share adventures full of everyday hopes and fears, mistakes and misunderstandings.

One day, when Christopher Robin and Winnie-the-Pooh and Piglet were all talking together, Christopher Robin finished the mouthful he was eating and said carelessly: "I saw a Heffalump today, Piglet."

"What was it doing?" asked Piglet.

"Just lumping along," said Christopher Robin. "I don't think it saw me."

"I saw one once," said Piglet. "At least I think I did," he said. "Only perhaps it wasn't."

"So did I," said Pooh, wondering what a Heffalump was like.

"You don't often see them," said Christopher Robin carelessly.

"Not now," said Piglet.

"Not at this time of year," said Pooh.

Then they all talked about something else, until it was time for Pooh and Piglet to go home together. At first as they stumped along the path which edged the Hundred Acre Wood, they didn't say much to each other; but when they came to the stream, and had helped each other across the stepping stones, and were able to walk side by side again over the heather, they began to talk in a friendly way about this and that, and Piglet said, "If you see what I mean, Pooh," and Pooh said, "It's just what I think myself, Piglet." And then, just as they came to the Six Pine Trees, Pooh looked round to see that nobody else was listening, and said in a very solemn voice:

"Piglet, I have decided something."

"What have you decided, Pooh?"

"I have decided to catch a Heffalump."

Pooh nodded his head several times as he said this, and waited for Piglet to say "How?" or "Pooh, you couldn't!" or something helpful of that sort, but Piglet said nothing. The fact was Piglet was wishing that *he* had thought about it first.

From *Winnie-the-Pooh* by A. A. Milne

---

6 **to lump along** to move along slowly and heavily • 13 **to stump** to walk stiffly • 13 **to edge sth** to form the border of sth • 13 **acre** an area of land (*Morgen*) • 15 **heather** [heðə] *Heide* • 17 **pine tree** *Kiefer* • 18 **solemn** [sɒləm] serious

1.1 **Pick out all the past tense forms in lines 1-7, lines 12-18 and the very last sentence of the text. Then, referring to the Basic Rules, explain the author's use of simple and progressive forms.**

1.2 **Why do you think Christopher Robin's remark about the Heffalump made such an impression on Pooh and Piglet? What sort of animal do you think they were imagining?**

2 Do you recognize these?

2.1 Identify these past tense forms. What verbs do they come from?

rode lay flew laid felt bled tore struck rose beat bit fell wept paid drew

2.2 Complete the sentences with past tense forms from the word cloud above.

a Germany ______ England in the match on Saturday.
b Sam ______ his bike into a tree and ______ a big hole in his jeans – and his knee! It ______ so badly that he had to have it stitched.
c Our neighbour's chickens ______ these eggs.
d I ______ so tired that I ______ down on my bed to rest.
e Our dog ______ the postman yesterday.
f Mum ______ at my sister's wedding!

2.3 Which words are still left? Choose three and make your own sentences with them.

3 How to mow the lawn

3.1 **What does John Goodacre tell his wife, Jane, about their ingenious (*genial*) neighbour when she gets home in the evening? Use the past tense to tell his story.**
The notes below will help you.
You could start this way:
"Guess what happened this afternoon, Jane! I went out into the garden after lunch. As the grass …"

a go • out • garden • this afternoon • grass • get • a bit long • decide • mow • lawn • take • me • over an hour • feel quite tired • afterwards
b before • put • lawnmower • back • garage • look • over • hedge • into • the Wisemans' garden
c at first • only • see • Dave Wiseman • he • sit • deckchair • middle • their lawn • read book • look • very relaxed
d then • notice • something else • cannot • believe my eyes • grass • near • edges of their garden • look • very long • three sheep on a string • move • slowly • round • eat grass • Dave • hold • string • guide • them • round in a circle!
e after a while • Dave • see • me • ask • me • come round for a drink • we • sit • on • lawn • together • couple of hours • when • I • leave • three sheep • just • eat • last bits of grass • near • house
f when • I • get home • call • local farmer • order • couple of sheep • for us!

3.2 **Which forms did you use more often – simple or progressive? Can you explain why?**

4 Looking for the girl

Translate the text, paying particular attention to simple and progressive forms.
These words will be useful:

coin (2) • machine (2) • platform ticket (2) • to stand (3) • steps (leading to the platform) (3) • to look closely at (6) • to light (a cigarette) (9) • railing (10)

Ich kam ein paar Minuten zu spät zum Bahnhof, und während ich den Groschen in den Automaten für die Bahnsteigkarte warf, versuchte ich, mich an das Mädchen zu erinnern. Ich stellte mich an die Treppe zum Bahnsteig und dachte: blond, zwanzig Jahre, kommt in die Stadt, um Lehrerin zu werden; als ich die Leute, die an mir vorübergingen, musterte, schien es mir, als sei die Welt voller blonder zwanzigjähriger Mädchen – so viele kamen von diesem Zug her, und sie hatten alle Koffer in der Hand und sahen aus, als kämen sie in die Stadt, um Lehrerin zu werden. Ich steckte eine Zigarette an und ging auf die andere Seite des Aufgangs, und ich sah, dass hinter dem Geländer ein Mädchen auf einem Koffer hockte …

From *Das Brot der frühen Jahre* by Heinrich Böll

Generally speaking, the ***simple past*** is used ***much more often*** than the ***past progressive***.

5 Alice in the Duchess's kitchen

Alice opened the door and went in.

The door led right into a large kitchen, which was full of smoke from one end to the other: the Duchess was sitting on a three-legged stool in the middle, nursing a baby; the cook was leaning over the fire, stirring a large cauldron which seemed to be full of soup.

"There's certainly too much pepper in that soup!" Alice said to herself, as well as she could for sneezing.

There was certainly too much of it in the air. Even the Duchess sneezed occasionally; and the baby was sneezing and howling alternately without a moment's pause. The only things in the kitchen that did not sneeze, were the cook, and a large cat which was sitting on the hearth and grinning from ear to ear.

"Please would you tell me," said Alice a little timidly, "why your cat grins like that?"

"It's a Cheshire cat," said the Duchess, "and that's why."

"I didn't know that Cheshire cats always grinned; in fact, I didn't know that cats *could* grin."

"They all can," said the Duchess, "and most of 'em do."

"I don't know of any that do," Alice said very politely, feeling quite pleased to have got into a conversation.

"You don't know much," said the Duchess, "and that's a fact."

Alice did not at all like the tone of this remark, and thought it would be as well to introduce some other subject of conversation. While she was trying to fix on one, the cook took the cauldron of soup off the fire, and at once set to work throwing everything within her reach at the Duchess and the baby – the fire-irons came first; then followed a shower of saucepans, plates and dishes. The Duchess took no notice of them even when they hit her; and the baby was howling so much already, that it was quite impossible to say whether the blows hurt it or not.

From *Alice's Adventures in Wonderland* by Lewis Carroll

---

5 **cauldron** ['kɔ:ldrən] large open cooking pot • 8 **to sneeze** *niesen* • 11 **to howl** [haʊl] to cry loudly • 11 **alternately** [ɔ:l'tɜ:nətlɪ] in turns • 13 **hearth** [hɑ:θ] the place in front of an open fire • 14 **timid** shy • 24 **saucepan** ['sɔ:spən] cooking pot (with a lid) • 26 **blow** [bləʊ] *Schlag*

5.1 **Start by looking at the illustration. Then look at lines 2-13. Pick out all the sentences (or parts of sentences) that describe the scene in the kitchen as it is shown in the illustration. Which past tense form does the author prefer for this description? Why?**

5.2 **Look at lines 21-26. Describe the action in the kitchen after Alice's conversation with the Duchess. Explain the use of the past tense forms here.**

☆ **5.3** **At the end of the book, Lewis Carroll writes: "'Oh, I've had such a curious dream!' said Alice, and she told her sister, as well as she could remember them, all of these strange adventures of hers that you have just been reading about . . ." Imagine that you are Alice, and retell what happened in this part of the dream, picking out what you feel are the most important details. (Close your book for this if possible.)**

ADVANCED RULES AND EXERCISES

Different form – different meaning	
Ben **laughed** when I came into the room.	▸ *Meaning*: When I came in, he began to laugh. (= a new activity)
Ben **was laughing** when I came into the room.	▸ *Meaning*: When I came in, he was already laughing. (= an activity in progress)

1 Which form makes more sense?

Complete the following sentences with whichever form you find more suitable. Explain your choice, and say whether the other form would make sense or not.

a	The boys ____ off in the opposite direction when they saw us coming.	run
b	When we set off that morning, the sun ____.	rise
c	I ____ up when the alarm went off.	wake
d	We asked the girl to translate the menu for us, but unfortunately she ____ English.	not speak
e	She ____ a big pot of coffee when the visitors arrived.	make
f	They ____ out of the house when the telephone rang.	go
g	Whenever there was a thunderstorm, the dog ____ under the kitchen table.	hide
h	On the way home in the car last night, my brother ____ on the box of eggs we had bought at the farm.	sit
i	Please say exactly where you were and what you ____ when the murder took place.	do
j	When Mum got back from work, I ____ the table for supper.	set

2 Richard Cory

Whenever Richard Cory went down town,
We people on the pavement looked at him:
He was a gentleman from sole to crown,
Clean favored, and imperially slim.

And he was always quietly arrayed,
And he was always human when he talked;
But still he fluttered pulses when he said,
"Good morning," and he glittered when he walked.

And he was rich – yes, richer than a king –
And admirably schooled in every grace:
In fine, we thought that he was everything
To make us wish that we were in his place.

So on we worked, and waited for the light,
And went without the meat, and cursed the bread;
And Richard Cory, one calm summer night,
Went home and put a bullet through his head.

Edwin Arlington Robinson (1869-1935)

---

3 **crown** *here:* the top of the head • 4 **clean favored** *(not in modern use) glatt rasiert* • 5 **to array** *here:* to dress • 11 **in fine** *(not in modern use)* in a word

2.1 Use your dictionary to check any words you are not sure about. Then explain what you understand by:

line 7: he fluttered pulses
line 8: he glittered when he walked
line 10: he was … admirably schooled in every grace

2.2 Use the past tense to answer these questions:

a What sort of a person was Richard Cory?
b How did other people feel about him? Why?
c What couldn't they know about him?
d Why do you think he committed suicide?

☆ **2.3 This poem is an example of a text written in the past, in which the progressive form does not occur at all. Try to explain why the poet uses only the simple form.**

3 Present Perfect –
Simple and Progressive Aspects

CHECK-UP

1 Dear Annie

Decide which fits: present perfect simple or progressive?

http://www.

Fed up *Sun Sep 19th, 20:35 GMT*
Ever since my parents split up last year, I ___ with my mother. Everything was great at first, but now she ___ a new boyfriend, and I can only say our home life ___ for the worse. They ___ out together for about six weeks, and now he ___ coming round here regularly for meals. Mum ___ helping me with my homework, and since school started again last week, she ___ me to bed early so they can spend time alone together. I ___ enough of it! At least he ___ in yet, but who knows what they're planning? I ___ to talk to Mum several times about how I feel, but so far nothing ___. She says she ___ without a partner long enough so I just have to adapt. For a while now I ___ whether to go back to my dad. What do you think? Annie's answer

live
find
change · go
start · stop
send
have
not move · try
help · be
wonder

Unhappy parent *Sun Sep 19th, 20:30 GMT*
Help! Ever since our son, aged 13, got his new computer, he ___ up in his room, playing games, and he ___ his homework. What worries me most, though, is that he ___ going to basketball practice. In fact, apart from going to school, he ___ outside the house for days. The only positive aspect of all this is that he ___ watching TV. Annie's answer

sit
neglect
stop
not be
stop

Pig-in-the-middle *Sun Sep 19th, 20:29 GMT*
My problem is my two best friends. They ___ each other, and recently the situation ___ worse than ever. Whenever the three of us do things together, they start arguing. For months now I ___ to think of a way of solving the problem, but nothing I ___ of so far ___. Since their last big quarrel, I ___ them separately, which I thought might be the best solution, but they both ___ to this badly – each of them ___ me all the time for liking the other one better. What should I do? Annie's answer

like / never
be
try
think · work
meet
react · blame

2 At the station

Use the present perfect – simple or progressive – to explain the situation.

Example: A young man rushes onto Platform 3. The train is just leaving the station. → miss *He has missed the train.*

a A woman with a young child is sitting on a platform bench. She sat down there 20 minutes ago. → wait
b Two girls are in the station snack bar. Both had hamburgers on their plates, but now their plates are empty. → eat
c A young boy travelling alone is looking in all his pockets. He is very worried indeed. → lose
d The train at Platform 5 came in at 3.55. It is now 4.10, and it is still there. → stand
e A young woman is walking away from the bookstall. The magazine she wanted is sold out. → not buy
f A young man is leaving the station, alone. He is looking sad. → say good-bye

BASIC RULES AND EXERCISES

Simple present perfect	
The post **has come**. There are two letters for you. I'm afraid the post office **has** *just* **closed**. **Has** my parcel **arrived** *yet*? – No, it **hasn't been delivered** *yet/so far*. Please write that letter now – **I've reminded** you *a hundred times*! When are you going to post these cards? They**'ve been** on the hall table *for days/since the day before yesterday/all week*. **I've had** a lot to do *since I last mailed you*.	▸ to stress the **result of a past activity on the present** and for **activities only just completed** (together with *just, this very moment*) ▸ in questions and statements about whether something has **ever, yet, so far** taken place, especially with expressions of **frequency** (*five times, often, always, never*) ▸ to describe **states** that **began in the past** and have continued **into the present**, together with *for …* or *since …, all week*, etc. and together with clauses of time introduced by *since*

Present perfect progressive	
Is Dad still on the phone? He**'s been talking** *for ages*. (Will he never stop?) Ed seems to be away. **I've been trying** to contact him *since the weekend/since I got back from Italy*, but no one answers the phone.	▸ for **activities** that **began in the past** and have continued **into the present** (and may still continue), together with *for …, since …*, etc. ▸ for **activities** that have been going on **at intervals**, also together with *for …, since …*, etc., but never with expressions of frequency

Remember that certain verbs are normally used only in the simple form:

know	*like*	*see*	*be*	*have (= own)*
think	*love*	*hear*	*sound*	*contain*
believe	*hate*	*feel*	*look (=aussehen)*	*belong to*
remember	*want*	*notice*	*seem*	*consist of*
forget	*wish*	*realize*	*mean*	*cost*

1 Violent crime in the countryside

From burglary to arson, violent crime is rampant in the countryside. According to a survey of farmers this year, more than half have been burgled, 45 per cent have suffered vandalism, and 20 per cent arson. 10 per cent have even been attacked.

Rural crime first became a serious problem in the 1980s, when the M25 motorway was completed. Since then it has been getting steadily worse, and crime has been spreading across the countryside, following the expanding motorway network.

Because of the high level of police surveillance in urban areas, criminals are moving out to easier targets. The same criminal gangs who used to rob banks are now stealing farm machinery. William Day, whose family has been farming near Maidstone in Kent for generations, has been robbed twice in the last two months. "I have lost three tractors and a Land Rover so far this year," he says.

Animals are also stolen. Three years ago, Richard Longthorp, a Yorkshire farmer, had 260 outdoor pigs stolen in one night.

It is a mistake to believe that it is just animals and farm equipment being targeted. Lines of trees have been stolen, and stretches of dry-stone wall. Slates have even been taken off roofs and antique furniture has been stolen from farmhouses. Some farmers say they do not have a problem. But they should not think that because they have been safe up to now, they will be in the future.

Adapted from *The Times*

---

1 **arson** the crime of setting fire to sth • 1 **rampant** spreading in an uncontrolled way • 2 **survey** ['sɜ:veɪ] examination of facts or opinions by asking people • 11 **surveillance** [sɜ:'veɪləns] act of carefully watching sb or sth • 12 **target** ['tɑ:gɪt] sth you aim at • 21 **dry-stone wall** wall built with loose stones • 21 **slate** *Schiefer; hier: Schieferplatte*

1.1 **Look at lines 1-10 and pick out two examples of the present perfect simple, and two of the present perfect progressive. Explain why the different forms are used.**

1.2 **Look at lines 11-24 and find four examples of 'signal words' with the present perfect, noticing which form (simple or progressive) they are used with.**

1.3 **Give a description of some of the kinds of crime that have been reported to the police:**
Examples: arson: *Farm buildings have been set fire to.*
theft; violence towards farmers, etc.

Use the present perfect wherever you can.

1.4 **Explain why the countryside has become a target for crime.**

1.5 **Translate lines 14-17 (*William Day … he says.*) into German.**

2 American evangelists

Explain in English what it means to be an 'evangelist' in America, why they have been criticized – and what role Patty's faith plays in her life.

highlight (or: big day) (4) • belief / faith (7) • the teachings of Christianity (8) • to be born again (9) • to take on a new meaning (12) • interpretation (13) • to prove effective (14) • faith (17)

„Schon seit meiner Kindheit gehe ich regelmäßig in die Kirche", sagt Patty Schwarz aus Nashville, Tennessee. „Der Sonntag war für mich schon immer der Höhepunkt der Woche. Ich habe durch die Kirche auch viele Freunde gewonnen."
Patty und ihre Familie sind, wie Millionen andere Amerikaner, ‚evangelists'. Nach ihrem Glauben genügt es nicht, einfach die christliche Lehre zu akzeptieren; man muss ‚neu geboren' werden. Erst wenn man Christus persönlich als Herrn erkannt hat, ist man auch ‚neu geboren' worden – und das Leben hat einen neuen Sinn bekommen.
Seit vielen Jahren gebrauchen führende ‚evangelists' das Fernsehen, um ihre Auslegung des Wortes Gottes unter die Bevölkerung zu verbreiten. Dies hat sich als sehr wirkungsvoll erwiesen. Aber die sogenannten ‚televangelists' und ihre Sendungen sind häufig kritisiert worden, weil sie zu emotional und zu kommerziell erscheinen.
„Das alles hat aber mit meinem Glauben nichts zu tun", sagt Patty. „Für mich persönlich und meine Freunde hat sich nichts geändert."

3 Who likes going to the dentist's?

Complete these sentences sensibly, using verbs in the present perfect.

a "I'll have to make an appointment with the dentist. One of my fillings ___."
b "I'm not afraid of the dentist. I ___ twice a year ever since I can remember, and ___ so far."
c "Your face looks very swollen!" – "One of my wisdom teeth ___."
d "I really ought to go to the dentist's for a check-up. I ___ for ages."
e "The right toothpaste makes all the difference. I ___ for years, and I really can recommend it."
f The state of children's teeth ___ a lot since dentists ___ the use of fluoride.
g "Your toothbrush looks awful! How long ___?"

"It's your dentist, Charlie. He says it's been five years!"

ADVANCED RULES AND EXERCISES

Both aspects of the present perfect can be used without adverbials of time.
The simple form stresses the **result** of a past activity.
The progressive form stresses that **something has been in progress for a certain time** (for a while), usually until only a short time ago.

Dad **has been teaching** Jane to swim.	= They have been at the swimming-pool together – probably more than once, and he has helped her to learn, but she isn't perfect yet.
Dad **has taught** Jane to swim.	= Thanks to Dad, she can swim now.
You look hot! **Have** you **been playing** football with the kids?	= Have you been busy playing with them all this time?
I**'ve kicked** a ball through the neighbours' window.	= The window is broken. The 'event' was quickly over.
What's wrong with Jim and Susan? – They**'ve been fighting** again.	= Until a short time ago, they were shouting and hitting each other.
Susan **has knocked** Jim over.	= He's on the floor now.

1 Different situation – different form

Decide which form is more suitable in the following situations. Explain why.

a	"I won't let you drive home. You _____."	drink
b	"I'm afraid I _____ one of those new plates."	break
c	"_____ you _____ the book you were looking for?"	find
d	"Where have you been all this time?" – "I _____ the dog for a walk."	take
e	"What's the matter? _____ you _____?"	cry
f	"Do you know those French irregular verbs now?" – "Yes, I _____ them all."	learn
g	"My father _____ German at evening classes. He's slowly picking it up."	learn
h	"Can you lend me £5? I _____ all my money."	spend

2 Summing up the situation

Describe and comment on the situation in the cartoon.
Use the present perfect.

Tom has been having trouble with his parents.
So he has decided to leave home …

"I think he means it this time."

4 Past Tense and Present Perfect Contrasted

CHECK-UP

1 It's common knowledge

Form questions in the correct tense: past tense or present perfect (simple forms only).
(Just for fun try to give the answers, too – or work with a partner and try out the exercise as a quiz!)

Example: Which continent • Columbus • discover • in 1492?
Which continent did Columbus discover in 1492? → He discovered America in 1492.

a When • the Normans • conquer • England?
b Since when • the present British government • be • in power?
c How many times • Britain • be invaded • since the Norman conquest?
d Where • the potato plant • come from • originally?
e Where • the World Cup • take place • in 2010?
f How long • the present British monarch • be • on the throne?
g Who • first • climb • Mount Everest?
h In which century • the USA • become • independent of Britain?
i Which American president • be shot • after the Civil War?
j How many countries • become • members of the EU • so far?
k In what year • the Berlin wall • fall?
l What city • be chosen • for the next Summer Olympics?

2 Good to see you!

Choose the correct verb form: past tense or present perfect (simple or progressive).

A	MARK	There you are at last! I ___ for absolutely ages.	wait
	NINA	Sorry! – When ___ you ___ here?	get
	MARK	At least quarter of an hour ago. I ___ about in the rain all this time, and as you can see, I haven't got an umbrella. Look how wet I ___! Why ___ you ___ home earlier?	stand get · not leave
	NINA	Serena ___ just as I ___ my coat on. She ___ me on the phone till nearly half past. You know what she's like. Anyway, I'm sorry I ___ here at the time we ___, Mark.	call · put · keep not get · arrange
B	AUTHOR	Nice to see you. Er – ___ you ___ the book yet?	read
	FRIEND	Which book? Oh, you mean the one you ___ me a month or so ago. Your first novel. Ah yes, well, I ___ reading it last week, but I'm rather a slow reader really, so I ___ it yet. So far, I ___ it very much, though.	give start not finish like
	AUTHOR	How far ___ you ___?	get
	FRIEND	Oh, not very far yet, I'm afraid. – But tell me now, ___ you ___ work on another book yet? Last time we ___ you ___ you might write another.	start meet · say
	AUTHOR	Well, actually, I ___ ideas most of the time since then, so I ___ very busy. One of my best ideas ___ to me while I ___ the dog in the kitchen sink last weekend. I –	collect be · come · bath
	FRIEND	Sorry – I must rush. Tell me about it another time, OK?	

BASIC RULES AND EXERCISES

Past tense	Present perfect
My brother **moved** to Leeds three years ago.	We**'ve moved** house. (→ Have you got our new address?)
We often **went** to the theatre when we **lived** in London.	**Have** your visitors **gone** yet?
When **did** you last **see** Tom? – I **saw** him in Harrod's last week.	**Have** you **seen** Stuart lately? – I **haven't seen** him for ages.
Did you **hear** from Lucy at Christmas?	**Have** you **heard** from the Smiths since they left?
▸ The past tense is used for events and states in the past that are over, and are **not seen as related to present time.** Stress is laid on **the time or period of time at which the event took place.**	▸ The present perfect is used for events and states that happened or began at some time in the past, but are **closely related to present time. The result of the past event** is important, not the time when it took place.
Time adverbials that signal 'past tense': *yesterday, last week, a year ago*, etc.; clauses with *when*; questions with *when*	Time adverbials that signal 'present perfect': *so far, up to now, (not) yet, lately, since ..., for ...*

Past progressive	Present perfect progressive
What **were** you **doing** last night between nine and ten o'clock? – I **was watching** TV.	What **have** you **been doing** all the time since supper? – I**'ve been writing** e-mails. (= I haven't finished yet.)
▸ The past progressive stresses what was **in progress at a certain time in the past.**	▸ The present perfect progressive is used for activities that began in the past and **have continued into the present** (and may still continue further).

1 The bison are back

On the prairie, the past has returned. The rumbling noise of hooves over the Great Plains states has been absent for a century, but now the bison are back. In recent years their numbers have been slowly growing. Now the number of bison in commercial herds has risen to about 400,000. Another 30,000 now roam free – as they did in the days of Buffalo Bill.

There are several reasons for the return of the bison – or 'buffalo' (early French settlers called them 'les boeufs'). They have been bred by ranchers who were looking for a healthy alternative to beef cattle. And the Great Plains Indian tribes, whose reservations were wracked by alcoholism and unemployment, hoped that restocking their land with bison would put their people back in touch with their heritage.

For thousands of years, the Plains Indians' lives depended on the bison. Its meat fed them, its skin clothed them and gave them the leather for their teepees. They used its guts to string their bows and its horns to make cups and spoons. They worshipped the bison, and included it in their myths and legends. In 1804, it was estimated that 70 million bison were roaming the plains.

In 1902, there were only 23 animals left in the wild. Between these two dates, in an orgy of killing by white settlers and soldiers that was partly designed to deprive the Indians of their way of life, the bison was almost completely eradicated. Many Indians, who were hoping to trade skins and meat to the whites, also killed their sacred bison, which was gradually replaced on the plains by European cattle. Now, however, the bison has slowly but surely been reinstated on the prairie.

Adapted from *The Daily Telegraph*

11 **to wrack** *plagen* • 13 **heritage** a people's (historical and cultural) traditions • 16 **guts** *Darm* • 18 **to worship** *anbeten* • 20 **to roam** to wander (over) • 22 **to deprive sb of sth** to take sth away from sb • 23 **to eradicate** to destroy or remove • 24 **sacred** ['seɪkrɪd] holy

1.1 Use the past tense and the present perfect in your answers to these questions:

a What are the reasons for the return of the bison to the Great Plains states? (7-13)
b In what ways did the Plains Indians traditionally depend on the bison? (14-20)
c What happened to all the bison roaming the Great Plains in the 19th century? (21-25)

1.2 Which verb forms are used in

a the first four sentences (1-5);
b the third paragraph of the text (14-20)? Explain why the different forms are used.

☆ 1.3 What else do you know about the Native Americans? (What happened to them when the whites moved west? What has happened since then?)

2 The big decision

**Form sentences to describe the situation in the cartoon.
Choose carefully between past tense and present perfect forms.**

- **a** three weeks ago • two men • be • ship • middle of the ocean • when • terrible storm • come up • their ship • sink • near • desert island
- **b** they • manage • swim • island • make • raft • debris from ship • then • leave island • with • box of ship's provisions
- **c** now • be • on raft • together • for ten days
- **d** they • watch • horizon • all day • and • hope • see a ship
- **e** but • no ships • appear • so far
- **f** two days ago • finish • last bits of their food
- **g** since then • they • get hungrier and hungrier
- **h** now • one of them • have idea • how to solve the problem

"What we now have to decide is – which of us has run out of food?"

b **raft** *Floß* • b **debris** ['debriː] broken bits or rubbish • b **provisions** a supply of food

3 Going back to India

Choose the most suitable verb forms: past tense or present perfect (simple or progressive).

Dalbir is an ambitious businesswoman whose family ___ in Britain for over four decades. But like many others of her generation, she ___ Britain now and ___ back to India.
Just over 40 years ago, her newly-married parents ___ over from Delhi to London, where they ___ a small shop. At first, while they ___, they ___ of returning to India rich in the end. But after a while they ___ it wouldn't happen that way.
For their daughter Dalbir, however, the dream ___ true: since last year she and her husband ___ their own business in Bangalore. So far they ___ the decision to leave London. "It's strange," she says. "My parents ___ their home all those years ago to make a better life for themselves and their family, and that's exactly what we ___ – only the other way round!"
Like a lot of second and third generation Anglo-Indians, Dalbir and her husband ___ a good education when they ___ in Britain, and while they ___ in London, they naturally ___ bilingual and bicultural. "So, in a way, coming back to India is something we ___ for all our lives!"

live
leave
go
come
open · work · dream
realize
come
run · not regret
leave
do
receive · live
grow up · become
prepare

Based on an article in *The Times*

4 Adrian, the runaway

Sue Townsend's humorous books about Adrian Mole, written in diary form, quickly became bestsellers. In this extract from the second book, Adrian, who has been having trouble at home and is feeling generally unhappy and unwanted, has finally run away, taking the dog with him. He has now been away from home for four days …

Saturday April 2nd
Manchester Railway Station.
Got here by fish lorry.
10.31 a.m. I wonder what my mum and dad have bought me for my birthday. I hope they are not too worried.
3 p.m. Nobody has said "Happy Birthday" to me.
3.05 p.m. I'm not well (I've got a cold) and I'm not happy. In fact I'm extremely unhappy.
5.30 p.m. Bought myself a birthday card. Inside I wrote:
To our darling first-born child on his sixteenth birthday.
With all the love it is possible to give,
From your admiring and loving parents.
PS. Come home son.
6.15 p.m. There was nothing about me on the six o'clock news.
7.30 p.m. Can't face another night in the open.

9 p.m. Park bench.
I have asked three policemen the time, but none of them have spotted me as a runaway. It's obvious that my description hasn't been circulated.
9.30 p.m. Rang the police station, using a disguised voice. I said, "Adrian Mole, a sixteen-year-old runaway, is in the vicinity of the Blood Transfusion Headquarters. His description is as follows: small for his age, slight build, mousey hair. He is wearing a green school blazer. With him is a mongrel dog." The desk sergeant said, "April Fool's Day was yesterday, sonny."
10 p.m. Waited outside the Blood Transfusion place but there wasn't a policeman in sight. There is never one around when you need one.
11.39 p.m. I have walked past the police station twenty-four times, but none of the cretins in blue have given me a second glance.

Sunday April 3rd Easter Sunday
Still in Manchester. (St. Ignatius's church porch.)
1 a.m. It is traditional for the homeless to sleep in church porches so why don't vicars make sure that their porches are more comfortable? It wouldn't kill them to provide a mattress, would it?
7.30 a.m. Got up at six. Had a wash in a bird bath. Read the inscriptions on the gravestones. Then went in search of a shop. Found one; bought two Cadbury's creme eggs. Ate one myself, gave the other to the dog. The poor thing was so hungry, it ate the silver paper as well.

Monday April 4th

St Ignatius's church porch, Manchester.

6 a.m. For two days I have had the legal right to buy cigarettes, have sex, ride a moped, and live away from home. Yet, strangely, I don't want to do any of them now I'm able to.
Must stop. A woman with a kind face is coming through the gravestones.

10 a.m. Mrs Merryfield, the vicar's wife, has phoned my parents and asked them to come and fetch me. I asked Mrs Merryfield for my parents' reactions. She said, "Angry relief is the nearest I can get to it, dear!" I haven't seen the vicar yet. He is having a lie-in because of being so busy yesterday.

From *The Growing Pains of Adrian Mole* by Sue Townsend

---

18 **to spot** to notice • 20 **to use a disguised voice** [dɪs'gaɪzd] to speak in a different voice (so as not to be recognized) • 21 **vicinity** [vɪ'sɪnətɪ] neighbourhood • 23 **slight build** *here:* not very strong-looking • 24 **mongrel** (dog) ['mʌŋgrl] dog of 'mixed' parents • 29 **cretin** ['kretɪn] person of very low intelligence • 29 **glance** a quick look • 31 **porch** covered entrance-way • 33 **vicar** rector of a church • 37 **Cadbury's creme eggs** chocolate Easter eggs with creamy filling • 49 **to have a lie-in** to sleep later than usual

4.1 **Compare Adrian's diary entries at 3 p.m., 9 p.m. and 11.39 p.m. on Saturday with the one at 7.30 a.m. on Sunday, and explain the reason for the different tenses.**

4.2 **Translate the sentence beginning "For two days . . ." (Monday, 6 a.m.), and the one beginning "Mrs Merryfield . . ." (Monday, 10 a.m.). What do you notice?**

4.3 **Look carefully at the text and say what Adrian was doing at the following times. (You won't be able to quote from the text for this.)**

a 10 a.m. on Saturday
b 9 p.m. on Saturday
c 1 o'clock on Sunday morning

4.4 **Now write a short account of what happened to Adrian in Manchester (up to 1 a.m. on Sunday), using the simple forms of the past only. (Keep to the facts for this; do not include any description of Adrian's thoughts and opinions.)**

4.5 **Imagine what Mrs Merryfield might say to her husband about Adrian. Use the present perfect and the past tense to explain what (has) happened.**

5 Belfast's 30-foot 'peace wall'

Use the information in the text to explain why there is a 30-foot wall in Belfast, how the troubles started and what the situation is today. The following words will be helpful:

30-foot wall (1) • conflicting sections of the population (5) • to pull down / to demolish (8) • mistrust (12) • barrier (14) • to originate / to begin (16) • to oppress (18) • to contain (violence) (21) • Peace Agreement / Good Friday Agreement (22) • to make peace (25) • to lay down arms (25) • government of Northern Ireland (26) • troubles (26) • a thing of the past (27) • to claim lives (28) • to leave (permanent) scars (28)

Seit 1969 steht in Belfast eine 10 Meter hohe Mauer, die oft mit der Berliner Mauer verglichen worden ist. Sie wurde zwischen der katholischen *Falls Road* und der protestantischen *Shankill Road* errichtet, um die beiden verfeindeten Bevölkerungsgruppen voreinander zu schützen. Als 40 Jahre später zum ersten Mal davon die Rede war, diese ‚Friedensmauer' abzureißen, gab es unterschiedliche Reaktionen. Obwohl offiziell die Probleme Nordirlands größtenteils gelöst worden sind, ist es vielen Menschen noch nicht gelungen, ihr Misstrauen und ihre Ängste zu vergessen. Viele Bürger Belfasts leben schon so lange mit dieser Mauer und anderen ähnlichen Barrieren, dass sie gelernt haben, sie als notwendigen Schutz anzusehen. Es gibt immer noch viele, die noch nie ein Gespräch mit einem Angehörigen der anderen Religion geführt haben.

Die Probleme Irlands nahmen im 16. und 17. Jahrhundert ihren Anfang. Damals besiedelten protestantische Engländer und Schotten vor allem den Norden des Landes und begannen, die katholische Bevölkerung zu unterdrücken. Die Republik Irland – zu 95% katholisch – ist seit 1921 vom Vereinigten Königreich unabhängig. Nordirland – mit einer protestantischen Mehrheit – ist ‚britisch' geblieben.

1969 brach in Derry und in Belfast Gewalt auf beiden Seiten aus. Britische Soldaten versuchten, die Gewalt einzudämmen, aber eine dauerhafte Lösung der Probleme wurde nicht gefunden. Trotz eines Friedensabkommens im Jahre 1998 blieb das Misstrauen zwischen Protestanten und Katholiken unverändert.

Inzwischen haben die IRA (Irish Republican Army) und ihre britisch-protestantischen Gegner Frieden geschlossen und ihre Waffen niedergelegt. Sie arbeiten heute sogar seit einiger Zeit in der nordirischen Regierung zusammen. Fast jeder hat angefangen zu hoffen, dass die Unruhen nun endlich der Vergangenheit angehören. Aber ein Konflikt, der so lange angedauert hat (und mehr als 3.700 Tote gefordert hat), hat natürlich viele Narben hinterlassen.

ADVANCED RULES AND EXERCISES (I)

Past tense or present perfect with certain adverbials of time and frequency

Certain adverbials of time or frequency can be a signal for either the past tense or the present perfect, depending on the context. Look at these examples:

	Past tense	Present perfect
already	The children **were *already* sitting** at the table *when we came in.*	No more cake, thanks. I**'ve *already* had** three pieces!
just	We **were *just* having** tea *when Paul and Joanna called round.*	Are your visitors still here? – No, they**'ve *just* left.**
always	*When I was little,* I ***always* woke up** early on Christmas morning, but I don't now.	Of course we're not going out for Christmas dinner. We**'ve *always* had** it at home.
never	They ***never* served** Sunday lunch at the golf club *until a year or so ago.*	Let's have lunch at the Rose and Crown. We**'ve *never* been** there for a meal.
today	I **didn't go out** at all ***today*** – the weather was so bad. (It's too late in the day to go out now!)	No one**'s taken** the dogs out ***today***. Let's have a quick walk over the fields with them now. (The day isn't over yet!)
for (+ time)	We **lived** in London ***for six years** before we moved here.*	I**'ve been looking** forward to this trip ***for weeks***. Now the great day is here at last!

1 The right tense for the context

Complete these dialogues so that the tense fits the context.

a	– You're back early! – Yes. I ___ for 20 minutes, but Julie didn't turn up, so I decided to come home.	wait
b	– Where's Dad? – He ___ out into the garden.	go/just
c	– We overslept on Sunday morning. By the time we got downstairs, the others ___ breakfast.	have/already
d	– ___ you ___ Greg today? – Not yet, but he may call round later.	see
e	– Sally must have missed her train this morning. – No, she didn't, actually. It ___ in when we got to the platform. It was five minutes late! She ___ lucky with things like that.	come/just be/always
f	– Where ___ you ___ for your summer holiday this year? – Greece. We ___ Greece. But another time we'll go there in the spring. I ___ it as hot as it ___ this time.	go love/always know/never · be
g	– When my grandparents still lived in Cornwall, we ___ at their house for three weeks every summer. We ___ abroad.	stay/always go/never
h	– Let's watch 'Titanic' on TV tonight. – That old film? I ___ it at least twice.	see/already
i	– What's happened to Laura? Where is she? – When I last saw her, she ___ some e-mails in her room. I'll call her. She ___ up there for hours now.	write/just sit

ADVANCED RULES AND EXERCISES (II)

Past tense or present perfect in sentences without time adverbials

When no adverbial of time is used, choice of past tense or present perfect depends on other 'clues' from the context or on the personal 'perspective' of the speaker. Compare these examples:

Past tense (connection with past time)	Present perfect (connection with present time)
I **met** Paul at the tennis club dance. (*meaning*: when I was at the dance)	**Have** you **met** Melissa? (*meaning*: Do you know her?)
Mary's father **was** in the Army. (*meaning*: before he retired)	He **has been** all over the world. (*meaning*: He has a lot of travelling experience/is very cosmopolitan.)
We **parked** the car outside the library. (*meaning*: when we went down into the town)	Someone **has parked** their car in front of the garage. (*meaning*: I can't drive in/out.)
How many eggs **did** you **put** in the cake? (*meaning*: when you made it)	I **haven't put** any sugar on the strawberries. (*meaning*: You can still add some if you like.)

2 What does the speaker mean?

Comment on the choice of tense in the following sentences, by explaining the speaker's meaning.

a Have you seen Samantha anywhere?
b I bought these jeans at a little shop on Bedford Street.
c I'm afraid I forgot to post your letter.
d Don't worry – I haven't forgotten what you said.
e I'm surprised Jerry hasn't called.
f We caught the train from Exeter, and we were in London for lunch.
g Didn't you hear the telephone?
h Someone's taken my camera.
i Why haven't you packed your tennis shorts?
j I've put some cheese and tomato sandwiches in the fridge.
k You and Frank were at primary school together, weren't you?
l Why didn't you put any onions in the salad?

"Well, I've been in three or four documentaries, two feature films and loads of commercials, of course. Mostly as a dog."

5 Forms of the Future

CHECK-UP

1 Messages on the family fridge

Will-future or _going-to_-future? Decide which form fits best.

a

Hi Dad,
Pete Richards rang.
He says he ___ round when he finishes work. *(come)*
(That ___ probably ___ at about six, he thinks.) *(be)*
Jack

b

Sam!
I expect I ___ back late this evening – I ___ at the office all afternoon. *(be · stay on)*
Could you take some steaks out of the freezer for supper? Don't worry about vegetables – we ___ a tomato salad – that's quick. *(have)*
Love,
Jenny

c

MUM! Sue Barton rang up about your trip to London with her. As she can't get tickets for "Romeo and Juliet" she ___ seats for a musical. *(book)*
___ that ___ OK? *(be)*
(You ___ ring her when you get back.) *(have to)*
Tina

d

Hi Tina,
Freddy and I ___ out to the island this evening. Want to come with us? Ring me (at Freddy's) if so. *(sail)*
(There ___ room in the boat for Foxie, too, if you want to bring her along.) *(be)*
We ___ a picnic. *(take)*
Jack

e

Jack!! Thanks for your note. I ___ the evening at Moira's. She ___ me her photos of Austria (as planned – or didn't I tell you?). *(spend · show)*
Enjoy your picnic. Perhaps I ___ next time! *(come)*
Tina

2 It's all arranged

Present progressive, simple present, or _will_-future? Fill in the most suitable form.

TED	David and I ___ skiing for a week after Christmas. Like to come too?	go
JOHN	___ you ___ to the Alps?	go
TED	No – the Cairngorms. It ___ great! We ___ on Boxing Day.	be · set off
	The train to Edinburgh ___ in the morning. We ___ trains at	leave · change
	Edinburgh, and we ___ at Aviemore in the early evening. Our ski	arrive
	course ___ at ten the next morning. Look – I ___ you the catalogue.	start · show
JOHN	Hmm. What ___ you ___ if there ___ any snow – like last year?	do · not be
TED	There ___ plenty of snow, you just wait. According to the long-	be
	range forecast, we ___ a really hard winter this year. Temperatures	have
	___ all-time lows!	reach
JOHN	Well, as long as you believe it. Anyway, I can't come with you.	
	My French penfriend ___ here when you ___. He ___ Christmas	be · go · spend
	and New Year with us.	

3 **the Cairngorms** mountain range and skiing area in the Scottish Highlands

BASIC RULES AND EXERCISES

Will-future	
I can post that parcel after work. The Post Office **will** still **be** open.	▸ for predictions, and future events not influenced by the speaker's plans
I expect Tom **will do** the shopping on Saturday morning.	▸ for what the speaker supposes (often with *I expect, I'm afraid, probably,* etc.)
I'm ready! – Right, **I'll get** the car out. **I'll drive** carefully – don't worry!	▸ for spontaneous decisions and promises
Going-to-future	
Are you **going to book** a seat on the train?	▸ for plans and intentions, mostly in the near future
Present progressive	
We**'re collecting** Suzanne at half past eight this evening.	▸ for definite arrangements (often with an adverbial of time)
Simple present	
Our flight to Dublin **leaves** at 11.40. The meeting **starts** at 9 a.m.	▸ for timetable information and programmes of events
I'*ll ring* up when we **arrive**. If we **don't leave** soon, we'*ll be* late.	▸ in clauses with *if, when, as soon as,* etc. referring to future time. (Note the *will*-future in the main clause. See also Basic Rules p. 60.)

1 He's leaving home

Charles Webb's first novel, 'The Graduate', 1963, was a big success. It was filmed in 1967, starring Dustin Hoffman in the title role.
Benjamin Braddock has just finished college. All his life he has done what he's told: been successful at school, passed exams, done what people expect. Now everyone expects him to go to a graduate school and become a teacher. But Ben has other ideas …

In the morning, Benjamin got up earlier than usual. Mrs Braddock was in the kitchen.
"You're up early," she said.
Benjamin sat down at the table in front of his grapefruit. "I'm leaving home," he said.
"What?"
"I said I'm leaving home," he said. "I'm clearing out after breakfast."
"You're going away?"
"That's right."
"Well, where are you going?" she said.
"If you want the cliché," Benjamin said, looking up from his grapefruit, "I'm going on the road."

graduate school senior department of a US university • 8 **to clear out** (slang) to go away

"What? I don't understand this. You aren't just planning to throw your things in the car and leave, I hope."

"No. I'm hitchhiking."

"What?"

"Don't get excited, Mother. I'll be all right."

"You mean you're just going to pack your bag and go?"

"I'm not taking any luggage."

"What?"

"I'm taking what I have on."

"Well how much money are you taking?"

"Ten dollars."

"Oh," she said. "Then you won't be gone more than a day or two. – How long will you be gone?"

"I don't know. Maybe five years. Maybe ten. I don't know."

Mr Braddock came into the kitchen carrying the morning newspaper. "You're up early," he said.

"Ben, tell your father. Because I know he won't let you do it."

"What's all this about?" Mr Braddock said.

"I'm leaving after breakfast on a trip," Benjamin said. "I have no idea where I'm going. Maybe just round the country or the continent. Maybe if I can get papers I'll work around the world. So that's that."

Mr Braddock frowned at him. "This doesn't sound too well thought out," he said. "You just plan to work around? Bum around?"

"That's right."

"Well Ben," his father said. "I don't see anything wrong with taking a little trip. But this is the wrong way to go about it. How's this for an idea, Ben. Spend the summer picking out a graduate school in the East, then throw your things in the car and take a week or two driving back."

"No."

"What's wrong with that?"

"Because I'm finished with schools, Dad. I never want to see another school again. I never want to see another educated person again in my life."

"Come on, Ben."

"Dad," Benjamin said, "for twenty-one years I have been shuffling back and forth between classrooms and libraries. Now you tell me what the hell it's got me."

"A damn fine education."

"You call me educated? Well, I don't," Benjamin said. "I am through with all this. I'm sick of it. Do you know what I want? Simple people. I want simple honest people that can't even read or write their own name. I want to spend the rest of my life with these people."

"Ben."

"Farmers," Benjamin said. "Truck drivers. Ordinary people who don't have big houses. Who don't have swimming-pools. Real people, Dad. – I know how I feel."

They finished breakfast quietly. When it was over, Mr Braddock pulled a checkbook out of his pocket and began making out a check. He signed it and tore it out of the book. "Here," he said. "Take it. Cash it if you have to."

"I won't have to."

"All right. But Ben?"

"What."

"I have a feeling you'll be back here before you think you will."

"I won't." Benjamin stood. "Goodbye," he said, holding out his hand. His father shook it.

"Ben?" Mrs Braddock said. "Do you think you might be back by Saturday?"

"Mother."

"Because I invited the Robinsons over for dinner."

From *The Graduate* by Charles Webb

---

44 **to frown at** to look critically at • 46 **to bum around** (US slang) to fool around wasting one's time • 63 **to shuffle** to walk (aimlessly, without lifting one's feet)

1.1 Sum up Benjamin's arrangements and plans (8-23; 39-43):

He's leaving after breakfast. He ...

1.2 Why do you think Benjamin doesn't want to stay at college and become a teacher? Suggest some reasons:

If he stays at college, he'll just spend all day .../he won't ...
If he becomes a teacher ...
He's afraid that ...
He feels that ... probably ...
By breaking away, he expects that ...

1.3 What future form does the author use most, and why? What other form could have been used instead?

☆ **1.4 Imagine what will happen to Benjamin when he leaves home. How soon do you think he'll be back? Do you think he'll need the check? Why? Or why not?**

2 A meeting at the tennis club

Translate this conversation into English. More than one future form may sometimes be possible.

TINA Kommst du heute Abend zum Clubhaus? Es gibt nächstes Jahr wahrscheinlich eine neue Damenmannschaft, und wir wollen uns alle treffen, um die Einzelheiten zu besprechen.

JULIA Leider schaff' ich's diesmal nicht. Ich gehe heute abend zum Chor. Wir proben (to rehearse) mit dem Orchester für das Konzert am Samstag. Es gibt Ärger, wenn ich nicht hingehe.

TINA Wann fängt denn eure Probe (rehearsal) an?

JULIA Um halb acht. Sie geht vermutlich bis neun oder halb zehn. Bis dahin ist die Besprechung im Clubhaus sicher schon vorbei.

TINA Glaub' ich nicht! Wir treffen uns erst um halb neun. Wenn du also nach der Probe zum Clubhaus kommst, ist die Besprechung wahrscheinlich noch voll im Gang (in full swing).

JULIA Also gut. Ich komme, sobald die Probe vorbei ist.

3 An unexpected invitation

Erskine Childers' novel 'The Riddle of the Sands' was published in 1903. At the beginning of the story Carruthers, a diplomat, hears from an old friend, who invites him to go sailing with him. A pleasant invitation, it seems .... The exciting adventure described in the novel begins with a harmless letter ...

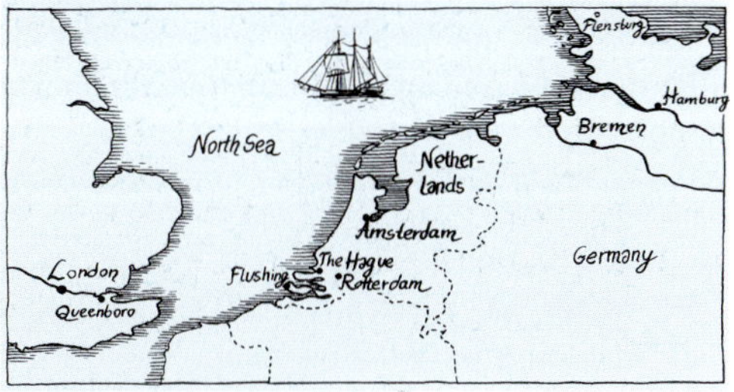

Yacht Dulcibella
Flensburg, Schleswig-Holstein, Sept. 21

Dear Carruthers,

I expect you'll be surprised to hear from me, as it's ages since we met. Probably what I'm going to suggest won't suit you, as I know nothing of your plans and you probably won't be able to get away from the Foreign Office. So I'm just writing to ask on the off-chance. Can you come out here and join me in a little yachting and duck shooting? There will be plenty of duck here soon, if it gets cold enough. My friends here are having to leave shortly, and I'll badly need someone else to help me, as I'm not putting the boat into dock for a bit. If you can come, a telegram to me at the PO here will find me. Flushing, and on by rail via Hamburg will be your best route – your boat for Flushing goes from Queenboro'.
I'm going to have a few repairs done here this week and will have them ready by the time your train arrives. Bring your gun and some oilskins. I hope you'll come. I'll be here when you get here.

Goodbye. Yours ever, Arthur Davies

Adapted from *The Riddle of the Sands* by Erskine Childers

Childers [ɪ] • **Carruthers** [kə'rʌðəz] • 5 **to suit sb** to fit in with sb's plans • 6 **Foreign Office** *Außenministerium* • 6 **on the off-chance** just in case (it may be possible) • 7 **yachting** ['jɒtɪŋ] sailing • 9 **badly** *here:* very much • 10 **PO** Post Office • 10 **Flushing** (Vlissingen) a town in Holland • 13 **oilskins** waterproof clothes

3.1 Work in groups to collect all the examples of future forms. Explain why each form you find is used.

3.2 Use suitable future forms in your answers to these questions:

a What are Davies's immediate plans?
b Why does he so badly want Carruthers to join him?
c What makes him think his suggestion may not suit Carruthers?
d Why does he tell Carruthers to bring oilskins?

3.3 Carruthers decides to go to Flensburg. Think of:

a questions he might want to ask at the railway station, about times, places, etc. (These words will help you: London station, leave, arrive, change, sleeping car, restaurant car, reservation, seat, ...)
Example: Which London station does the train to ...
b thoughts he may have about things to take with him and things to do there. (cold weather, warm clothes, map, camera, sailing shoes, writing paper, books, clothes for the evening, ...)
Example: The weather will probably ... so I'll need ...

ADVANCED RULES AND EXERCISES

More ways of expressing future time	
Tomorrow at this time, I'**ll be flying** over the Atlantic. Barry **will be coming** back from New York next month.	▸ The **future progressive** expresses • that an activity will be in progress at a certain time in the future;
I expect he'**ll be staying** with us for a few weeks.	• what the speaker expects to happen 'anyway', whether it is planned or not.
The waiter can't speak any English. It's **going to be** difficult to explain what we want. It's still quite a long walk to the theatre. We'**re going to miss** the beginning of the show.	▸ The ***going-to* future** can be used to express a logical conclusion (the speaker feels certain that something will happen because there are already signs that it is inevitable).
By the end of this year, we'll **have moved** into our new house.	▸ The **future perfect** expresses that something will have happened by a certain time in the future.

1 Our troubled planet

A In 2011 the world's population reached an incredible 7 billion (7,000,000,000!) – and it is still rising. Over 80 million more babies will be born this year, it is estimated. That means about 225,000 extra mouths to feed each day, day after day, with no end in sight. If the present rate of growth continues, the population of the planet is going to increase by another 50% by the year 2050. Amazing to realize that during the two minutes you take to read just this page, approximately 300 new babies will have come into the world.

B It seems certain that global warming is a reality, and that increases in man-made emissions of carbon dioxide over the past 250 years are at least partly responsible. Scientists expect global temperatures to have risen anything between 3°C and 5°C by 2100. Whatever we do to limit emissions, sea levels are predicted to continue rising over the next two centuries. If the giant ice sheets of Greenland and parts of Antarctica should disintegrate, it is going to be impossible to prevent most of the world's big cities from being flooded by the sea. Around the coast of Australia, rising sea levels are already becoming a problem.

C More and more of the Earth's wealthier inhabitants now eat meat regularly, and as long as this trend continues, more and more of the Amazon rainforest is going to be cut down to make room for cattle ranches and land for growing animal feed. Most people do not realize that meat production is also responsible for 18% of greenhouse gas emissions, which is a lot more than the 13% that comes from traffic!

14 **ice sheet** thick ice covering a large area of land • 15 **to disintegrate** to break up into small bits

D 25 % of all grain crops grown in the USA is used to produce ethanol for cars instead of food. At the same time, food prices have risen and the number of hungry people in the world has increased to over 1 billion. The fertile land available per person for growing crops in the world's poorest regions has decreased dramatically in the last three decades. This is partly because of the rise in population, and partly because of extreme weather conditions and desertification.

25 **grain** *Getreide*

1.1 **According to statistics, how large is the world's population going to be by the middle of the 21st century? (Text A) How will it have developed just one year from now?**

1.2 **How will global temperatures probably have changed by the end of this century? (Text B) If melting ice sheets have caused sea levels to rise massively by then, what geographical changes will have resulted?**

1.3 **What effects can wealthier people's eating habits have on the future of our planet? (Text C)**

1.4 **What kind of problems are there going to be in poorer parts of the world if present trends continue? (Text D)**

1.5 **What predictions can you make about the future of our planet? (Think of world oil, gas and coal reserves, alternative forms of energy, advances in technology, political or social changes, etc.) Use the Internet to discover facts to support your ideas. Imagine what will be happening – or will have happened – by the year 2050.**

2 It's inevitable!

What might you say in these situations?

Example: Big black clouds are coming across the sky from the west.
"It's going to rain soon." / "I think we're going to have some rain."

a A car is overtaking a lorry on a narrow road. Another car is coming the other way.
b There is a lot of blossom on the apple trees in your garden.
c England has to play against Germany in the final of the World Cup.
d There is a very strong wind. You have just got on the cross-Channel ferry at Dover.
e It is December 23rd. It has turned quite cold and a few snowflakes are beginning to fall.
f You are waiting for the London train. Crowds of other people are also on the platform.

3 Gone! A Victorian melodrama

3.1 Look at the picture. What seems to have happened?

3.2 Read the dialogue that has been written to describe what the scene is about.

COOK Here, dear, drink some of this! *(She holds out a glass of water.)*

HENRY Louisa's gone! She's gone! She'll never come back. *(He groans.)* She said she hated me. She threw my presents out of the window. Look! *(He points with great drama to some jewels lying in the dust.)* We were going to be married next month!

COOK *(patting him on the shoulder)*: There, there. Don't worry. Where's she gone, then?

HENRY She's just gone on without me. I had to jump out of the cab to get the jewels. The cab was going quite fast, and I fell over. Look at my clothes!

COOK Don't you worry about her. She's no good. Forget her. *(The young man sighs.)* Why don't you come into the house? I'll make you a nice cup of tea. *(She helps the young man to his feet, picks up the jewels for him, and they go slowly into the house.)*

---

2 **to groan** to make a noise in pain • 8 **cab** taxi (*here:* horse-drawn).

3.3 Now answer the questions, using your imagination to think of as many possibilities as you can.

a What will be happening in one minute? And in five minutes?
b What will have happened an hour later? Six months later? What will Louisa be thinking and doing then? And Henry?

6 Sequence of Tenses

CHECK-UP

1 In town

Put in the missing verb forms. Think carefully before deciding which tense to use.

- **a** "When Dick Randall ___ out of the cinema last Thursday evening, he couldn't remember which street he ___ his car in." — come · park
- **b** "I wanted to walk back along the river, but when I got to the bridge, I ___ that they ___ the public footpath." — discover · close
- **c** "The play starts at 7.30. If we ___ here at half past six, we ___ plenty of time. I expect we ___ at the theatre shortly after seven." — leave · have · arrive
- **d** "There were so many people waiting for the Underground at Waterloo, it ___ as if we ___ onto the train at all!" — look · not get
- **e** "You ought to try the King George. I ___ lunch there several times recently. They ___ excellent pub food." — have · serve
- **f** "Sorry we're late. We ___ to the station in good time, but the train ___ late." — get · be

2 Jenny's A-level results

Our holiday in Normandy was over, and I knew what would await me when we got home. My A-level results. A little white envelope – or would it be a postcard? – from the school would be on the mat with all the other letters that had come while we'd been away.

All through the holiday, I had been trying to forget all about it. But now the day of truth had finally arrived! I worked out in my head what I would do when we got home. I'd take the envelope up to my room, then I'd lock the door and read the results on my own.

I knew my parents were expecting me to do well, but I also knew that my Biology teacher hadn't been very impressed with my efforts before the exams … The worst thing in a way was that I knew I hadn't done as much revision as some of my friends. How would their grades compare with mine? I knew I needed straight A's, because if my grades weren't good enough, I wouldn't get into University – which had always been my dream.

Answer the questions, referring in detail to the lines given in brackets, and using the present as the basic tense.

Start like this: **a** Why is Jenny nervous about coming home from holiday? (1-3)

She knows what will await her when she and her parents get home. Her A-level results. A little white envelope – or will it be a postcard? – from the school …

- **b** Has she often thought about her exam results during the holiday? (4)
- **c** What does she plan to do when she and her parents get home? (5-6)
- **d** What do other people think of her chances ? (7-8)
- **e** What worries Jenny most? (8-9)
- **f** What have her results to do with her future – and why are they so important to her? (10-11)

BASIC RULES AND EXERCISES

The two *basic tenses* in English are the *present tense* and the *past tense*. The use of all the other tenses depends on which *basic tense* is chosen. This fundamental relationship is called the *sequence of tenses*.

Present tense sequence

present perfect: "up to now"
past tense "before"
basic tense = present tense "now"
***will*-future "later"**

It **is** hard to believe that the young woman of today – or tomorrow – **will** ever **return** to the hampering clothes of her great-grandmother. She **is** a different sort of person and **lives** in a different world. Women in the 1920s **were thought** very daring to expose their legs to the knee, but we **have reached** a degree of permissiveness in society which even the Twenties never **attained**. It **is** fairly certain that the main lines of 'emancipated' costume **will remain**.

From *A Concise History of Costume* by James Laver

2 **to hamper** to hinder • 3 **to expose** *here*: to show • 4 **permissiveness** tolerance • 4 **to attain** to reach, to achieve

The present tense sequence is used when referring to present time, e.g. in everyday conversation. It is also often used in summaries, comments, essays, etc.

Past tense sequence

past perfect "up to then"
past perfect: "before that time"
basic tense = past tense "then, at that time"
conditional (would + infinitive) "later"

Maxim **was not** in love with me, he **had** never **loved** me. Our honeymoon in Italy **had meant** nothing to him, nor our living here together. What I **had thought** was love for me, for myself as a person, **was not** love. He **did not belong** to me at all, he **belonged** to Rebecca. He still **thought** about Rebecca.
He **would** never **love** me because of Rebecca … Rebecca, always Rebecca. Wherever I **walked** in Manderley, wherever I **sat**, even in my thoughts and in my dreams, I **met** Rebecca.

From *Rebecca* by Daphne du Maurier

The past tense sequence is used to describe real past events. It is also used in most novels, short stories, and in other fictional narratives.

The past tense sequence is also used in **indirect speech** if the introductory verb is in the past tense.

- "Work **has begun** on the new leisure centre. I **spoke** to the architect on Monday. It **will be finished** in the spring."
- The mayor **said** that work **had begun** on the new leisure centre, and that he **had spoken** to the architect on Monday. He promised that it **would be finished** in the spring.

(see Basic Rules p. 70)

Other forms of the future have equivalent forms in the past tense sequence.

- I'**m meeting** Amy at ten. We'**re going to look** round the shops together.
- Julie and Mike were excited. They **were flying** to Cape Town next morning. Their mother **was going to take** them to the airport.

(see Basic Rules p. 46)

1 Sleep: How much do you need?

Complete the sentences with verb forms belonging to the present tense sequence.

Millions of Americans wake up feeling tired when the alarm ___ in the	go off
morning. In Europe, too, countless people try to manage regularly on six	
hours sleep or less, although it ___ by recent tests that most adults ___	be proved · need
about eight hours – teenagers at least nine! A simple test to check that you	
___ the sleep you ___: You don't need an alarm clock to wake you if you	get · need
___ enough sleep.	have
People mistakenly believe that as long as they ___ themselves more time in	allow
bed at weekends, their bodies ___ for the sleep they ___ during the week.	compensate · lose
Everybody knows that people sometimes feel irritable simply because they	
___ too little sleep the night before. More seriously, fatal road accidents can	have
be caused by exhausted drivers – especially truck drivers – who ___ asleep	fall
while they ___. When questioned later by police, they often simply ___ how	drive · not remember
it ___.	happen
Another common problem is insomnia: many people find it difficult to sleep	
after they ___ a very active or stressful day. Some people even ___ the	have · hate
thought of going to bed because they ___ so afraid that they ___ badly.	be · sleep
Instead of sleeping-pills, doctors recommend that people who ___	suffer
regularly from insomnia should do something really relaxing before they	
___ to bed.	go
Why not have an early night tonight? You ___ fitter tomorrow if you ___!	feel · do

2 Tourist saves tour guide's life

Use the notes below to write a short newspaper report, using the past tense sequence.
Here's how you can start: *A tourist was enjoying his ...*

a tourist • enjoy • "Swim with the Dolphins" snorkelling trip • off the coast • Western Australia • when • the 20-year-old tour guide • be attacked • shark;
although • tourist • never • see • shark • before • somehow • know • instinctively • how • help the girl;
after • grab • 10-foot Great White • by its tail • and • pull • it • off her • drag • her • surface • and • swim • with her • to the boat;
back on shore • tourist • not want • be called • hero;
just hope • girl • soon recover • from • terrible • attack;
later • he say • very glad • be able to help • but • not be sure • whether • ever • go snorkelling • again.

to drag to pull (with difficulty) • **surface** the top (of the water)

3 The newcomer

In Jack London's short story 'To Build a Fire', a man fights – unsuccessfully – to survive in the bitter cold of the Yukon.

Day had broken cold and gray, exceedingly cold and gray, when the man turned aside from the main Yukon trail. He paused for breath. It was nine o'clock. There was no sun, though there was not a cloud in the sky.
The man flung a look back along the way he had come. The Yukon lay a mile wide and hidden under three feet of ice. On top of this ice were as many feet of snow. It was all pure white.
He was a newcomer in the land, a *chechaquo*, and this was his first winter. The trouble with him was that he was without imagination. Fifty degrees below zero meant eighty-odd degrees of frost. Such fact impressed him as being cold and uncomfortable, and that was all. That there should be anything more to it than that never entered his head.
As he turned to go on, he spat speculatively. There was a sharp explosive crackle that startled him. He spat again. And again, in the air, before it could fall to the snow, the spittle crackled. He knew that at fifty below spittle crackled on the snow, but this spittle had crackled in the air. Undoubtedly it was colder than fifty below – how much colder he did not know. But the temperature did not matter. He was bound for the old claim on the left fork of Henderson Creek, where the boys were already. They had come over across the divide from the Indian Creek country, while he had come

the Yukon ['ju:kɒn] part of Canada, east of Alaska; also the name of a river • 5 **to fling/flung/flung** to throw • 9 **trouble** *here*: fault • 10 **zero (Fahrenheit)** = -17.8° C (-50° F = ca. -46° C) • 10 **eighty-odd degrees of frost** about 80° (Fahrenheit) below freezing point (= 32° F) • 13 **to spit/spat/spat** *spucken* • 13 **speculatively** ['spekjʊlətɪvlɪ] *here*: in order to form an opinion • 13 **crackle** sound like dry sticks burning • 13 **to startle** to shock, to surprise • 17 **bound for** on the way to • 17 **claim** piece of land 'belonging' to a (gold) miner • 17 **creek** (AE) small river • 18 **divide** line of high land between two rivers

the roundabout way to take a look at the possibilities of getting out logs in the spring from the islands in the Yukon. He would be in to camp by six o'clock; a bit after dark, it was true, but the boys would be there, a fire would be going, and a hot supper would be ready.
At the man's heels trotted a dog, a big native husky. The frozen moisture of its breathing had settled on its fur in a fine powder of frost. The animal was depressed by the tremendous cold. It knew that it was no time for traveling. Its instinct told it a truer tale than was told to the man by the man's judgment. In reality, it was not merely colder than fifty below zero. It was seventy-five below zero.

From *To Build a Fire* by Jack London

19 **roundabout way** long way round • 22 **heel** back of the foot • 22 **moisture** ['mɔɪstʃə] slight wetness • 23 **fur** (animal's) thick hair • 23 **tremendous** [trɪ'mendəs] great, extreme • 25 **merely** only • 25 **seventy-five below zero** = ca -60° C

3.1 Pick out the past perfect forms in lines 1-8 and lines 14-20 and explain why they are used.

3.2 Why are conditional forms used in lines 20-21?

3.3 Why didn't the man realize the danger he was in on his journey? Refer to the weather, the man's past experience, his character, and the length of time he expected the journey to take. These words will help you:

extremely cold • man • never • be • Yukon • before • not realize • temperature • not imagine • what • happen • if • walk • long way • not know • how foolish • outside • nine hours

3.4 The dog with him was a 'native' of that part of Canada. In what way did this make it wiser than the man? Use these words to help you:

live • cold climate • for years • know • because • experience • low temperatures • before • also • know by instinct • dangerous

3.5 Decide which are the most important points in the text, and arrange them freely as a summary, using the present tense sequence. Start like this: *A man is walking through the icy cold of the Yukon. He has left the main trail, and he wants ...*

ADVANCED RULES AND EXERCISES

The past tense as an alternative to the past perfect

David was tired when he arrived home that evening. It **had been** a long day. He **had left** London early in the morning, and heavy traffic on the motorway **(had) made** the journey seem longer than ever. The weather **(had) turned** wet in the afternoon, and then it **(had)** even **started** to snow.	It is sometimes possible to use the past tense instead of the past perfect. Once the 'time before' relationship to the narrative has been made clear, it is common to change back to the past tense in order to avoid a long run of past perfect forms.
They went to bed as soon as their visitors **(had) left.** A few moments after she **(had) switched** the light off, the baby started crying again.	In clauses with *as soon as, once, before* or *after*, the past tense is often used instead of the past perfect. As the time relationship is made clear by the conjunction, the past perfect is not absolutely necessary.

"Poor Eric, he had got within two yards of the Princess when her private detective stamped on him."

1 North America's First People

Decide which verb form is needed: past tense or past perfect. When you think there are two possibilities, try to explain why.

a When Europeans first ___ to America at the end of the 15th century,	come
they ___ the land that they ___ the 'New World'.	call · discover
b But for the American Indians, who ___ there for many thousands of years,	be
the land ___ 'new' at all.	not be
c By the first century AD, Indians ___ in many different areas, and by about	settle
1500, they ___ all over America.	spread
d Long before the Europeans ___, the American Indians ___ a wide range of different cultures.	come · develop
e When the whites ___ into contact with the Indians, they ___ that the	come · notice
various tribes ___ their own languages. They ___ different ways of fighting and different forms of religion.	develop · develop/also
f Once the whites ___ to settle on Indian land, however, their traditional	start
way of life ___ threatened.	become
g The whites' treatment of the Indians ___ devastating consequences.	have
In 1500, it is estimated that there ___ about a million Indians in North	be
America. By the end of the 19th century they ___ altogether. Many ___	die out/almost · die
in battle, others ___ the mass extermination of the buffalo, which they	not survive
___ for food and clothing.	rely on
h The journey to the reservations that the whites ___ for the Indians ___	choose · be/often
long and exhausting. Before they ___ reach the journey's end, many	can
of the weaker ones ___. Many more ___ after their 'new' lives on the	die/already · die
reservations ___.	begin

7 Conditional Sentences

CHECK-UP

1 Sunday trip to the seaside

Fill in the correct verb forms.

MOTHER	Let's go to the seaside tomorrow. If the weather ___ nice,	be
	we ___ a great time, I'm sure!	have
FATHER	OK. But if I ___ you, I ___ the forecast first.	be · check
DAUGHTER	Well, I'm afraid I ___ to get up all that early if I ___ to Dan's party tonight.	not be able · go
MOTHER	You and your parties. If you ___ to so many parties, you ___ a lot better at school, you know.	not go · do
DAUGHTER	Oh, Mum! If you ___ all the time, I ___ much more like trying!	not complain · feel
SON	I'm sick of hearing about school. – What about Whitby then?	
	If you ___ me the map now, Dad, I ___ out the best route.	give · work
12.30 next day:		
MOTHER	If we ___ earlier, we ___ stuck in that awful traffic jam back there.	leave · not get
SON	Well, we ___ to start in time if 'Sleeping Beauty' ___ so long in the bathroom.	be able · not spend
DAUGHTER	That's not true! Anyway, we ___ into that stupid traffic jam at	not get
	all if we ___ to the traffic news on the radio like I suggested.	listen
FATHER	Now then, now then. If Junior here ___ his bathing trunks,	not forget
	we ___ to go back, and we ___ that half hour to begin with.	not need · not waste
MOTHER	And who forgot to fill the tank up yesterday?	
FATHER	Well, let's not worry about whose fault it all was. We've still got a nice day – hm – afternoon – on the beach to look forward to.	
	If this rain ___, we ___ a great time, I'm sure!	stop · have

2 In the news today

First read the text, then complete the sentences below.

There was a terrible accident on the M6 near Birmingham last night, in which 40 cars and lorries were involved. The police say that the drivers were surprised by sudden fog, and so were unable to slow down in time. The road was icy, making driving conditions extremely difficult. A lorry had broken down shortly before, so one of the lanes was blocked. A spokesman for the Department of Transport said after the accident: "Drivers simply don't take enough notice of weather conditions. That's the reason for so many road accidents. People must learn to be more responsible behind the wheel. Otherwise drastic fines will be the only answer."

a If the drivers hadn't been surprised by the fog, …
b Driving conditions wouldn't have …
c If the lorry …
d There would be fewer accidents if …
e Drastic fines will be the only answer if …

BASIC RULES AND EXERCISES

Type I	This condition may be fulfilled
If Tom **practises** a lot, But if he **doesn't play** regularly,	he **will get** very good at tennis. he **won't improve** much.
if-clause : **present tense**	main clause: **will-future**

Type II	This condition cannot be/isn't likely to be fulfilled
If Tom **was** a year younger, If he **had** a different coach,	he **would** still **be** in the junior team. he **would** perhaps **feel** more motivated.
if-clause: **past tense**	main clause: **conditional**

Type III	This condition can no longer be fulfilled
If he **had won** more matches last year, If he **hadn't broken** his leg in the autumn,	he **wouldn't have lost** interest so easily. he **would have had** more practice.
if-clause: **past perfect**	main clause: **conditional perfect**

If Tom wins against Ralph on Sunday, he **can** really **be** proud of himself.
- In **Type I**, *can*, *must*, *needn't* or *may* can be used instead of *will*.

If he tried hard enough, he **could get** really good.
If he hadn't injured his leg, he **might have won** the tournament.
- In **Types II** and **III**, *might* or *could* can be used instead of *would*.

1 Do you know this joke?

Fill in the correct verb forms.

a *Salesman (selling parrot to young boy):*
If you ____ the string on his right leg, he ____ "Good morning", and if you ____ the string on his left leg, he ____ "Good night". (pull · say / pull / say)
Boy: What ____ if I ____ both strings together? (happen · pull)
Parrot: I ____ off the perch, you idiot. (fall)

perch branch etc. on which a bird can rest

b PATIENT What do you charge for pulling a tooth?
DENTIST Ten dollars.
PATIENT What! Ten dollars for only two minutes' work?
DENTIST Well, if you ____, I ____ it very slowly. (prefer · pull)

to charge to ask for money (in return for goods or services)

c A boy cut a cake into one small piece and one huge piece. Then he put the huge piece on his plate.
GIRL How greedy of you! If I ____ that cake, I ____ the smaller piece. (cut / take)
BOY That's OK then, you've got it anyway!

d "Don't apologize," said the baby-sitter to the parents who came back late. "If I ____ a kid like yours, I ____ home either." (have / not hurry)

2 I'm in a 'What if' mood today

2.1 **Which of the three types of conditional sentences does Garfield use? Why does he use this one?**

2.2 **Use the other two types instead. In what way does the situation change?**

2.3 **Can you add any further ideas to Garfield's thoughts?**
Example: *If we had a huge wedding, it would cost a lot of money / we'd get all sorts of useless presents.*
If we had kittens … If I stayed on my own … If Arlene wasn't …
Go on.

3 Things would be much better if …

3.1 **Complete the conditional sentences below and say how things could be/could have been improved.**
Example: *I would be much happier if Kevin didn't always complain about everything.*

- a You might feel better if …
- b If we hadn't bought that expensive car, …
- c If I spent less on clothes, …
- d If I wasn't so lazy, …
- e If you hadn't eaten up all the biscuits, …
- f Monday mornings would be less bad if …
- g If we'd got up a bit earlier, …
- h You would have passed your driving-test if …

Careful with commas! When the *if*-clause comes first, use a comma. When the main clause comes first, don't.
"If it stops raining, I'll take the dog out."
"I'll take the dog out if it stops raining."

3.2 Now use conditional sentences to express complaints or regrets in the following situations:

- a You got a bad grade in your last English test.
- b Yesterday your father forgot to wake you up in the morning.
- c Your English teacher never calls on you.
- d Your friend didn't want you to copy her homework.
- e Tom didn't pass the ball to you.
- f You always have to hunt through piles of stuff on your desk before you find the things you need.
- g You didn't get any tickets for the pop concert – you forgot to ring up.
- h You have had a nasty fall – the brakes on your bike didn't work.

"If you didn't spend so much money on cameras, we might be able to afford a real holiday."

4 Once upon a time

4.1 Do you still remember the old fairy tales? First put together a simple summary of the story of *Little Red Riding Hood.*

4.2 Then think – It all might (could / probably would) have happened quite differently if ...

If Grandmother hadn't been ill, Little Red Riding Hood's mother wouldn't have baked a cake for her.
If Little Red Riding Hood hadn't stopped to pick some flowers, she might not have met the wolf.

Go on. Think of ...

the Wolf being able to talk • Little Red Riding Hood getting into conversation with him • the Wolf being so hungry • the Wolf wearing Grandmother's nightclothes • Little Red Riding Hood being so naïve • the Hunter coming to the rescue ...

Use conditional sentences; you needn't be too serious.

"When did you first feel the need to wear women's clothing?"

☆ 4.3 Choose one of the following fairy-tales and comment on it, using conditional sentences.

Snow White • Sleeping Beauty • Hansel and Gretel • Rumpelstiltskin • Cinderella

5 Writing to an English penfriend

You might want to express these ideas in English. Be careful with the German *wenn* – decide whether to put *when* or *if* in English.

- a Wenn du ankommst, holt dich meine Mutter am Flughafen ab.
- b Wenn du dann bei uns bist, kannst du dich erst einmal ausruhen.
- c Wenn ich am Freitag aus der Schule komme, können wir etwas zusammen unternehmen.
- d Wenn das Wetter am Wochenende schön ist, gehen wir schwimmen.
- e Wenn du nichts dagegen hast, können wir am Abend in eine Disco gehen.
- f Wenn du vor zwei Wochen gekommen wärst, hätten wir uns eine tolle Picasso-Ausstellung (exhibition) anschauen können.
- g Wenn ich ‚The Lord of the Rings' gelesen habe, schicke ich es dir zurück.
- h Oder willst du es mitnehmen, wenn du kommst?
- i Wenn dein Flug Verspätung hat oder sonst etwas dazwischen kommt (come up), kannst du mich anrufen.

ADVANCED RULES AND EXERCISES

In both **written** and **spoken** English you will also find **other types of conditional sentences.**
Look at these combinations of *if*-clauses and main clauses.

If you **want** more information, **write** to the address below.	**Imperative** in the main clause – for **advice and instructions**
If you **should not like** the book, we'**ll** take it back.	*Should* (like *sollte*) makes the condition **less likely**.
If you **buy** on credit, you **have** more time to pay.	**Present tense** in both clauses – for a general statement (not restricted to the future).
If you **had ordered** the car in June, you **would be** able to drive it now.	A **mix** of Types II and III, producing a variation in meaning.
If you **were** a millionaire, you **would be living** a completely different life.	**Progressive forms** (here: of the conditional) are sometimes used.
Unless you **start** saving now, you'**ll** never **have** enough to buy that house.	*Unless* is a common alternative to *if not*.

When you read authentic texts, your may find other combinations not mentioned here. But generally speaking, for your own work it is safer not to vary too much from Types I, II and III.

1 The language of advertising

1.1 Try to put the two parts together correctly – so that these extracts from advertisements make sense.

1 If a man has money,
2 And if we may draw a conclusion from five generations of experience,
3 If and when 'Your 6 numbers' come up,
4 If all this seems like yesterday,
5 If you think it's expensive,
6 If you should see furniture like this in a shop,
7 How can you meet the right person
8 If you should prefer to drive,

a think again.
b it would probably cost at least twice as much.
c you'll find a free parking space reserved for you.
d unless you're already meeting the right people?
e see what tomorrow could bring.
f it will be this: choose once but choose well.
g you will share in a guaranteed minimum of $1,000,000,000 in tax-free cash.
h it's usually a sign that he knows how to take care of it.

1.2 Can you guess what these extracts might be advertising – or what sort of person they are trying to attract?

Example: *I think extract number 1 might be advertising … / could be from an advert for … / is supposed to attract people who want …*

☆ 1.3 Think of ways to advertise the following products, using suitable conditional sentences. Work in groups to collect ideas.

jeans • toothpaste • mountain bike • mobile • deodorant • sportscar

2 Say it with *if*

Use sentences with *if* to express these ideas differently.

Example: Sorry I can't come with you to the cinema tonight, but I've got so much work to do!
→ *If I didn't have so much work to do, I'd come / I might come with you to the cinema tonight.*
→ *I'd come / I might come with you ... if I ...*

a I hope I can help you install that new e-mail programme. Maybe I'll still have time.
b I don't think I'm going to buy these jeans after all – look how expensive they are!
c I haven't got a present for Jackie. Why on earth didn't you tell me it was her birthday today?
d Maybe Dad won't like the pullover I've chosen for him. Oh well, I suppose he can always change it.
e I'd like to get some nice steaks for dinner on Sunday. Does your friend eat meat?
f Please stay at home tonight so I can show you the photos I took in Normandy.
g We didn't know the McLarens' address, so we weren't able to visit them while we were in Scotland.
h Never try cooking popcorn without a lid! Don't you know what happens?
i Now we can't go to that concert this evening – tickets are sold out! Why didn't we think of ringing up to book tickets earlier?
j I'm not good at baking. So I haven't made a cake for you, I'm afraid.

3 The 'ifs' of history

3.1 How different the results would have been! Think of historical events, and say what would, could or might have happened / be the case 'if' …

Example: *If the Romans hadn't conquered Britain, many names of places in Britain would be different today. / Hadrian's Wall wouldn't have been built. / …*

a If Harold had defeated the Normans in 1066, …
b If Columbus hadn't discovered America, …
c If the Great Armada hadn't been defeated in 1588, …
d If the American colonists had been represented in the English Parliament, …
e If all the Indian tribes had united against the white man, …
f If the economy of the Southern states of the USA had not depended on cotton, …

3.2 What if the causes of historical events had been different? Complete the sentences as logically as you can.

Example: *Henry VIII might not have broken with Rome if the Pope had agreed to his divorce.*

a Britain would not have been able to found so many colonies if …
b Slavery in the United States might have continued even longer if …
c The Americans might not have landed on the moon if …

☆ **3.3 Go on. Talk about other 'ifs' of history.**

4 If only she knew the boy's name

Jane Purdy, 15, lives in a small American town. More than anything, she wants to have a boyfriend – and to feel really grown-up and confident. One afternoon, while she is babysitting at the Nortons' house, a nice-looking boy comes into the kitchen to deliver meat for the dog. Jane likes him immediately – and wonders how she can get to know him. That evening, when Jane suggests getting a dog, or even having meat delivered for their cat, her parents are puzzled …

Mrs Purdy looked curiously at her daughter. "What's come over you tonight?" "Oh, nothing," said Jane, realizing that she had better be careful what she said, or her mother would start asking a lot of tiresome questions like who was the boy's family and a lot of things she couldn't answer until she got to know him. If only she knew the boy's name she could look him up in the telephone book and just happen to walk by his house, and he might just be outside washing the car or something. She would glance at him as if she had seen him someplace but couldn't quite remember where. And he would look up and say, "Why, hello. Aren't you the girl who was baby-sitting at the Nortons'?" And she would say … But she did not know his name and even if she did, he was probably so new in town that his family would not be listed in the telephone directory yet.

3 **tiresome** annoying, irritating

Or she could happen to walk by the Nortons' house about three o'clock on Friday afternoon when he might be delivering Cuthbert's food again. Jane thought this over and decided the plan had both advantages and disadvantages. She could easily go for a walk in the Nortons' neighbourhood without looking out of place. However, the truck would not arrive at exactly three o'clock and she could not very well walk up and down in front of the Nortons' as if she were picketing their house. The neighbours would begin to wonder what she was doing. Nevertheless, a leisurely stroll up their street next Friday afternoon could do no harm. He might happen to drive by and see her and think, "Why, there's that girl I spoke to at the Nortons'." He would stop the truck and say, "Hi, there. Going to Sandra's house? If you are I'll give you a lift." And she would say …

And then Jane had an even better idea. If she were baby-sitting with Sandra she would be sure to see him. She turned this over in her mind. Could she stand another afternoon of Sandra – another afternoon of trying to manoeuvre her into doing what she was supposed to do when Sandra was so clever at outwitting sitters? To see that boy again, yes. It would not be easy but she could do it. The boy would arrive with Cuthbert's food and say, "Hi! I didn't expect to see you here again," and of course he would look as if he were glad she was there again. And she would laugh and say …

From *Fifteen* by Beverly Cleary

---

12 **Cuthbert** the Nortons' dog • 15 **to picket** to guard, to watch in order to prevent people from going in or out • 16 **a leisurely stroll** ['leʒəlɪ] an unhurried walk • 23 **to outwit** to defeat sb or to gain an advantage over sb by behaving in a clever or tricky way

4.1 Use conditional sentences to say what would / could / might happen or be the case …

a if Jane wasn't very careful what she said (3-5),
b if she knew the boy's name (5-6),
c if she just walked past his house (6-9),
d if the boy's family was new in town (9-10),
e if she went for a walk in the Nortons' neighbourhood (11-16),
f if he saw her there (17-19),
g if she spent another afternoon looking after Sandra (20-25).

4.2 Look at the progressive forms in lines 12 and 20. Try to explain why they are used.

4.3 Try to imagine Jane's thoughts. How might she finish these sentences?

a "I could easily go for a walk in the Nortons' neighbourhood if …"
b "I wouldn't mind babysitting with Sandra too much if …"
c "It would be fantastic if …"

5 Britain's new high-speed rail network

5.1 Explain in English what the plan is, and when the project is expected to be finished. What are the main arguments for and against the plan?
These words will help you:

route (1) • high-speed train (1) • to reduce / to cut journey times (3-4) • considerably (3) • to pull down / to demolish (7) • track (7) • viaduct (7) • to spoil an area of outstanding natural beauty (8) • high-definition video conferencing unit (10) • to equip with (10) • business travel (11) • superfluous (11) • supporters (12) • railway nation (12) • (it's) a disgrace (13) • to keep pace with (14)

Wenn alles nach Plan läuft, wird eine neue Strecke für Hochgeschwindigkeitszüge zwischen London und Birmingham gebaut werden. Diese Linie wird die erste Phase eines Netzwerks sein, das die Reisezeiten zwischen der Hauptstadt und den größten Städten Großbritanniens wesentlich verkürzen soll. Es wird aber alles eine Weile dauern: falls bis 2017 tatsächlich mit dem Bau der Birmingham-Linie begonnen werden sollte, fahren frühestens 2026 die ersten Züge!

Viele kritisieren den Plan. Wenn er Wirklichkeit würde, müssten in London und Birmingham Hunderte von Häusern abgerissen werden. Neue Schienen, Tunnels und Viadukte müssten durch die Chiltern Hills gebaut werden und würden eine einzigartige Naturlandschaft zerstören. Außerdem finden viele das Projekt zu teuer – und unnötig. Wenn man das gleiche Geld ausgäbe, um alle britischen Firmen mit hochmodernen Videokonferenzmöglichkeiten auszustatten, wären viele Geschäftsreisen überflüssig.

Die Befürworter aber erinnern daran, dass Großbritannien das erste Eisenbahn-Land der Erde war, und sie sagen, es wäre eine Schande, wenn Großbritannien im 21. Jahrhundert mit anderen europäischen Ländern nicht Schritt hielte. Was wäre passiert, wenn man auf die Kritiker, die gegen den Bau der ersten Eisenbahn im 19. Jahrhundert waren, gehört hätte?

5.2 Look at the cartoon. Rephrase the sign under the window, using a conditional sentence.

8 Indirect Speech

CHECK-UP

1 An interview

First read the text, then complete the sentences below.

Sue wants to work for a few weeks during the summer holidays. She sees an advert in the local paper for a temporary job at a care home, and decides to apply for it. Mrs Beale, who is in charge of the home, invites her to come for an interview.

MRS BEALE Sit down, Sue. Right. Before I can promise you the job, I'd like to ask you one or two questions. – Why did you apply for this kind of work?
SUE Well, firstly, I like the idea of helping other people. And I think I'd enjoy the work.
MRS BEALE Have you ever worked with elderly people before?
SUE No, I haven't. But I don't think I'll have any problems.
MRS BEALE Where do you live? Will you be able to start work at seven-thirty most mornings? That's when the night nurse goes off duty.
SUE I'll easily be able to manage it by then. I live quite near.
MRS BEALE Fine. – Can you cook?
SUE Er … well! I often help to get meals ready at home, but I haven't often cooked a whole meal by myself.
MRS BEALE Don't worry. You won't have to cook whole meals without help. But I do need someone with a bit of experience in the kitchen. You would also have to do jobs like vacuum-cleaning, washing, setting tables and so on.
SUE I see. – When will you be able to tell me whether I can have the job, Mrs Beale?
MRS BEALE Well, a young man's coming to see me in the afternoon, so naturally I can't make a decision until I've talked to him, too. Call me tomorrow morning and I'll let you know then.

That evening, Sue talks to her friend Jessica about the interview.
"What happened?" Jessica asks.
"Well, Mrs Beale told me to ___, and then she asked me why ___, and so I told her ___ and ___. Then she asked ___, and of course I said ___, but that ___. She also wanted to know ___, and asked ___. I told her ___ as ___. Then she asked me ___, so I said ___, but that ___. She told me ___ about that, and explained that ___, but that ___. She also told me ___."
"When will you know if you've got the job?" Jessica asks.
"Well, Mrs Beale said ___, so ___. She told me ___ to find out."

---

temporary opposite of permanent • **care home** old people's home • 4 **elderly** old or getting old (of people)

BASIC RULES AND EXERCISES

Direct speech	Indirect speech (introductory verb in the **past**)
"I **like** your new jacket." "I'**m looking** for a pair of warm boots for the winter."	She said that she **liked** my new jacket. He said he **was looking** for a pair of warm boots for the winter.
present tense ⟶	past tense
"Dad **looked** at hundreds of pullovers, but he **didn't buy** one."	She told me that her father **had looked** at hundreds of pullovers, but that **he hadn't bought** one.
past tense ⟶	past perfect
"You'**ve spent** enough on clothes for one day!"	I told her she **had spent** enough on clothes for one day.
present perfect ⟶	past perfect
"The shops **will be** closed on Monday."	He told us the shops **would be** closed on Monday.
future ⟶	conditional
"**Where**'s the men's department, please?" "Do you sell umbrellas?"	I asked the assistant **where** the men's department was. I asked them **whether/if** they sold umbrellas.
Questions Repeat the 'question word' (*where*, *when*, etc.). If there is no question word use *whether* or *if*.	
"**Try** on the trousers you like best. **Don't buy** them if they're too tight."	She told me **to try** on the trousers I liked best. She advised me **not to buy** them if they were too tight.
Imperatives Use the infinitive with *to/not to*.	

"Saturday morning **is** the worst time for shopping."	I reminded her that Saturday morning **is/was** the worst time for shopping.
If the speaker states a fact that does not change (or is generally accepted as true), the tense in indirect speech need not necessarily be changed.	
"I **hadn't thought** of that." "I **would prefer** to go to town on Monday."	She said she **hadn't thought** of that. I told her I **would prefer** to go to town on Monday.
Past perfect and conditional remain unchanged in indirect speech.	

"I'll **pick** you up at six thirty."
▸ Ben said he'll **pick** us up at six thirty.

"We **saw** John and Mary at the cinema."
▸ Lucy said they **saw** John and Mary at the cinema.

Don't be surprised if you hear – or read – examples like these. In fact, English-speaking people tend to use the 'backshift of tenses' less and less. However, when you write your own texts, it is safer – and more correct – to keep to the rules that you have learnt.

1 Waiting

Mrs Foster was always terribly afraid of missing a train or a plane. Her fear was made worse by her husband, who had a habit of keeping her waiting unnecessarily. Mrs Foster sometimes wondered if he did this intentionally. On the day of her long-awaited journey to Paris to visit her daughter and grandchildren, her flight from New York was put off because of fog, and was finally arranged for eleven o'clock the next day. A car was ordered for nine o'clock, to take Mrs Foster to the airport and to drop Mr Foster at his club on the way …

Next morning, Mrs Foster was up early, and by eight-thirty she was ready to leave.
Shortly after nine, her husband appeared. "Did you make any coffee?" he asked.
"No, dear. I thought you'd get a nice breakfast at the club. The car is here. I'm all ready to go."
"Your luggage?"
"It's at the airport."
"Ah yes," he said. "Of course. And if you're going to take me to the club first, I suppose we'd better get going soon, hadn't we?"
"Yes!" she cried. "Oh, yes – please!"
"I'm just going to get a few cigars. I'll be right with you. You get in the car."
She turned and went out to where the chauffeur was standing, and he opened the car door for her.
"What time is it?" she asked.
"About nine-fifteen."
Mr Foster came out five minutes later. As on the day before, he paused to examine the sky. The weather was still not quite clear, but there was a wisp of sun coming through the mist.
"Perhaps you'll be lucky this time," he said as he settled himself beside her in the car.
"Hurry, please," she said to the chauffeur. "Please get going. I'm late." The man went back to his seat behind the wheel and started the engine.
"Just a moment!" Mr Foster said suddenly. "Hold it a moment, chauffeur, will you?"
"What is it, dear?" She saw him searching the pockets of his overcoat.
"I had a little present I wanted you to take to Ellen," he said. "Now, where on earth is it? I'm sure I had it in my hand as I came down."
"I never saw you carrying anything. What sort of present?"
"A little box wrapped up in white paper. I forgot to give it to you yesterday. I don't want to forget it today."
"A little box!" Mrs Foster cried. "I never saw any little box!" She began hunting frantically in the back of the car.

14 **a wisp of sun** a little sunshine • 14 **mist** fog • 23 **to wrap up** to pack (in paper) • 25 **frantic** excited (with worry)

Her husband continued searching through the pockets of his coat. "Confound it," he said. "I must've left it in my bedroom. I won't be a moment."

"Oh, please!" she cried. "We haven't got time. Please leave it! You can mail it."

"Stay here!" he commanded. "I'm going to get it."

"Be quick, dear! Oh, please be quick!"

She sat still, waiting and waiting.

"Chauffeur, what time is it?"

"I make it nearly nine-thirty."

"Can we get to the airport in an hour?"

"Just about."

At this point, Mrs Foster suddenly spotted a corner of something white wedged down in the crack of the seat on the side where her husband had been sitting. She reached over and pulled out a small paper-wrapped box, and at the same time she couldn't help noticing that it was wedged down firm and deep, as though with the help of a pushing hand …

From *The Way Up to Heaven* by Roald Dahl

---

27 **Confound it** Damn it • 37 **to spot** to notice • 37 **to wedge** to squeeze or push tightly • 37 **crack** *Ritze* • 39 **she couldn't help noticing** it was impossible for her not to notice

Retell what happened, using indirect speech. You need not always give a word-for-word report.

When Mrs Foster's husband came downstairs, he asked her ___ (2), but she explained that ___. She told him that ___ and that ___ (3). He wanted to know ___ (4), and she reminded him that ___ (5). Just when they seemed ready to leave, he told her that ___ (9). So he went upstairs again, telling her that ___ and instructing her ___ (9).

By the time Mr Foster reappeared, it was 9.20. When he had got in the car, she told the chauffeur ___ (16), because ___ (16). But no sooner had the man started the engine than Mr Foster ordered him ___ (18). Mrs Foster wanted to know ___ (19), and he explained that ___ (20). He felt sure that ___ (21). His wife asked him ___ (22), and he explained to her ___, which ___ (23). After searching through his pockets, Mr Foster announced that he ___ probably ___ (27-28). He wanted to go and look for it, but his wife begged him ___, reminding him that ___ (29). He took no notice of her, however, and said ___ (30). By this time, it was almost 9.30, and Mrs Foster was wondering ___ (35). While her husband was in the house, Mrs Foster suddenly noticed the box in the crack of the car seat. When she saw it wedged down so deep, she wondered ___ (39-40).

2 Disappointments and misunderstandings

Things don't always turn out as we expect, do they? Sometimes other people disappoint us – or we misunderstand what they meant in the first place, or …
Complete these pieces of dialogue with your own ideas. Use indirect speech.

"I won't be able to get to your party till ten at the earliest." → "But you said you would come at eight-thirty."
"Donna's been dropped from the volleyball team." → "But I thought she was their best player!"

a "I've decided to give Betsy a box of chocolates for her birthday." → "But you told me …"
b "Your photos aren't ready yet, unfortunately." → "But when I was here on Friday …"
c "Dr Singh is very busy this morning. Please take a seat in the waiting-room." → "But …"
d "Have you heard? Ted has failed all his A-levels." → "That's strange …"
e "I'm going to stay with my aunt in Melbourne." → "Really? You never told me …"
f "John's getting married next Saturday." → "What! I never even knew …"
g "My Dad's in the USA on business. He's got a big meeting in Toronto." → "Uh? I thought …"

3 Unusual criminals

A Some unusual evidence came to light at the trial of Terry Greenwood, a repentant burglar. He admitted in court that he had written to his victims after the break-ins and had advised them how to improve their security. Letters to ten different householders were shown to the judge, in which Terry had apologized for stealing from them. In the letters he gave advice about not leaving keys in obvious places in future, and telling his victims to install window locks and better alarm systems. He assured them that a good burglar alarm would keep them safe, and asked them to forgive him for what he had done to them.

B An unconventional armed robber ran into a small shop and ordered the shopkeeper to hand over the money from the till, threatening to shoot him if he did not do so. The shopkeeper, however, who was very observant, asked the man where his gun was. The robber had to admit that he didn't actually have a gun, but if there was any more trouble he would go out, get one and come back. Warning the shopkeeper not to call the police because he was a violent man, he then left the shop and was never seen again.

Text B adapted from *The Return of Heroic Failures* by Stephen Pile

---

1 **evidence** *Beweismaterial* • 1 **trial** *Gerichtsverfahren* • 1 **repentant** *reuig* • 9 **till** *Ladenkasse*

Text A:

3.1 What exactly did Terry Greenwood admit in court? Use direct speech.

3.2 Imagine one of Terry's letters being read out to the judge. What exactly would the letter say?

Text B:

3.3 Reconstruct the dialogue between the 'armed robber' and the shopkeeper. Add extra details where it seems appropriate.

4 Remember how you once told me . . .

4.1 **Look at the cartoon. Why does Calvin's mood change so suddenly?**

4.2 **Make up a dialogue between Calvin and his dad that might have taken place a few months earlier. Start like this:**

DAD How's your schoolwork going, Calvin? Is your teacher pleased with you?
CALVIN I'm not sure, Dad. I guess if she starts giving us grades, mine won't be that great.
DAD Why's that, Calvin?

4.3 **Imagine what Calvin might say to his dad now. "That's not fair! Remember how you once asked me how my schoolwork . . .? Go on, using the dialogue you have written as a basis.**

5 Missing

Adverbials of time (e.g. *this morning, today, next week*) and place (e.g. *here*) sometimes have to be changed in indirect speech. This is only necessary when the report is made at a time or place at which use of the original adverbials would not apply.

Tom (Cornwall, July 26th): "We're having a lot of rain **down here this week**."
▸ *Mother (Leeds, to friend, August 12th):* "When Tom phoned us from their holiday cottage in Cornwall, he said they were having a lot of rain **down there that week**."

Mr and Mrs Bassett of Leeds gave the following statement to the police on August 3rd:
"Everything seemed quite normal this morning. Mark, our 15-year-old son, went out today, as he often does on Saturdays. He wanted to go to a football match, and we expected him back for tea this afternoon. But he hasn't come back. We didn't want to call the police unnecessarily, but when he still hadn't appeared by nine o'clock tonight, we decided to ring up and report him missing."

At the beginning of November, Mrs Bassett was interviewed by a local newspaper reporter: "Tomorrow it will be three months since Mark went missing. We have no idea what has happened to him. It was Mark's birthday last week. I bought him a present, as usual, hoping he would come home, but he still isn't here. We're going to talk to the police again next week, but they've discovered nothing up to now. It's the uncertainty that's so difficult to bear. One day I think to myself, 'Perhaps tomorrow at this time he'll come walking in the door and everything will be all right.' And another day I wonder if we'll ever see him again."

The following January, there was an article in the paper about young people missing from home: Each year, about 100,000 under-16s in Britain go missing from their homes. Many of them return to their families of their own accord, others are found by the police; a few are found dead. But a large number of these missing youngsters disappear altogether. The following example is just one of many. In August last year, Mr and Mrs Bassett of Leeds reported the disappearance of their son Mark. They told police that everything had seemed quite normal that morning ...

15 **of one's own accord** without being asked or told

Go on with the report, including the November interview with Mrs Bassett.

6 Big cats on the moors

Translate the text. These words and expressions will help you:

big cat (1) • remote area (1) • to sight (2) • lion tamer (3) • on the moors (4) • to release [s] (4) • spokeswoman (8) • RSPCA (Royal Society for the Prevention of Cruelty to Animals) (8) • indigenous [ɪn'dɪdʒɪnəs] (9) • species ['spiːʃiːs] (9) • to be at risk (10) • plausible (12) • to breed in the wild (13)

Schon seit Jahren gibt es immer wieder Berichte über Raubkatzen, die in abgelegenen Gegenden Großbritanniens gesichtet worden sind. Alles nur Märchen? Oder kann so etwas möglich sein? Leslie Maiden, 63, der früher Löwenbändiger war, sagte, er habe vor mehr als 20 Jahren auf dem Hochmoor in Derbyshire zwei Raubkatzen freigelassen. Er sagte, die Tiere seien ihm von Leuten gegeben worden, die sie wegen neuer strengerer Gesetze nicht länger halten konnten. Er betonte, es sei damals noch nicht illegal gewesen, solche Tiere freizulassen. Er selbst habe mehrere Leute gekannt, die ihre ‚Haustiere' so losgeworden seien.
Eine Sprecherin des britischen Tierschutzvereins sagte, es sei aber jetzt illegal, Tiere in Großbritannien freizulassen, die nicht einheimisch sind. Solche Arten würden für andere Tiere eine Gefahr darstellen, oder könnten selbst gefährdet sein.
Mike Thomas, der Direktor des Newquay Zoo, sagte, solche Berichte über freigelassene Tiere seien eine glaubwürdige Erklärung für die vielen Fälle, in denen Raubkatzen heute gesichtet werden. Er erläuterte, es sei gut möglich, dass die Tiere sich damals in freier Wildbahn fortgepflanzt hätten.

Based on an article in *The Times*

ADVANCED RULES AND EXERCISES

Reporting in summarized form

Roger talking to Mark on the phone: Hello, Mark. Roger here. Look, I know this is a bit sudden, but I was wondering if you and Ann would like to come to Osmotherley and spend the weekend with us at the cottage? The weather forecast sounds quite promising, so it should be ideal for walking on the moors.	*Mark later, talking to Ann:* Roger rang up this morning and invited us to spend the weekend with them at Osmotherley. He said they were planning to do some walking on the moors.

In most situations, it is natural **not** to give a word-for-word report of what has been said. Often it is enough to give a **summary** of the most important points.

1 Mr Van Huyten makes an offer

Vic Brown is twenty. He works as a draughtsman for a big engineering works in the North of England. On Saturdays he earns a little extra money working in Mr Van Huyten's music shop, a job he enjoys. One day Mr Van Huyten talks to him …

"How do you like your work, Victor?" he asks me all of a sudden, and I give a shrug.

"I liked it well enough for the first two or three years," I tell him, "but now, just lately … I've been a bit unsettled, as you might say. I want something different altogether. I feel I want to meet different people …"

"You like it in the shop on Saturdays?"

"I enjoy it. It's grand."

"Have you ever considered doing something like that full time?"

I'm a bit embarrassed at this. "Well, to tell you the truth, Mr Van Huyten, I don't think the money's there."

He nods. "I agree. The money isn't very good for the ordinary shop assistant. One must have er … an interest in the business for it to be worthwhile."

He sits back in his chair. "I'm an old man, Victor," he says. "I have a sound business which looks as though it will continue to prosper. I'm an old man," he says again, "and I have no living relatives." He stops for a minute. "Victor, you're still a very young man … But I will say in all honesty that I'm very fond of you and have every faith in your character and ability. You've become rapidly familiar with the business even though you spend only one day a week with us …"

draughtsman ['drɑːftsmən] technischer Zeichner • 2 **to give a shrug** to move one's shoulders up (as a sign of indecision, etc.) • 15 **sound** solid, financially safe • 15 **to prosper** to be a success

I'm wondering what he's driving at. Is he trying to tell me he wants to leave me the shop? I begin to feel excited, and a bit scared at the same time.

"The immediate problem, Victor, is that I'm going to be compelled to take on a full-time assistant in the shop. I want someone whom I can like and trust, someone to whom eventually I can hand over the day-to-day running of the business."

"What you're saying, Mr Van Huyten, is that you'd like me to come and work full-time in the shop."

He nods again. "Correct. Now assuming the money was, shall we say comparable, and there were prospects of a future when you wouldn't be just a shop assistant in a dead-end job, what would you say then?"

"I don't know, Mr Van Huyten." I think about it for a minute. "I rather fancy the idea ... Thanks very much for your offer, Mr Van Huyten, and I'd like to think it over, please."

"Well done," he says. "A very reasonable answer. The last thing I wanted was for you to jump to a decision without considering every side of the matter."

"I'll have to talk it over at home, you see."

"Of course, of course. Naturally."

From *A Kind of Loving* by Stan Barstow

---

24 **to be compelled** to be forced • 26 **eventually** in the end • 31 **prospects** good chances for future success • 34 **to fancy** to feel keen on, to like

Think out what Vic might say to his parents that evening. Before you start his summary of the conversation, pick out the most important points, from Vic's point of view.

The summary might start like this:

"I was talking to Mr Van Huyten today, and he suddenly asked me about my work – you know, whether I enjoyed it. Well, I had to admit that I was feeling a bit unsettled ..."

2 The anonymous letter

Inner monologue

Many authors use '**inner monologue**' as a way of showing their characters' unspoken thoughts and feelings. For this style of writing, the '**backshift' of tenses** is used, as in indirect speech; but mostly, the introductory verb is left out and word order is the same as in direct speech.

When Ed gets home, his wife Greta shows him an anonymous letter, both unpleasant and threatening, which has come while he was at work. It is the third he has received …
All have been signed 'Anon'.

As he let the water rinse away the soap, he thought, I'm washing my hands of the subway and also of that damned letter. Who was writing the letters? Someone who lived in his neighbourhood, probably. Ed two weeks ago had asked George, one of the doormen downstairs, if any stranger had asked for his name, if he'd seen anyone odd hanging around, male or female, and George had said no. Ed was sure George had asked the other doormen the same question. Was it someone in his office? Inconceivable, Ed thought. Yet one never knew, did one? A poison-pen letter-writer didn't necessarily stare at you, wouldn't be obviously an enemy. On the other hand, Anon's letters seemed genuinely dim-witted, not like anyone at C. & D., even the clean-up men. The letters annoyed Ed, but they frightened Greta, and Ed didn't want to show even his annoyance too much, lest it augment her fear. And perhaps he was a little afraid, too. Someone had singled him out to write to. Or was he the only recipient? Were there other people in his neighbourhood just as annoyed as he was?

From *A Dog's Ransom* by Patricia Highsmith

6 **inconceivable** impossible to imagine • 8 **dim-witted** stupid, unintelligent • 9 **lest it happen** for fear that it might happen • 9 **to augment** to make greater • 11 **recipient** person who receives sth (e.g. a letter)

2.1 **Pick out all examples of direct speech, indirect speech and inner monologue in the text.**

2.2 **Put the inner monologue into direct speech, then into indirect speech, using suitable introductory verbs (e.g. *think/wonder/suppose/realize*). Explain the differences.**

☆ **2.3** **Try to describe the stylistic effect of inner monologue in this text. What impression does it make on you?**

9 The Passive Voice

"Ever since we were burgled he's become much more security conscious."

CHECK-UP

1 Police kicked and beaten in quiet area of Canterbury

Add the passive forms (in the correct tense) to this newspaper article.

Two policemen ____ as they tried to break up a fight in a quiet area of Canterbury in the early hours of Sunday. The trouble ____ by two rival gangs. Within seconds the peace and quiet of Surrey Road ____ by the noise of breaking glass and shouting. Police officers Sean Murphy and Bob Wilcox arrived at the scene only after considerable damage ____. When they tried to make arrests, they ____ and ____. Hospital treatment ____, however, and they were able to remain on duty.
They ____ by more police officers who arrived before any further damage ____. So far, seven people ____. They ____ in court next month. Further investigations ____ still ____, and witnesses ____ to pass on any information that might help the police.

attack
start
shatter

do
beat · kick · not require

help · do
arrest · hear
carry out · ask

2 The by-pass

Change the active structures (in *italics*) into the passive.
Decide where a 'by-agent' is necessary.

Last night the villagers of Botesdale in Suffolk met to protest against the Department of Transport's decision to postpone the building of the A143 by-pass between Wattisfield and Wortham. *The county council had passed the plan for the new road* two years ago. The construction of the by-pass was to begin next year, but now *the Department of Transport has informed the council* that it *cannot finance the project* for at least five years.
"*We need the by-pass now,*" said a speaker at the meeting. *"Enormous numbers of cars use the existing road through the village* on their way to the East Coast. *The constant noise of traffic badly affects people living on Botesdale High Street.* Over the past six years *lorries driving at high speed have killed or seriously injured nine people. Inhabitants no longer consider Botesdale a safe place for children,* who are especially at risk; not surprisingly, *house-owners are selling property here at an alarming rate. We must save our village community* before it is too late."
At the end of the meeting, *the villagers decided on a course of action. They asked people to sign a petition,* which *they will send to the Department of Transport* before the end of the month.

---

by-pass a road leading traffic round a town or village • 2 **to postpone** to put off until a later time • 10 **property** houses/land owned by sb • 11 **rate** *here*: speed

BASIC RULES AND EXERCISES

How the passive is used

The question of the origin of the universe **is** often **discussed.**	▸ The passive is preferred when the 'doer' is obvious, unimportant, or unknown.
Aristotle's idea of the earth as the centre of the universe **was** first **doubted** *by Copernicus* in 1514.	▸ The '*by*-agent' is used if it is important to say by whom (or by what) something is done.
At the London 'Planetarium', *visitors* **are shown** a vivid picture of how stars and planets are born – and die. Thanks to modern telescopes, fantastic new opportunities **have been given** *to scientists studying outer space.*	▸ Certain verbs with two objects (e.g. *give, show*) are often used with a 'personal' subject in the passive. The alternative construction with *to* is only used if the indirect object is emphasized, or especially long.
Signs of life on other planets **have** long **been searched for** with the help of radio telescopes.	▸ Prepositions closely linked to verbs (e.g. *search for, look after, break into*) remain in the same position in the passive.
More research will need **to be done** before a manned mission to Mars can **be attempted.**	▸ The passive also has an infinitive form (with or without *to*).
All the time, new discoveries about the nature of the universe **are being made.**	▸ Progressive forms of the passive can be used in the present and past.

"Is that a science fiction story you're reading?"
"Yes, it's about a spaceship that **gets attacked** by aliens."

The passive with *get* is often used in spoken English to express that an event is unintended or unexpected.

"Doesn't it make you sick? Our baggage has been sent to Jupiter!"

1 Hallowe'en is being abused

Children throughout Britain have been asked not to play 'trick or treat?' pranks on old people on Hallowe'en. In recent years an increasing number of complaints have been made by older people about children and teenagers who abuse this traditional American custom. Now police warn that action will have to be taken against any young people who make threats if they are not given the money they demand. Last night on BBC TV a police spokesman for the West Yorkshire Constabulary, Inspector George Stevens, said: "There have been incidents in the past in which flower-pots were kicked over or windows smashed. Sometimes fireworks even get thrown through letterboxes. We don't think old people should have to put up with behaviour like that." Inspector Stevens added that especially old people living alone could get badly shaken when doorbells were rung late at night – or if they opened their doors in the evening and were surprised by a group of youngsters wearing strange masks. "The custom has been misunderstood by a lot of youngsters," commented Inspector Stevens. "Old people's helplessness is being taken unfair advantage of."

to abuse to use in the wrong way • 1 **prank** foolish trick • 5 **to demand** to ask for sth you expect to get

1.1 Find examples of the use of the passive as described in the Basic Rules.

1.2 Use the passive to describe

a what complaints the police have received;
b what kind of incidents there have been;
c what will happen if there is more trouble.

1.3 Use passive forms (choosing from the given verbs) to complete what these people said about Hallowe'en when they were interviewed by a reporter for BBC television.

deal with • hear of • look after • make too much of • pay for • take advantage of

a "Incidents of this kind ___ never ___ when I was a teenager."
b "I don't think hooliganism ___ strictly enough – by parents or by the police."
c "Most of these pranks are harmless. They shouldn't ___."
d "Windows even got broken in our road last year. Damage of this kind must ___."
e "It's no joke when old people ___ like this."
f "This sort of thing wouldn't happen if kids ___ properly. Parents these days don't give them enough of their time."

1.4 Find the two examples of the *get* passive in the text. Remembering that this form is often used to describe an unintended or unexpected event, complete the sentences with these suggestions.

get run over • get stung • get stolen • get thrown away • get broken

a Where's yesterday's paper? – No idea! It must have ___.
b Don't leave your bike unlocked. It might easily ___.
c Are there only three wine glasses? – I'm afraid so. All the others ___.
d Anna goes crazy if she sees a wasp! She always thinks ___.
e Sally, our dog, had a lucky escape yesterday. She nearly ___ by a bus.

2 The new Noah

In 'The new Noah', Gerald Durrell describes his experiences as an animal collector in many parts of the world, and the unusual situations in which he found himself during his travels.

Before starting out on a collecting trip you have to know what wild animals are wanted by the zoos; then you choose those areas in which not only the specimens required are to be found, but other rare creatures as well. Zoologists and biologists, generally, have not the time or the money to travel to these distant corners of the earth to find out about wild life on the spot. Therefore, the animals have to be caught and brought back to them, so that they can be studied more conveniently in the zoo. Now the larger and commoner creatures from most parts of the world are well represented in nearly all zoological collections, and quite a lot is known about them. So it was the smaller and rarer beasts, about which we know so little, that I wanted to collect.

From many points of view it is sometimes the small animals in a country that influence man more than the large ones. At home, for instance, the brown rat does more damage every year than any of the larger creatures. It was for this reason that I concentrated during my collecting trips on the smaller forms of life. For my first expedition I chose the Cameroons, a small, almost forgotten corner of Africa. Here, in the gigantic rain forests, the animals live their lives as they have done for thousands of years.

It is of great value to get to know and study these wild creatures before they are influenced by civilisation, for wild creatures can be affected just as much by change as people. One of the results of cutting down forests, building towns, damming rivers, and driving roads through jungle, is an interference with their way of life, and they have either to adapt themselves to the new conditions or die out.

I landed at the little port of Victoria. A great many things had to be done before I could start on the actual work of collecting. There were Africans to engage as cooks or house-boys, various stores to buy and a great many other things as well. Also the necessary permits to hunt and capture the animals I was after had to be obtained, for all the animal life in the Cameroons is strictly protected and, unless you obtain Government permission, you are not allowed to capture or kill any animals and birds. Eventually, when all this had been done, a lorry was hired and the food and equipment piled into it, and I set off.

From *The new Noah* by Gerald Durrell

---

2 **specimen** ['spesɪmən] a single animal or plant which is an example of a particular kind • 5 **conveniently** *here*: easily • 18 **interference** [ˌ--'--] unwanted attempt to influence others' affairs • 23 **to obtain** to get • 24 **to capture** to take as a prisoner, to catch

2.1 Use the passive wherever possible in your answers to the following questions:

a What first has to be done before rare animals can be studied in zoos? (1-6)
b Why did Durrell specialize in collecting smaller animals? (6-12)
c Why were the Cameroons chosen for his first expedition? (12-14)
d Why are so many wild animals in danger of dying out? (15-19)
e What preparations had to be made before Durrell could set off into the interior of the Cameroons? (20-26)

2.2 Put these sentences into the passive:

a We know so little about the smaller and rarer beasts.
b Small animals sometimes influence man more than larger ones.
c The brown rat does more damage every year than any of the larger creatures.

2.3 What do you think? Should animals be kept in captivity? Use some of the verbs below – in the passive – to help express your opinion.

see✓ • look after • spend (money) • be born • improve • lock up • feed • allow • treat • keep (in natural/unnatural surroundings) • transport • crowd (in small cages) • give • show • leave

Example: *Zoos can be very educational. All sorts of interesting animals, which most people would normally never meet, can be seen in zoos.*

3 Having it done

"Has your house been repainted?" – "Yes, we **had it repainted** last year. We **had it done** by Carter's."

- A passive idea can sometimes be expressed by a construction with *have* + past participle.
  This is used when a person causes an action to be done by someone else.
  The '*have*-passive' can also be used with a '*by*-agent'.

Complete these mini-dialogues, using suitable forms of the '*have*-passive'.

a "Your hair's getting a bit long." – "Yes, I really ought ____."
b "That big birch tree in front of the window makes this room very dark." – "Why don't you ____?"
c "There's something wrong with my MP3 player." – "Well, don't throw it away! Perhaps you ____."
d "This is a nice photo of Sally! Who took it?" – "We ____ by ____."
e "Don't look so worried – you're only going to the dentist's!" – "I've got to ____."
f "Did you put up the wallpaper yourselves?" – "Yes, we did. It would have cost the earth if we ____ professionally."

ADVANCED RULES AND EXERCISES (I)

Other forms of the passive	
There are also passive forms of	
▸ the *ing*-form (gerund and present participle)	**making → being made**
▸ the perfect *ing*-form	**having made → having been made**
▸ the perfect infinitive	**(to) have made → (to) have been made**

1 In and out of hospital

Look at the passive structures in the following sentences. Then translate the sentences into German.

a Medical students sometimes feel faint when they watch an operation being done for the first time.
b These instruments ought to have been sterilized, nurse.
c Many people dislike being prescribed strong drugs, as they are afraid of being affected by unpleasant side-effects.
d The cut on John's knee has healed well in spite of not having been stitched.
e Having been given a local anaesthetic, the patient was able to carry on a conversation with the doctor while being operated on.
f The girl being wheeled into the operating theatre just now was involved in a terrible road accident.

2 Killed by a crocodile?

Use the right passive forms to complete the text.

Amy, an 18-year-old British student whose body ___ from a lake in Kenya	recover
by divers yesterday, may ___ by a crocodile.	attack
She was paddling in Lake Chala with two friends when she disappeared. One	
of them says she saw Amy ___ under the water, but the other girl is not sure.	drag
After ___ by locals that the lake was safe, the three girls had decided to go	tell
swimming. But later a Kenyan police spokesman said crocodiles ___ to ___	know · see
in the lake on several occasions. The body, which ___ now ___ as Amy's,	confirm
apparently showed signs of ___ by a crocodile. But it still remains ___	attack · establish
whether this was before or after she died.	
Amy was doing a year's voluntary work in Kenya after school, ___ a place	offer
to study geography at Edinburgh University next year. Other young Britons	
planning to go out to Africa ___ that there is no reason at all for ___ working	tell · put off
in Kenya. But the two friends who were with Amy at the lake and who ___	treat
now ___ for shock, ___ ___ from the area.	expect · remove
The Nile crocodile, which ___ to reach a length of up to six metres and	know
to weigh over a tonne, can ___ in many watery parts of Africa.	find

Based on articles in *The Weekly Telegraph* and *Associated Newspapers*

ADVANCED RULES AND EXERCISES (II)

Passive forms in English – active in German

▸ The dinosaurs **are said to have died out** when a huge meteorite crashed into the earth.	▸ *Man sagt, die Dinosaurier seien ausgestorben …*
▸ In the days of Columbus, the earth **was thought to be** flat.	▸ *… dachte man, dass die Erde flach sei.*
▸ **It remains to be seen** how much world population will grow this century.	▸ *Es bleibt abzuwarten, …*

Passive constructions are sometimes used in English where you would find active constructions in German – especially with *man*.
Common phrases: be said to / be supposed to / be thought to / is to be expected / remains to be seen

3 The sense of smell

Translate into English.

a Man sagt, dass der Geruchssinn Erinnerungen schneller heraufbeschwört als unsere anderen Sinne. → to evoke
b Man nimmt an, dass die meisten Menschen etwa 4.000 Gerüche unterscheiden können. → to differentiate between
c Leute mit besonders empfindlichen Nasen sollen sogar 10.000 verschiedene Düfte erkennen können! → sensitive
d Frauen sind vermutlich geruchsempfindlicher als Männer. → sensitive to smell
e Man weiß, dass ein Baby im Alter von einem Monat seine Mutter an ihrem Geruch identifizieren kann. → to identify sb by sth
f Vor kurzem hat man auch entdeckt, dass Mütter in der Lage sind, die T-Shirts ihrer Kinder am Geruch zu erkennen. → to recognize sth by sth
g Bis zum 19. Jahrhundert hat man Körpergeruch nicht als unangenehm empfunden. Ob er je wieder in Mode kommt, bleibt aber abzuwarten. → body odour · to consider
h In der heutigen Zeit von Deos und Parfüms ist eine solche Entwicklung aber kaum zu erwarten! → in these days of deodorants and perfumes

10 Modal Auxiliaries

CHECK-UP

1 Summer time

For part A, choose between *can, can't, will, won't, may* and *may not*.
For part B, choose between *must, may, mustn't* and *needn't*.

A "Let's go down to the beach now. It ___ be so sunny later, you never know."
"OK. Wait – I ___ find my sunscreen."
"You ___ use mine. – Hey, whose are those flippers over there?"
"John's. But we ___ take them. He ___ let *anyone* borrow his things."
"Hmm. This snorkel here ___ be his, too, I suppose?"
"Yes. Oh come on! Swimming ___ be just as much fun *without* all this equipment."
"OK. You ___ be right."

B "How much further do you plan to go? We ___ have walked miles along this beach by now!"
"All right. We ___ go any further. Let's put our things down and go in the water here."
"Have you seen that sign? 'No swimming beyond this point.' We ___ swim over there, then."
"I wonder why. It ___ be because of the river mouth. There ___ be some reason."
"I'll have a swim later. ___ I borrow your camera to take a photo of those birds?"
"OK, but you ___ wade out to those rocks with it! I know what you're like."
"You ___ worry. I won't go near the water – even if you're drowning!"

---

3 **flippers** Schwimmflossen

2 Life in the days of Queen Victoria

Fill in suitable positive or negative forms of *have to, be able to* and *be allowed to*.

In the 19th century many poor people (including children) ___ work long hours in factories and down coal mines. There were no trade unions, so they ___ protest against the terrible conditions. Middle-class families ___ suffer in this way, but even their 'comfortable' way of life would seem strange now. The Victorian father was 'head of the house' and everyone ___ treat him with great respect. At meal times the children ___ talk unless they were spoken to by a grown-up. Their mother, often with ten or more children, ___ work hard to organize the household. Even with servants to help, she ___ relax for long.

On Sundays the maid ___ get up an hour later than usual and ___ relax a little during the day. But nobody ___ play games or read books (except the Bible and other religious books). Everyone ___ go to church.

Until 1870 very few working-class children ___ read or write. When Parliament finally decided that now all children ___ go to school from age 5 to 13, many parents were angry, arguing that if their children ___ go to school, they ___ earn money, so their families would be poorer than ever!

---

2 **trade union** organization that represents workers *(Gewerkschaft)* • 8 **maid** female servant

BASIC RULES AND EXERCISES (I)

1 What modal auxiliaries express

Common modal auxiliaries:	How to use them:	When to use them:
will / would can / could may	**Will/Would/Can/Could** you open the window, please? **May/Can** I sit here? – Yes, of course you **may**. You **can** have the window seat if you like. I **can** see the lights of New York already.	▸ when asking someone to do something ▸ when asking for permission ▸ when giving permission ▸ when talking about abilities
must / mustn't needn't	You **must** fasten your seatbelt. You **mustn't** smoke in here. I **must** apply for a new passport. You **needn't** show your ticket. Only your boarding card.	▸ when instructing someone – to do sth – not to do sth ▸ when talking about a duty or necessity ▸ when explaining that something is unnecessary
should / ought to shouldn't / ought not to	You **should/ought to** read this article. I really **should/ought to** send Grandma a postcard. You **shouldn't/ought not to** spend so much money on souvenirs.	▸ when giving advice ▸ when talking about a moral obligation ▸ when expressing a criticism
may / might / could must / will	There **may/might/could** be a good view from that bridge. Look at that ruin. It **must** be the castle mentioned in the guidebook. – Yes that'**ll** be it. We **could** go to the National Gallery this afternoon.	▸ when expressing – a possibility – a strong probability ▸ when making a suggestion

I've asked him twice, but he **won't** change his mind.	Refusal to do something can be expressed by *won't/will not.*
We **ought to have left** earlier. The train **may have arrived** by now.	Perfect forms (e.g. *ought to have/could have/ may have + past participle*) are also commonly used.

2 Substitutes

Modal auxiliaries only have a present and / or past tense form.
For other tenses, verbs with similar meanings are used as substitutes.

can/ could	be able to	Perhaps we'**ll be able to** swim to the island tomorrow.
may mustn't	be allowed to not be allowed to	**Were** you **allowed to** look through the coastguard's telescope? We **weren't allowed to** use the swimming-pool while it was being cleaned.
must needn't	have to not have to	The Beach Hotel **has had to** close down. The Old Swan isn't so busy on Sunday evenings. We **won't have to** book a table.

Guests **have to** sign the Visitors' Book.
The hotel staff **aren't able to** provide breakfast before 7.30.

Substitute forms can also be used in the present tense.

1 In human hands

Money can buy many things, including the basics to which every human being on the planet has a right, but there are lots of things it can't guarantee. Money alone can't guarantee our health and fulfilment, nor can it guarantee the future of the giant panda or the Bengal tiger, the fish in the sea or the quality of our drinking water.

Many things have to change, to ensure that life remains worth living. We have to stop believing that what we can take from the planet is limitless; that there will always be more. There are no new places to look for vast untapped resources.

In practical terms, this means using resources as carefully and sparingly as possible. If human beings didn't take more than their fair share, we wouldn't have chronic pollution and starvation. Left to its own devices, nature will not tolerate lasting imbalances. Far-reaching global imbalance such as currently exists is a uniquely human phenomenon.

Luckily, the chance of solving this dilemma is also in human hands. But we must act decisively, and act now. When faced with impending disaster, psychologists tell us, many people are able to continue functioning only by denying the signs of catastrophe. Part of the denial process is becoming numbed into a state where people believe that even though things aren't going as well as they should be, there is little they can do about it.

In fact, nothing could be further from the truth. And many of us are beginning to recognize that every action we take can affect the well-being of the planet. Some things we can do on our own, whereas others require groups of like-minded people. There is no end to the things we can do. And of course they don't all have to be done at once. You can begin in small ways, taking it one step at a time.

From *How to be Green* by John Button of 'Friends of the Earth'

---

7 **untapped** not yet made use of • 8 **in practical terms** expressed in a practical way • 10 **left to its own devices** left alone • 11 **currently** at the present time • 13 **impending** threatening to happen • 14 **to deny sth** to say sth is not true • 15 **to numb** [nʌm] to put into a state without feeling • 19 **like-minded** of the same opinion

1.1 Work in groups, going through the text to find as many examples of different modal auxiliaries (including substitute forms) as you can.

1.2 What's wrong here? Correct the statements by changing the auxiliaries.

a We needn't continue to take as much as we like from the planet.
b Nature may tolerate unlimited pollution.
c We mustn't save our world before it is too late.
d Some people think we shouldn't do much to improve the situation.
e Naturally, we must change our ways overnight; things ought not to be done step by step.

1.3 Use future forms of modal auxiliaries to complete these sentences.

a We ______ solve global problems with money alone.
b In future people ______ get used to a simpler lifestyle.
c When laws to protect the planet become stricter, people ______ only ______ build zero-emission houses.

1.4 **Use *can, could, should(n't), must(n't)*, etc., to suggest ways of protecting the planet.**

energy in the home • food • the 'throw- away' mentality • free time and holidays • respecting the countryside • transport • chemicals

Examples: *People should eat food that is grown locally instead of expensive imported food.*
A lot of energy can be saved by insulating houses properly.

2 The right thing to say

Choosing the right auxiliary in everyday situations can be quite important. If you want someone to shut the door, for example, it is much more polite to say, *"Could / Would you shut the door, please?"* than simply *"Please shut the door."* Decide what to say in the following situations:

a You are sitting in a non-smoking area, and someone gets out a cigarette.
b The shop assistant shows you a nice pair of jeans and you want to know if they'll fit.
c You want to recommend a book to someone.
d A friend gives you quite an expensive present, which you feel was unnecessary.
e Someone is standing in your way, so it is difficult for you to get past.
f The coffee you have ordered is cold.
g You see a child putting her hand into a monkey's cage at the zoo.
h You haven't quite understood what someone means.
i You need a longer straw for your drink.

"Do you have a longer straw?"

3 What went wrong?

The perfect forms *must have …, may have …, might have …* are often used to express possible explanations of unexpected situations, while *should have, ought to have …* and *could have …* can express criticism or regret. Think what you might feel like saying in the following situations. Try various possibilities.

Examples: You hang up your jacket in a café, but when you want to leave, the jacket is gone.
→ *"Someone must have taken it by mistake."*
You get to the station late and your train has just left.
→ *"I ought to have left home earlier."*

a There is an unexpected tailback on the motorway.
b You and a friend have decided to go to a concert, but when you get there, you are told the tickets are sold out.
c You have arranged to meet a friend at the swimming-pool, and are disappointed when she doesn't turn up.
d It is 11 p.m. There is no reply when you ring your friend's number.
e You want to cut out an article you have read in yesterday's paper – but you can't find the paper.
f Your cat likes to go out at nights. One morning, it does not come back home.
g There is a delicious cake for tea, and you have five pieces. Later, you feel sick.

tailback long line of cars in a jam

BASIC RULES AND EXERCISES (II)

Equivalents of German *sollen*

You really **ought to/should** try this cheese – it tastes great!	*Ought to / should* is used to **give advice**, etc. (see Basic Rules, p. 73).
Shall I put the flowers on this table? **Shall we** have wine with our meal?	*Shall I … / Shall we …?* is used to **ask what someone else would like** or **advise you to do**, or to **make a suggestion**.
Are we **supposed to** hand our keys in? Dogs **are not to** be taken into the hotel dining-room. Our visitors **were (supposed) to** arrive at six.	*Be supposed to / be to* expresses ▸ a **rule** or **obligation** that someone else has decided on; ▸ a **previously arranged plan**.
I don't like fish, although it's **supposed to** be / **is said to** be very good for you.	*Be supposed to / be said to* are used to express what is **generally accepted as true**.

4 Doctor, doctor …

Fill in the appropriate equivalents of *sollen*. Give more than one equivalent whenever it seems possible.

a *Patient:* Doctor, doctor, what ___ I do? My little boy has swallowed my pen.
Doctor: Use a pencil till I get there.

b There were two snakes in the jungle. One snake said, "Do you know if we ___ be poisonous?"
"Why?" said the other snake.
"Because I've just bitten my lip."

c *Piano tuner*: Good morning, sir. I ___ tune your piano.
Man: Oh? But we didn't send for you.
Piano tuner: No, sir, but your neighours did.

d *Sam*: One of my ancestors ___ have died at Waterloo.
Ted: Really? Which platform?

e *Teacher*: You're late! You ___ have been here at 9 o'clock.
Boy: Why, sir – what happened?

5 For the last time!

What else could he have said?
Use equivalents of *sollen*.

"For the last time!
I will not have him inside
this house until you've
done your homework."

ADVANCED RULES AND EXERCISES

Combining different modal auxiliaries and substitutes

Different modals are often linked together in one sentence:
We **ought to** ***be able to*** reach the Pole by next week.
We **may** ***have to*** turn back if this blizzard continues.
Those tourists **should** never **have been** ***allowed to*** join the Everest expedition.
In better weather conditions they **might have** ***been able to*** reach the summit.

1 Strange – but true!

A care worker, aged 30, had been trying to find a new job for months – but without success. In desperation she hit on a new idea, and put this unconventional advert in the local paper:
I want a well-paid job. I have no imagination, I am uncreative, anti-social and untalented.
After that, she got countless phone calls and job offers. The best one came from a company offering a much higher salary than she had ever earned before.

Adapted from *Oddly Enough*

1 **care worker** *Pflegekraft*

Complete what this "talentless" woman told a friend after the successful job interview.

may have to • might never have been able to • shouldn't have had to • ought to be able to

Well, for ages I thought to myself: "I _____ find a job I really like." But nothing worked out. Then I thought: "Perhaps I _____ try a different approach." I suddenly had this new idea! It seemed crazy, but why not? And now, just look what's happened – I've had this fantastic offer! Better than my wildest dreams! If I hadn't put that crazy advert in the paper, I _____ get a really well-paid job. It just shows how strange life can be! But on the other hand, in order to get a good job offer like this one, I _____ describe myself like that. Oh well, who cares? Main thing is, I've got the job.

2 Working in Antarctica, the coldest place on earth

**Explain what construction workers find so attractive about work in Antarctica.
What are the dangers? What role do colleagues play?
These words and expressions will help you:**

construction worker (2) • southernmost (5) • research centre (5) • to maintain (7) • accommodation and food (11-12) • to be provided (12) • to be awed by sth (17) • to go walking off (21) • penguin (26)

Sonnenanbeter werden es kaum glauben können: es soll Dutzende von Bauarbeitern geben, die sich nichts besseres vorstellen können, als vier Monate lang in der Antarktis zu arbeiten. Dort muss das südlichste britische Forschungszentrum während des kurzen Polarsommers instand gehalten werden. Die Antarktis ist der kälteste Kontinent; selbst in der Sommerzeit können die Temperaturen bis auf -28 °C sinken. Die Arbeit dort wird aber gut bezahlt, man muss sich um nichts kümmern: Kleidung, Unterkunft und Verpflegung werden gestellt – und man kann natürlich nirgends Geld ausgeben. Für diejenigen, die sich dafür entscheiden, in dieser eisigen verlassenen Landschaft zu arbeiten, muss es aber andere Gründe geben als den Wunsch, Geld sparen zu können.

Für die meisten ist die Zeit in der Antarktis das Abenteuer ihres Lebens. „Ich war von der Landschaft völlig ergriffen," sagt Linda Capper, die selbst drei Monate dort arbeitete. „Ich hatte schon so viele Fotos gesehen und so viel darüber gelesen, aber nichts hätte mich auf die Gefühle vorbereiten können, die ich erlebte, als ich den Kontinent mit eigenen Augen sah. Es ist dort unglaublich schön."

Aber es kann auch gefährlich sein. Man darf zum Beispiel nicht einfach alleine loslaufen. Aber die größte Gefahr ist wohl die, dass man sich in den Kontinent verliebt. Wenn die vier Monate zu Ende gehen, soll es viele geben, die nicht mehr zurück nach Hause wollen.

„Die Beziehung zu Kollegen ist dort auch ganz anders," sagt Mrs Capper. „Man muss sich auf sie – auch als Freunde – verlassen können, weil es keine anderen Menschen dort gibt. Die nächsten Nachbarn sind 30 km entfernt – und das sind Pinguine."

Based on an Article in *The Guardian*

11 The Infinitive

CHECK-UP

1 The dinner party

Complete the sentences with infinitives. Decide whether to use the active or the passive infinitive, with or without *to*.

The guests were expected _____ at eight o'clock. The Fergusons didn't want them	arrive
_____ late as they had arranged for some delicious Chinese food _____ by that time.	be · deliver
And, of course, they didn't want it _____ cold. The first _____ was Major Winterbottom.	get · arrive
It was, of course, easy for him _____ on time as he was the Fergusons' next-door	be
neighbour. He said he would love _____ in the kitchen, but Mrs Ferguson made him	help
_____ down and invited him _____ a drink.	sit · have
At 8.30 the Chinese takeaway rang up _____ that their driver had no idea where _____	say · deliver
the food, and that he would like _____ of the exact address. A few minutes later they	inform
heard a car _____ in their drive. But it was only someone that had used their drive	stop
_____ in. Then they heard the telephone _____ again. It was the MacAlisters, announcing	turn · ring
that their babysitter had let them down. They were wondering whether _____ or	come
not, as they didn't want _____ the children at home on their own. At nine the	leave
Chinese takeaway rang _____ them _____ that it was now impossible for them _____	let · know · come
because their driver had somehow managed _____ into one of the trees on the High	run
Street, so they wanted _____ if the Fergusons wouldn't like _____ the food themselves.	know · collect
While the Fergusons were discussing what _____, the phone rang again.	do
It was Sue Jones, saying that she and Mike had been delighted _____ to their party	invite
next Friday. But what time exactly were the Fergusons expecting them _____?	come

9 **drive** Einfahrt • 11 **to let down** to disappoint (unexpectedly)

2 Christopher Columbus

Replace the phrases in italics by infinitive constructions.

a Christopher Columbus was not *the only sailor that explored* the oceans in the 15th century.
b But while others had sailed south, he was *the first explorer that thought* that west was *the direction one should take.*
c Columbus was certainly not *the only person who believed* the earth was round.
d But most people thought it *was impossible that any ship could make* the 10,000-mile journey from western Europe to Asia.
e Columbus, however, *decided he would travel* west and *expected that he would get* to India and China in the end.
f He asked several European monarchs for help. A lot of money was needed *so that he could buy and equip* the ships for the expedition.
g Columbus greatly underestimated *the distance that had to be covered.*
h When they had sailed far beyond where they *had hoped they might find land*, Columbus' men *told him he should turn back.*
i He *promised that he would give up* the search if they had not discovered land by October 12th.
j When they finally sighted land, Columbus was *relieved when he saw* the joy in his men's faces!

g **to underestimate** to make a calculation that is too low • g **to cover (a distance)** to travel

BASIC RULES AND EXERCISES

The infinitive without *to*	
Manchester City *must* **play** Everton in the next round. The match *might* **be shown** on BBC 1.	▸ after most auxiliaries
The new coach *makes his players* **work** very hard. (= forces/tells/orders them to work …) Aston Villa *let their lead* **slip** away in the second half. (= allowed/permitted it to slip …)	▸ after *make* + direct object ▸ after *let* + direct object
The home crowd were shocked when they *heard the referee* **blow** his whistle and then saw him **point** to the penalty spot.	▸ after verbs of perception + direct object
The infinitive with *to*	
Leeds *hope* **to play** in their new stadium next year. It won't be *easy* **to get** tickets for the Cup Final. Bell was *lucky* **to be included** in the team. The fans couldn't understand Arsenal's *decision* **to sell** three of their best players.	after certain ▸ verbs (*expect, want, would like, try, manage, promise*, etc.) ▸ adjectives (*difficult, hard, ready, happy, lucky*, etc.) ▸ nouns (*attempt, plan, wish*, etc.)
At the press conference the team manager did not know *what* **to say**. (= what he should say.) Liverpool were *the first* (*team*) **to score** in a very exciting match. (= the first team that scored …) Some of the crowd stood on their seats (*in order*) **to get** a better view. (= so that they would get …) This is *the game* **to win** if we want to stay in the Premier League. (= that we must/should win …)	instead of subordinate clauses: ▸ after question words (*what, where, how*, etc.) ▸ after *the first, the last, the only one(s)* ▸ instead of a clause of purpose ▸ instead of a relative clause with an auxiliary

The coach *wanted all his players* **to take** fitness tests.	*Want, wish, would like, expect, tell, advise, ask* and *invite* can be followed by an object + infinitive construction.
Wales *is expected* **to win** on Saturday.	*Expect, tell, advise, ask* and *invite* can also be used in the passive.
It is *unusual for local matches* **to attract** big crowds.	After certain expressions, e.g. *It's easy, important*, etc., a construction with *for* + object + infinitive is used.

"Hello! He's coming over to consult the linesman."

1 How they can help

Say how the following people and things can help you. Use infinitive constructions with question words.

Examples: *A travel agent will help you if you can't decide where to go on holiday.*
If you don't know which road to take you can look at a map.

a travel agent ✓
b map ✓
c recipe
d careers officer
e police officer
f dictionary
g skiing instructor
h railway timetable
i best friend

2 The right to decide?

Many people are in the care of others – think of people in hospital, children, old people. Should they be allowed to decide everything for themselves? Use infinitives with question words to complete the following ideas. Think of as many sensible variations as you can.

when • whether • where • how • what

a People in hospital would often prefer to decide for themselves …
b Old people don't like being told …
c Children should have the right to decide …
d Small children …
e People in prison …
f Disabled people …

3 Psychological warfare

Describe what is happening in this cartoon. Use infinitive constructions, deciding whether to use an object or not.

a Normally, it is easy for a player ____ from the penalty spot. — score
b And Kevin Robson hopes ____. — score
c Of course, his teammates expect ____. — get a goal
d But the Rovers' supporters don't want ____. — succeed
e Those not directly behind the goal are pretending ____. — be frightened
f They don't want ____ by the ball. — be hit
g They would like ____. — win
h Their intention is ____ and so to make ____. — make … nervous · miss
i But the home fans directly behind the goal want ____. — see … score a goal
j The goalkeeper hopes ____ the ball. — save
k The Rovers' supporters have managed ____ unsure of himself. — make … feel
l Kevin Robson looks as if he no longer wants ____ the responsibility. — take on
m He doesn't seem ____ what ____ any longer. — know · do

4 In and out of school

Translate into English. Remember: German constructions with *dass* sometimes correspond to infinitive constructions in English.

a „Wollen Sie, dass wir den ganzen Text übersetzen?"
b „Ich möchte, dass Sie ein Gedicht aussuchen, das Ihnen wirklich gefällt."
c „Es ist wichtig, dass das Labor nach dem Unterricht abgeschlossen wird."
d „Meine Eltern wollen nicht, dass ich Kunst studiere. Sie erwarten von mir, dass ich den Familienbetrieb übernehme."
e „Ich will, dass du das Radio ausschaltest. Es ist unmöglich, dass du bei dem Lärm deine Hausaufgaben machen kannst."

"Right! Now I want each of you to describe the weather in your own words."

5 Dr Watson at work

In this short extract from 'The Hound of the Baskervilles', Dr Watson has been sent ahead by Sherlock Holmes to watch the house of the naturalist, Stapleton. Stapleton, the villain of the story, is preparing to attack Sir Henry Baskerville, his guest, with an enormous dog he has locked up in the outhouse. From his hiding place, Dr Watson can look straight into the dining-room …

As I watched them, Stapleton rose and left the room, while Sir Henry filled his glass again and leaned back in his chair, puffing at his cigar. I heard the creak of a door and the sound of boots upon gravel. The steps passed along the path on the other side of the wall under which I crouched. Looking over, I saw the naturalist pause at the door of an outhouse in the corner of the orchard. A key turned in a lock, and as he passed in, there was a curious scuffling noise from within. He was only a minute or so inside, and then I heard the key turn once more, and he passed me and re-entered the house. I saw him rejoin his guest and I crept quietly back to where my companions were waiting to tell them what I had seen.

From *The Hound of the Baskervilles* by Sir Arthur Conan Doyle

---

naturalist botanist • **villain** ['vɪlən] the 'bad' character • **outhouse** shed • 2 **creak** groaning sound (e.g. of a door opening) • 3 **gravel** ['grævl] very small stones used to make paths • 3 **to crouch** [aʊ] *kauern* • 4 **orchard** ['ɔːtʃəd] piece of land where fruit trees grow • 5 **a scuffling noise** sound like the quick movements of an animal

5.1 Find examples in the text of object + infinitive after verbs of perception.

5.2 Use objects and infinitives wherever you can, to describe more details of what Dr Watson saw / noticed / heard.
Start like this: He watched Stapleton get up and …

6 The invention of the fast food restaurant

Explain in English what the reasons were for the radical changes the McDonald brothers made to their original restaurant in California. What sort of customers did they hope to attract? What further developments followed? These words will help you:

to overhaul (7) • to work efficiently (8) • to mass-produce hamburgers (9) • low income (10) • chain restaurant (16) • outskirts (23) • to dominate (25)

Wo essen Sie, wenn Sie keine Zeit haben zu kochen oder zu beschäftigt sind, sich gemütlich in ein Lokal zu setzen? Richtig, in einem Fast-Food Restaurant. Heute muss man nicht lange nach einem solchen Restaurant suchen. Das war aber nicht immer so.
Maurice und Richard McDonald waren in den 40er Jahren des 20. Jahrhunderts Besitzer eines erfolgreichen Drive-in-Restaurants in San Bernadino, Kalifornien. Sie verdienten genug Geld, um sich jedes Jahr einen neuen Cadillac kaufen zu können. Aber im Jahre 1948 beschlossen sie, ihr Restaurant zu schließen, um es völlig zu überholen. Papierteller wurden eingeführt, um das Geschirr zu ersetzen. Die Brüder zeigten ihren Angestellten, wie sie ökonomischer arbeiten konnten. Sie brachten sie dazu, Hamburger wie am Fließband herzustellen. Das neue Restaurant wurde der Ort, wo man hinging. Denn zum ersten Mal konnten es sich selbst Familien mit geringem Einkommen leisten, ein Restaurant zu besuchen. Dort konnte man auch davon ausgehen, dass das Essen immer gleich aussah, gleich schmeckte und das gleiche kostete.
Die Brüder McDonald waren die ersten, die die Chancen von Fast-Food-Restaurantketten und Hamburger-Fabriken erkannten. Aber sie waren nicht die Einzigen, die diese Idee nutzten. In den 50er und 60er Jahren begannen Fast-Food-Restaurants das Gesicht amerikanischer Städte zu verändern. Besonders die Außenbezirke scheinen heute von den Fast-Food-Restaurants beherrscht zu sein.

ADVANCED RULES AND EXERCISES

Different ways of expressing causing and allowing with *let* and *make* and their alternatives

Active	Passive
The immigration officer **made us open** all our bags. One of the stewards **told John to tighten** his seat belt.	All passengers **are made to show** their passports when they check in. We **were forced to spend** the night at the airport.
The flight attendant **let me put** my hand luggage under the seat in front. They won't **allow anyone to block** the gangways.	You **are allowed to leave** your seat when the seat-belt signs are switched off. Passengers **are not permitted to** smoke on board.
The following verbs can be used instead of **make** and **let** in the active form. Unlike **make** and **let**, they are always followed by the infinitive with *to*. **make**: *tell, order, force, etc.* **let**: *allow, permit, etc.*	**Make** can be used in the passive. Then it is followed by the infinitive with *to*. The passive forms *be forced to* and *be compelled to* give stronger emphasis.
	Let (= *allow*) cannot be used in the passive. The passive forms *be allowed to* and *be permitted to* (formal) are used as substitutes.

The smell of those steaks on the barbecue **makes me feel** hungry!

Make + object + infinitive often describes the effect something has.

1 The 'let and make thriller'

Translate the 'thriller', using *let* or *make* for German *lassen*.
These words will help you:

to sit up (1) • ghostly (2) • torch (4) • to hold one's breath (5) • throat (5) • to feel calmer (8) • to jump (8)

Ein plötzliches Geräusch ließ Bonner im Bett hochfahren. Das Licht der elektrischen Uhr ließ das Gesicht seiner Frau gespenstisch erscheinen. Bonner ließ sie weiterschlafen und ging nach unten. Die Holztreppe ließ seine Schritte schrecklich laut klingen. Die Angst ließ sein Herz schneller schlagen. Hatte der Hund Einbrecher hereingelassen? Das Licht einer Taschenlampe im Wohnzimmer ließ Bonner den Atem anhalten. Er ging zum Telefon. Seine trockene Kehle ließ seine Stimme unnatürlich klingen. „Lassen Sie den Einbrecher [ruhig] weitermachen“, sagte der Polizist, „tun Sie nichts, was ihn veranlassen könnte, gewalttätig zu werden.“ Die Stimme des Polizisten ließ Bonner ruhiger werden. Aber was war das? Ein Schrei ließ ihn zusammenzucken …

2 Chief Joseph

Chief Joseph's story is typical of the way American governments treated the Native Americans. The Nez Perce were peace-loving Indians. For many years they had let white explorers and settlers travel through their land without ever attacking them. Chief Joseph never let his people sell any land to the whites because he believed the land was sacred. But when gold was found in the mountains of western Idaho in 1860, the government wanted to make the Nez Perce give up their land. They told Chief Joseph that he and his people had to leave within a month – to be resettled later on a reservation in Oregon. Joseph had only 55 men of fighting age. This made him realize that he would have no chance against the whites.

On their way to Oregon, a few angry Nez Perce killed some white settlers. Troops were sent to capture them, but Chief Joseph tried to escape to Canada with his small band. For months they managed to escape from thousands of soldiers. When, at last, they had reached the Bear Paw Mountains, only thirty miles from the Canadian border, Joseph let his exhausted people rest. It was then that the cavalry attacked. After holding out for four days, the Indians were made to surrender. Rather than letting the children freeze to death and his people starve, Joseph decided to give up the struggle and let the government do with his people what they wanted.

The government of the US made the Nez Perce settle on a barren reservation in Oregon, but they didn't let Chief Joseph stay with his people. He was made to live on a reservation in Washington state. There he died in exile. Officially he was said to have died of a broken heart.

---

2 **Nez Perce** ['nez'pɜ:s] • 6 **sacred** ['seɪkrɪd] holy • 13 **to capture** ['kæptʃə] to catch • 18 **to starve** to die of hunger • 20 **barren** too poor in quality to grow anything on

2.1 Replace the constructions with *let* and *make* by constructions with *allow*, *permit*, *order*, *force*, *tell* or *compel*.

2.2 Work in groups to translate the sentences with *let* and *make*. (Can you always use *lassen* in German?)

2.3 "The government of the US ... stay with his people." (lines 20-21) Put this sentence into the passive.

3 Advice from a US President

What do you think of Harry Truman's advice? Express your opinion in a few sentences. You may find these phrases with infinitives useful:

> make / let sb do sth • tell / advise / expect / allow sb to do sth • want / prefer / plan / decide to do sth • important / best / (not) easy for sb to do sth • tell sb what to do • unusual for parents to ... • the best thing to do is to ...

> *"I have found the best way to give advice to your children is to find out what they want and then advise them to do it."*
> (Harry Truman, President of the United States, 1945-1953)

4 Another April

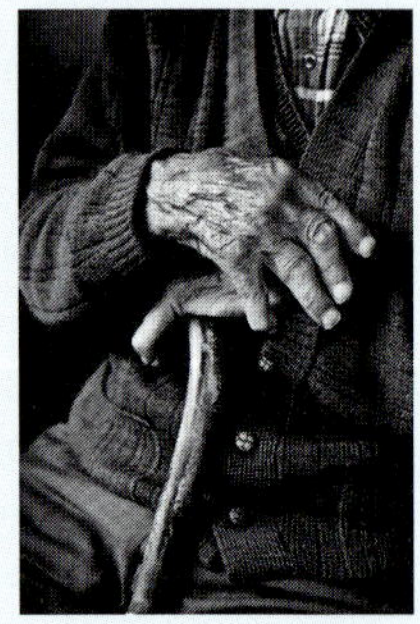

"How long has Grandpa been with us?" I asked Mom. "Before you's born," she said. "Pap has been with us eleven years. He was eighty when he quit cuttin' timber and farmin': now he's ninety-one."

I had heard her say that when she was a girl he'd walk out on the snow and ice barefooted and carry wood in the house and put it on the fire. He had shoes but wouldn't bother to put them on. And I heard her say that he would cut timber on the coldest day without socks on his feet. I had heard her tell how he'd sweat and how the sweat in his beard would be icicles by the time he got home from work on the cold winter days. Now Mom wouldn't let him get out of the house for she wanted him to live a long time.

As I watched Grandpa go down the path toward the hog pen he stopped to examine every little thing along his path. Once he waved his cane at a butterfly as it zigzagged over his head, its polka-dot wings fanning the blue April air. Grandpa would stand when a puff of wind came along, and hold his face against the wind and let the wind play with his white whiskers. I thought maybe his face was hot under his beard and he was letting the wind cool his face. When he reached the hog pen he called the hogs down to the fence. They came running and grunting to Grandpa just like they were talking to him. I knew that Grandpa couldn't hear them trying to talk to him but he could see their mouths working and he knew they were trying to say something. He leaned his cane against the hog pen, reached over the fence, and patted the hogs' heads. Grandpa didn't miss patting one of our seven hogs. There wasn't anything his dim blue eyes missed. He stopped under a redbud tree before he reached the garden to break a tiny spray of redbud blossoms. He took each blossom from the spray and examined it carefully.

"Gee, it's funny to watch Grandpa," I said to Mom, then I laughed. "Poor Pap," Mom said, "he's seen a lot of Aprils come and go. He's seen more Aprils than he will ever see again."

From *Another April* by Jesse Stuart

---

1 you's born you were born • **2 to quit**/quit/quit *here:* to stop • **3 timber** wood used for building • **8 to sweat** [e] *schwitzen* • **8 icicle** long thin piece of ice • **11 hog** AE = pig • **11 pen** small piece of land enclosed by a fence esp. for keeping animals in • **12 cane** walking stick • **12 butterfly** *Schmetterling* • **13 polka-dot wing** *getupfter Flügel* • **13 to fan** *here:* to beat (the air) • **14 whiskers** hair on a man's face, esp. on the sides • **16 to grunt** to make the sound of a pig • **20 dim** not bright • **21 redbud** (tree) American tree with red buds *(Knospen)* • **21 spray** small branch with its leaves and blossoms • **21 blossom** the flower of a tree or bush

4.1 The author uses various infinitive structures to make the three characters in the story come alive. Find places in the text where he expresses that …

a the boy knows a lot from his mother about the time Grandpa was younger
b the boy's mother is worried about her father's health
c Grandpa loves nature
d the boy is amused by his grandfather's behaviour
e the boy's mother regrets the fact that her father is so old and will only have a few more years to live

4.2 Talk about the story, using infinitive constructions.

a The little boy is too young to …
b His mother tries to …
c His grandfather examines everything in detail in order to …
d The author manages to …

Go on.

12 Gerunds

CHECK-UP

"Just keep on taking the tablets and stop worrying about the side-effects."

1 At the doctor's

Fill in suitable gerunds, together with prepositions when appropriate.

a "Twenty cigarettes a day, Mr Miller?! I think it would be better if you stopped ...... altogether.
b And you should also avoid ...... too much meat."
c "But I'm not keen ...... nothing but salads and vegetables. And I always look forward ...... a drink when I come home from work."
d "Well, well. How ...... muesli for breakfast now and then instead ...... egg and bacon every morning?
e And I'm afraid you're a bit overweight. Have you ever thought ...... weight? How ...... some exercise?"
f "But I've always hated ...... around in a tracksuit or ...... in some crowded pool."
g "Well, if you go on like this you might be in danger ...... a heart attack."
h "Hm, perhaps I'll give up ...... to work in the car. I might get used ...... my old bike again. Oh, and another thing, doctor. I don't seem to get enough rest at night. I have difficulty ...."
i "What ...... for a nice walk before you go to bed? That may help.
j And carry on ...... those red pills. They'll also help you to relax. See you again on Wednesday then, Mr Miller."

2 The successful politician

Rewrite the following sentences, using gerund constructions.
Choose from the expressions on the right.

Example: The successful politician quickly manages to get a seat in parliament. — succeed in
→ *The successful politition quickly succeeds in getting a seat in parliament.*

The successful politician ...
a ... doesn't find it difficult to remember people's names.
b ... is not nervous when she or he speaks in public.
c ... expects to become a government minister after the next elections, and is very pleased about this.
d ... is an expert hand-shaker and baby-kisser.
e ... never disagrees with her or his party bosses.
f ... is very happy to appear in TV discussions or chat shows.
g ... praises her or his party's achievements again and again.
h ... is not frightened when she or he has to answer awkward questions.
i ... is a great actor.

f **chat show (BE)** talk show

avoid • be afraid • be good • be good • enjoy • get tired • have difficulty • look forward • worry
about • at • at • in • of • of • to

BASIC RULES AND EXERCISES

	The gerund is used
Driving one's own car used to be very popular in the 20th and 21st centuries.	▸ as a subject
People even *enjoyed* **going** on holiday in their cars.	▸ as an object – after verbs without a preposition (*avoid, stop, suggest,* etc.)
Young people *looked forward to* **getting** a so-called 'driving licence'. But by the beginning of the 21st century people were *getting tired of* **waiting** in endless traffic jams and **breathing** in the polluted air. They had begun to realize they were in real *danger of* **destroying** their own environment.	▸ after verbs / adjectives / nouns + prepositions
Apart from causing environmental problems, cars were unnecessarily using more and more of the world's oil supply.	▸ together with a preposition as an adverbial phrase (*instead of, by, without,* etc.)

What about **going** by bike?	The gerund is also used after *how about? / what about?, it's no use, it's no good, it's worth.*
At first most people objected to *the government* **putting** more tax on petrol. Many were also against *them* **closing** city centres to private cars.	The gerund can have a **subject of its own.**

1 Fowl play!

A featherless fowl has been developed by scientists in Israel. By crossing a small, bare-skinned bird with a regular broiler chicken, they've produced a hybrid designed especially for hot climates.
Broiler chickens generate so much heat as they grow that they can overheat and die if not kept properly ventilated.
It is hoped feather-free chickens will direct their energy into growing larger rather than keeping cool. Their meat should be succulent and low in fat.
After creating several dozens of the bald, bright red birds, Dr Cahaner, the geneticist at the Hebrew University of Jerusalem said: "Feathers are a waste. The chickens are using feed for producing something that has to be dumped …

'You think you've got problems, I've started laying fried eggs'

2 **broiler chicken** chicken that is bred for roasting or grilling • 7 **succulent** juicy and delicious • 8 **bald** [ɔː] without hair (or feathers) • 10 **to dump** to get rid of, to throw away

fowl [faʊl] a bird, especially a chicken

"Our next challenge will be breeding featherless birds with as much meat on them as regular broiler chickens."

His naked birds could save poultry farmers large sums spent on electric fans, used to prevent overheating. And the lack of feathers would mean saving time and resources used for plucking.

But a spokesperson for the RSPCA said: "Genetically engineering a chicken in such a way is totally unacceptable. By taking away its feathers you are taking away its natural defences and preventing it from regulating its temperature.

"Featherless chickens will be in danger of getting skin diseases and have no water-proofing or protection against the sun. Many birds recognize each other by identifying feathers and feather patterns. This trait will also be lost."

Mr Cahaner concedes not everywhere would suit the chickens. They might be in danger of catching colds in chillier climates.

He said: "It would harm them if we forced them to be outside in cold weather. They are not designed for running around on the open fields of England in winter."

Adapted from the *Daily Express*

---

13 **poultry** [əʊ] birds that are kept on farms • 13 **fan** *Ventilator* • 14 **to pluck** to pull out feathers • 15 **RSPCA** Royal Society for the Prevention of Cruelty to Animals • 21 **to concede** to admit

1.1 Work in groups to find examples in the text of gerunds as they are described in the *Basic Rules*.

1.2 Use gerund constructions to answer these questions:

a	How did the Israeli scientists develop the featherless chicken?	... by ...
b	What can happen to chickens when they get too hot?	... in danger of ...
c	What will the 'naked' chickens put their energy into?	... instead of ...
d	What are Dr Canaher's aims in the future?	... look forward to ... / ... think of ...
e	What would the widespread introduction of the new chickens mean for poultry farmers?	... mean ...
f	According to the RSPCA the featherless birds are at a disadvantage. What problems will they have?	... in danger of ... and ... difficulty in ...
g	Why are the 'new' chickens only suitable for warmer climates?	... not designed for... and ... in danger of ...

1.3 Talk about the pros and cons of genetic engineering. Use some of these expressions:

the idea of ... • the risk of ... • the danger of... • I'm sick of ... • scientists should stop ... • people should avoid ... • I wouldn't worry so much about ... • scientists should be ashamed of ... • I personally don't mind ... • I have nothing against ... • animals should be able to enjoy ... • I suggest ... • humans will never succeed in ... • governments should insist on ... • instead of ... • apart from ... • it's no use ... • it's worth ...

2 Different parents – different attitudes

Complete the sentences, using gerunds with subjects of their own.

Tom's parents make life difficult for him. His father is very strict – and his mother tends to be anxious. Tom complains:

a "They don't approve of TV, except for the news. So, of course, they're always against …
b Dad never lets me stay out late. In fact, he insists on …
c Mum doesn't want me to get a motor-bike. That's because she's worried about …
d I haven't got any brothers or sisters. So I suppose that's the reason for …
e Katie is my new girlfriend. She's great! But, of course, my dad objects to …
f My mum can't bear to think about the time when I leave to start university. She seems to be keen on …"

Katie's parents are quite the opposite. Tom explains:

a "They allow Katie to stay out as long as she likes. They don't mind her …
b They don't mind when she sleeps as long as she likes on a Sunday. They honestly don't object to …
c Her mum thinks her daughter is old enough to look after herself. She automatically relies on …
d Katie's opinions are sometimes extreme, and especially her father disagrees. But he doesn't mind …
e Her parents never complain if Katie wants to spend a weekend away with her friends. They are quite happy about …
f Katie has become an independent person, so her parents see no danger in …"

3 Rewards and punishments

The danger in rewarding a child is not as extreme as that of punishing him, but the undermining of the child's morale through the giving of rewards is more subtle. Rewards are superfluous and negative. To offer a prize for doing a deed is tantamount to declaring that the deed is not worth doing for its own sake.

From *Summerhill* by A. S. Neill

2 **to undermine** [--'-] to weaken or destroy gradually • 2 **morale** [mə'rɑːl] • 3 **subtle** ['sʌtl] not immediately noticeable, difficult to explain • 4 **superfluous** [-'---] unnecessary • 5 **tantamount to** having the same value or effect as

3.1 Use gerund constructions with prepositions to rewrite the following sentences. (Choose from the prepositions on the right.)

Example: Adults may think they can make children try harder if they promise them rewards.
→ Adults may think they can make children try harder *by promising them rewards.*

a Giving 'prizes' can create envy between children, and it can also cause big disappointments.
b All true artists work 'for fun' – they do not think of financial rewards.
c It is wrong to imagine that one can develop a person's interest in a thing if one offers a prize.
d In the world of sport, successful people sometimes receive enormous sums because they have won a certain event.
e But although they are worth so much money, these prizes are not the 'real' reward.
f The winner of a sporting event takes pride in the achievement, but does not consider the prize important in itself.

inspite of
as well as
without
instead of
by
for

☆ 3.2 What do you think of Neill's opinion and of the arguments expressed in 3.1? Consider some of the points made.

ADVANCED RULES AND EXERCISES

Other forms of the gerund

Perfect form My brother didn't get far in the tournament, but he's very proud of **having taken** part in it.	▸ The perfect form is generally only used in formal style. (Less formal alternative: *proud that he took part …*)
Passive form I don't mind **being corrected** if I make a mistake, but I hate **being criticised** unfairly.	▸ The passive form is used frequently, in both formal and informal English.

Were you surprised about *Lewis* **being dropped** from the team?

Both of these forms can be used with subjects of their own.

1 Making it flow

Connect or rewrite the sentences, using gerund constructions to make them flow.

a The Robsons' daughter has won a scholarship to Oxford. Her parents are very proud of her.
b It's very encouraging to be praised. All children naturally like it.
c Sophie's dog was run over yesterday. We were all so sorry to hear about it.
d Too many discarded clothes are thrown in the dustbin. They could be recycled instead.
e My uncle and his family have moved out of the city. They are having second thoughts about it now.
f Our car was stolen. Apart from that, our holiday was a great success.

a **scholarship** *Stipendium* • d **to discard** to get rid of

2 Spotlight on a public figure

When Barack Obama was elected President of the United States in November 2008, *Dreams from My Father*, the book he had written some years earlier, became a bestseller. People – not only in America – wanted to know more about this fascinating man and his roots (he was born the son of a black African father and a white mother). In the book Obama describes the phenomenon of belonging to two different worlds, without ever having felt he really belonged to either of them.

Write a short text about Barack Obama – or about any other famous person or celebrity you admire. First, get a few basic facts together, e.g. from magazine articles or the internet. Use gerund constructions whenever they seem the most suitable way of expressing your ideas. If you choose to write about Obama, for example, you could include how he might have felt about some of these things:

having a white mother and a black father • growing up in Hawaii with his mother and grandparents • his father going back to Africa • never having really known his father well • having a half-sister and other African relatives in Kenya • being the first black US president • moving into the White House • his wife becoming First Lady • some black Americans calling him "not black enough"

13 Participles

CHECK-UP

1 Proverbs

Complete these English proverbs with either present or past participles.

a A ____ dog never bites. — bark
b A penny ____ is a penny ____ . — save · earn
c A ____ stone gathers no moss. — roll
d Let ____ dogs lie. — sleep
e Once ____, twice shy. — bite
f First come, first ____ . — serve
g First impressions are the most ____ . — last
h There's many a good tune ____ on an old fiddle. — play
i A trouble ____ is a trouble ____ . — share · halve
j ____ we stand, ____ we fall. — unite · divide
k If you want a thing ____ well, do it yourself. — do
l Well ____ is half ____ . — begin · do

"Jack believes in letting sleeping dogs lie!"

2 Finnegan's rest

First read the text. Then rewrite it, using participle constructions where possible.

Example: Inspector Finnegan had had a tough day at the police station. He felt exhausted.
Having had a tough day at the police station, Inspector Finnegan felt exhausted.

a He wanted to relax after supper, so he sat down on the sofa and switched on the TV.
b On the screen he could see two men. They were getting into a car.
c With heavy eyes he watched them as they drove slowly away.
d The man who was driving the car looked very much like Franco Costellini.
e Finnegan leaned back on the sofa and closed his eyes.
f His beer stood on the table next to him. It was untouched.
g He heard some soft voices. They were talking about something he couldn't quite make out.
h Then he noticed a third man. He was standing in front of a bank. He was waiting for someone.
i As Finnegan had never seen him before he tried to concentrate on the other two.
j Then he suddenly found himself in some dark room. He was lying on a bed.
k He lay there and was covered with some sort of blanket.
l He didn't know where he was. So he felt frightened.
m Then he heard that someone was opening a door somewhere.
n When he tried to get up, he noticed that someone was standing in front of him. – Costellini!?! –
o He jumped up in panic and screamed for help.
"Sorry, darling, I didn't mean to wake you up," said his wife.

BASIC RULES AND EXERCISES

present participles active in meaning → a **crying** baby *ein schreiendes Kind*
past participles passive in meaning → a **broken** leg *ein gebrochenes Bein*

Present participles → active in meaning	Past participles → passive in meaning	
The weather forecast for the **coming** week doesn't sound very **promising**.	The weather in Scotland was rather **mixed**, and we even had an **unexpected** fall of snow.	▸ used as adjectives
We got back in the car and *sat* **waiting** for the rain to stop. The hotel porter *came* **running** up to us with an umbrella.	With so little snow this winter, most ski runs will probably *remain* **closed**.	▸ after verbs describing a position (*sit*, *lie*, etc.) or movement (*come*, *go*, etc.)
We *watched* the clouds **racing** across the sky.	When we got down to the beach, we *found* our boat **damaged** by the storm.	▸ after verbs of perception and observation (*see*, *hear*, *notice*, etc.)
Rain **spreading** from the west will reach most areas tomorrow. (Rain which will spread …)	A woman **hit** by falling branches was badly injured. (A woman who was hit …)	▸ instead of relative clauses
Knowing that the roads would be icy, many commuters went by train. (As they knew …) **Having reached** the top of the hill, I sat down in the sunshine. (After / When I had reached …) The guide led us through the fog, **warning** us to keep to the path. (… he warned us to keep to the path.)	**Covered** in snow, the landscape looked quite different. (As it was covered in snow, …) A flash of lightning lit up the sky, **followed** by a loud clap of thunder. (… It was followed …)	▸ instead of adverbial clauses or main clauses • without conjunctions (reason, time, circumstances)
While **taking** photographs of the enormous waves, a man was swept off a cliff.	*Though* badly **shaken** by the earthquake, the skyscraper did not collapse.	• with conjunctions (*while*, *when*, *though*, *if*, *as if*, etc.)

There will be outbreaks of rain, *some of the showers* **falling** as snow over the Scottish hills.
It will be a cold day **with** *frost* **returning** to many places during the evening.
With so *many roads* **blocked** by the snow, traffic broke down in many areas.

Participle constructions can have subjects of their own. These constructions can also be introduced by *with*, which makes them sound less formal.

"The Joneses are having disappointing weather in Malaga."

1 The Great Plague

There were several disasters in the reign of Charles II. In 1665, a hot summer and the filthy streets caused a fever known as the Plague, or the Pestilence, to spread quickly, and thousands of Londoners died. A man named Samuel Pepys kept a secret diary at this time, written in shorthand. Here are some of the things he wrote down:

Samuel Pepys

June 7th
This day I did in Drury Lane see two or three houses marked with a red cross upon the doors and "Lord have mercy upon us" writ there, which was a sad sight to see.

June 21st
I find all the town almost going out of town, the coaches and waggons being all full of people going into the country.

People leaving London.

People who were ill with the plague were taken away in closed litters or coaches to a kind of hospital known as a pest-house. At night men with carts collected the dead.

Lord! how sad a sight it is to see the streets empty of people and two shops out of three, if not more, shut up.

One day, Pepys saw a naked child being passed out of the window of a house:

It was the child of a citizen in Gracious Street, a saddler, who had buried all the rest of his children of the plague, and he and his wife being now shut up in despair of escaping, did desire only to save the life of this little child; and so prevailed to have it received, stark naked into the arms of a friend, who brought it, having put it into new fresh clothes, to Greenwich; where we did agree it should be permitted to be received and kept in the town.

The dead were taken outside the walls and buried in the fields.

When the winter came, the plague grew less, but next year, 1666, another disaster happened: The Great Fire of London.

From *Looking at History* by R.J. Unstead

---

1 **reign** [reɪn] period of ruling (of a king, queen) • 3 **Pepys** [piːps] • 7 **mercy** pity and forgiveness • 7 **writ** written • 9 **all the town almost** most of the town • 13 **litter** a kind of bed for transporting sick pleople • 24 **in despair of escaping** having given up all hope of escaping • 25 **to desire** to wish strongly • 26 **prevailed to have it received** managed to have it accepted, succeeded in handing it over • 26-27 **(stark) naked** ['neɪkɪd] without clothes on

1.1 Before you start this exercise, form groups and make a list of all the participles or participle constructions in the text.

a Find an example of a participle used as an adjective (13). What verb is it derived from?
b Look at lines 6 and 9 to find one example each of present and past participles used after verbs of perception. What is the difference in meaning?
c There are several participle constructions used instead of relative clauses. (e.g. lines 2, 3, 4, 11 and 14) Change them into 'normal' relative clauses.
d Look at line 28 and change the clause with the perfect form of the present participle into an adverbial clause of time.
e Translate the two sentences that include participle constructions with subjects of their own. (lines 9-11; lines 21-25)

1.2 Look at the pictures and describe what you can see.
Example: *In the first picture you can see people leaving London ... / people can be seen leaving ...*

2 Get away from it all!

Write your own advertisement for a weekend break at one of the comfortable 'Castle Hotels' in Britain. Use present and past participles to make your advert sound effective.
Example: *Enjoy the view of the clouds sailing over the peaceful Yorkshire moors. Appreciate the taste of our own oven-baked bread.*

Use these ideas:

SIGHT see • rainbow / sun • **rise / build up / form / set** • on the horizon • watch • silvery moon • **shine** • on the sea • look at • eagles • **fly** • over the Scottish hills

SOUND hear • birds • **sing** • in the trees of Sherwood Forest • listen to • village church bells • **ring** • in a Welsh valley

TOUCH feel • soft wind • **blow** • in your hair

TASTE enjoy • **locally grow / home-cook** • specialities of our kitchen • taste • **beautifully serve** • delicious meals • try • **specially pick** • fruit • from our own gardens

SMELL find • lovely flowers • **perfectly arrange** • for you in your room • be woken up by • aroma • **freshly make** • coffee or delicious chocolate • rediscover • smell • open fire • **burn** • in our bars • be tempted • homely smell • **beautifully cook** • traditional English breakfast

3 My room

In this extract from 'Room at the Top', Joe Lampton, the hero of the novel, has just arrived in Warley and is being shown his new room. Moving into a room of his own is the first step on the way from his working class background to the 'top'.

Complete the text with these participles:

burning • chosen • cream-painted • depressing • extending • feeling • fitted • following • hanging • impressed • leaving • meaning • wanting

Now, ______ Mrs Thompson into my room, I was moving into a different world. "It's marvellous," I said, ______ the inadequacy of the words and yet not ______ to appear too ______: after all, I hadn't been living in the slums. I looked at it with incredulous delight: wallpaper vertically striped in beige and silver, a bay window ______ for almost the whole length of the room with ______ cushions along it, a divan bed that looked like a divan and not like a bed with its ______ daylight intimations of sleep and sickness, two armchairs, and a dressing-table, a wardrobe and writing-table all in the same pale satiny wood. On the ______ bookcase was a bowl of anemones and there was a fire ______ in the grate, ______ an aromatic smell, faintly acid and faintly flowerlike, which I knew but couldn't quite place.

"Applewood," Mrs Thompson said. "Thanks to the coal shortage we're becoming connoisseurs. There's an electric fire but I thought a real one would be more cheerful on a miserable day like this." There were three small pictures ______ on the far wall: *The Harbour at Arles*, a Breughel skating scene, and Manet's *Olympe*.

"Especially ______ in your honour," Mrs Thompson said. "Medici reproductions. We have quite a picture library – you just slip in new ones when you become tired of them."

"I like the skaters," I said, ______ I liked it best.

Adapted from *Room at the Top* by John Braine

---

to extend to stretch, to continue • **fitted** *here*: genau passend • 2 **inadequacy** if something is inadequate, it is not good enough or fitting • 4 **incredulous delight** unbelievable joy • 5 **bay window** *Erkerfenster* • 6 **divan** (bed) [dɪ'væn] *Liege* • 7 **intimation** suggestion • 10 **anemone** [ə'neməni] • 11 **grate** *here*: *Kamin* • 11 **acid** (unpleasantly) sour • 14 **connoisseur** [ˌkɒnə'sɜː] person who knows a lot about something

ADVANCED RULES AND EXERCISES

Participle constructions suitable for formal and for informal English

Seeing / Having seen the lorry approaching on the brow of the hill, she braked quickly enough to avoid a collision.	**Very formal:** Participle constructions used instead of adverbial or main clauses.
The guide led the way into the cathedral, *a stream of tourists* **following** behind.	**Very formal:** Participle constructions with subjects of their own.
Watch out! *There's* a car **coming**! *There were* two coaches **parked** outside the hotel.	**Informal:** Participles after *there is / there are* are very common in everyday spoken English.

The other uses of the participle (page 107) are common at all stylistic levels.

1 I was Vermeer

The fascinating biography "I was Vermeer", by Frank Wynne, tells the true story of Han van Meegeren of Amsterdam, the most famous forger in history. Forgery is, in fact, very common in the art world. Up to 40% of all major works offered for sale are thought to be fakes!

Han spent six months working on *The Supper at Emmaus* and, for all its faults, it is perhaps his finest work.
It is a simple group portrait: Christ faces the viewer, his eyes half-closed in prayer, his right hand raised to bless the bread he is about to break. On his left sits Cleopas, who gazes in awe at the risen Christ. Facing him, an unnamed disciple, wearing a rough-hewn tunic, looks towards Jesus, his back to the viewer, his face a sliver of profile. Behind the disciples stands a serving girl, her face as serene and as simple as a Madonna, her hand reaching towards the jug of wine.

'It is a wonderful moment in the life of a lover of art when he finds himself suddenly confronted with a hitherto unknown painting by a great master, untouched, on the original canvas, just as it left the painter's studio! And what a picture! Neither the beautiful signature "I.V.Meer" nor the *pointillée* on the bread which Christ is blessing, is necessary to convince us that we have here a – I am inclined to say *the* – masterpiece of Johannes Vermeer of Delft.' (Abraham Bredius, a respected art critic)

From *I was Vermeer – The Legend of the Forger Who Swindled the Nazis* by Frank Wynne

forger *Fälscher* • **fake** *Fälschung* • 2 **Emmaus** [em'eɪəs] • 6 **bless** *segnen* • 8 **awe** *Ehrfurcht* • 9 **disciple** [dɪ'saɪpl] *Jünger* • 9 **rough-hewn** [hjuːn] *grob* • 11 **a sliver** [ɪ] **of profile** *kleiner Ausschnitt des Profils* • 13 **serene** calm (quiet) • 16 **canvas** *Leinwand* • 18 **pointillée** small spots of pure colour • 19 **inclined** *geneigt*

1.1 **Look at the 'formal' participle constructions in the description of the painting. Then describe the painting in your own words, without using formal participle constructions. (You can use 'informal' constructions.) For example, you could start like this:**
In this famous forgery by Han van Meegeren, there are three people sitting together …

☆ **1.2** **Imagine you are working as an official guide in an art gallery. Choose a picture you like (ideally, with lots of lively and interesting details), and write a description of it, this time in formal style, with suitable participle constructions. (You could work in small groups for this; each of you describes your picture to the others in your group.)**

☆ **1.3** **How do you think Bredius, the art critic, must have felt when *The Supper at Emmaus* was found to be a fake? Think of past participles (used as adjectives) to describe his feelings.**
Example: He probably felt absolutely amazed.

2 Film choice

THE TERMINATOR (1984) CS, 9 pm *****

This thrilling action adventure stars former real-life muscle-man and once Governor of California, Arnold Schwarzenegger. *Directed and co-written by the Oscar-winning James Cameron* (of Titanic and Avatar fame), The Terminator is a dazzlingly high-tech tale *featuring Arnie as a violent cyborg sent from a future society ruled by machines. His task being to track down and kill a woman* whose as yet unborn son will overthrow the rule of the robots, Schwarzenegger, as an unstoppable and murderous man-machine, goes about his job ruthlessly and methodically. *Searching for his intended victim,* he wreaks havoc in the 20th century. Linda Hamilton, *playing the intended victim,* shows true grit as his unfortunate target.
With some superb special effects added as a bonus, this violent action fantasy will keep you gripped until the very end.
Though having made better films since, Cameron has never recaptured the brilliant simplicity of this one.

5 **dazzling** impressive, spectacular • 6 **cyborg** creature that is partly human and partly machine • 10 **ruthless** having no pity • 11 **to wreak havoc** to cause a lot of damage and destruction • 13 **grit** courage and determination

Complex sentences with participle constructions are typical of formal texts. Explain to a friend what 'The Terminator' is about, using adverbial, relative, or main clauses instead of the passages in *italics*.

> As a general rule, it is best to avoid complex constructions when you write your own texts. By keeping your sentences clear and simple, you will find it easier to avoid mistakes.

3 Journey of the Magi

"A cold coming we had of it,
Just the worst time of the year
For a journey, and such a long journey:
The ways deep and the weather sharp,
The very dead of winter."
And the camels galled, sore-footed, refractory,
Lying down in the melting snow.
There were times we regretted
The summer palaces on slopes, the terraces,
And the silken girls bringing sherbet.
Then the camel men cursing and grumbling
And running away, and wanting their liquor and women,
And the night-fires going out, and the lack of shelters,
And the cities hostile and the towns unfriendly
And the villages dirty and charging high prices:
A hard time we had of it.
At the end we preferred to travel all night,
Sleeping in snatches,
With the voices singing in our ears, saying
That this was all folly.

Then at dawn we came down to a temperate valley,
Wet, below the snow line, smelling of vegetation;
With a running stream and a water-mill beating the darkness,
And three trees on the low sky,
And an old white horse galloped away in the meadow.
Then we came to a tavern with vine-leaves over the lintel,
Six hands at an open door dicing for pieces of silver,
And feet kicking the empty wine-skins.
But there was no information, and so we continued
And arrived at evening, not a moment too soon
Finding the place; it was (you may say) satisfactory.

---

the Magi ['meɪdʒaɪ] the three wise men who brought gifts for the baby Jesus • 5 **the very dead of winter** the middle of winter • 6 **galled** [gɔ:ld] with their backs made sore by the saddle • 6 **refractory** stubborn and difficult to control • 8 **to regret** *here*: to miss • 9 **slope** rising ground • 10 **silken** *here*: wearing silk (Seide) • 10 **sherbet** kind of lemonade • 11 **to curse** to swear • 12 **liquor** ['lɪkə] any strong alcoholic drink • 13 **lack** absence • 13 **shelter** covered place that protects against rain, wind, etc. • 14 **hostile** ['hɒstaɪl] unfriendly • 15 **to charge** to demand (as payment) • 18 **to sleep in snatches** to sleep for short periods only and to wake up often • 20 **folly** stupidity • 21 **dawn** daybreak, sunrise • 21 **temperate** neither too hot nor too cold • 25 **meadow** [e] field of grass • 26 **lintel** a piece of stone or wood across the top of a door (part of the frame) • 27 **to dice** *würfeln*

All this was a long time ago, I remember,
And I would do it again, but set down
This set down
This: were we led all that way for
Birth or Death? There was a Birth, certainly,
We had evidence and no doubt. I had seen birth and death,
But had thought they were different; this Birth was
Hard and bitter agony for us, like Death, our death.
We returned to our places, these Kingdoms,
But no longer at ease here, in the old dispensation,
With an alien people clutching their gods.
I should be glad of another death.

T. S. Eliot (1888-1965)

39 **agony** great pain • 41 **at ease** feeling comfortable • 41 **dispensation** a particular religious system or order • 42 **alien** ['eɪljən] foreign; strange and frightening • 42 **to clutch** to hold very tightly

3.1 Look at the structure of the sentences in the first part of the poem (1-20).
Is there anything that strikes you as unusual?
What effect is created by this style?
How does the tone differ in the last part (32-43)?

3.2 Write a prose version of the first part. Do not use any participles.
Start like this:
In the poem T.S. Eliot describes the 'Journey of the Magi' to Bethlehem: The weather was very bad. The camels did not want to go on and they lay down in the snow. The men ...

4 Non-finite Verb Forms: Mixed Exercises

CHECK-UP

1 96-year-old fined for speeding

Fill in the correct non-finite verb forms – infinitives, gerunds or participles.

A motorist of 96 was fined £20 yesterday – for _____ – his first offence in 70 years of _____. Mr Dale was warned _____ more carefully in future but was not ordered _____ a _____-test. He was caught by a radar trap, _____ 49 mph in a 30 mph area, while _____ near his home in Folkestone. He refused _____ his age to police when _____, but later wrote a letter to a newspaper, _____ about the radar trap. He said he was 96 and was looking forward to _____ around Brands Hatch on his 100th birthday.

speed
motor · drive
take · drive · do
travel · give
stop · complain
go

Police Constable William Holton, one of the men _____ the radar trap, said: "We heard an engine _____ and then saw him _____ round the corner. He appeared _____ in some hurry."

operate
roar · come
be

Mr Dale said: "Oh, I'm 96 all right, but I'm fit. I've no doubt that I could _____ any test they might have asked me _____. I remember _____ my first motor-bike when I was 25. More than 70 years of trouble-free _____ is not a bad record, and I've got no reason _____ _____ that I'm one of the safest drivers on the road. But I'm still annoyed about _____. On that particular stretch of road _____ _____ 30 mph is absurd. I take regular medical check-ups, and my heart and lungs are first class. I do _____ glasses, and I don't _____ as well as I used to, but that won't make me _____ of _____ my licence, I'm still fit enough _____."

pass · take · drive
motor
stop · think
be caught
have to · do
need
hear · think · hand in
drive

1 **offence** breaking of a rule or law • 7 **Brands Hatch** a race track south-east of London

2 On holiday

Complete the sentences, using either infinitives or gerunds.

a	Look, it's stopped _____. We can go back to the beach.	rain
b	What a fantastic view! Let's stop _____ some pictures.	take
c	We must remember _____ Aunt Agatha a postcard from the States.	send
d	I'll always remember _____ New York for the first time.	see
e	I forgot _____ my shorts. How silly of me.	pack
f	I'll never forget _____ Ben Nevis. What an experience!	climb
g	We should try _____ to the hotel before 8 p.m. if possible.	get
h	My skin burns so easily! Try _____ some of my sunblock. That may help.	use
i	The flight leaves at 8.20. That'll mean _____ quite early.	get up
j	I've heard so much about Australia. I really mean _____ there soon.	go

BASIC RULES AND EXERCISES

Gerund and infinitive: no difference in meaning

The dog **started barking** when it saw the cat.	The cat **started to climb** the nearest tree.
Start, begin, continue and ***like, love, hate, prefer*** can be followed by a **gerund** or an **infinitive**.	

Note We **would like to have** a dog, but our flat is too small.

After ***would (should) like/love/prefer*** the **infinitive** must be used.

Gerund and infinitive: different meaning

We must have annoyed our parrot. He has **stopped saying** "Good morning" to us. Even after the postman had left, the dog **went on barking**.	There's a pet shop over there. Let's **stop to get** some bird food. First we taught Polly to say "Hello". Then we **went on to teach** her a song.
The **gerund** after ***stop*** expresses an action which has come to an end. After ***go on***, it expresses the continuation of an action.	The **infinitive** after ***stop*** expresses the intention to do something else. After ***go on***, it expresses the next step in a series of actions.
I can't **remember taking** that photo of Bonzo. Do you know when I took it?	We must **remember to feed** the budgie before we go.
The **gerund** after ***forget*** and ***remember*** expresses that something has been done/has happened.	The **infinitive** after ***forget*** and ***remember*** expresses an intention to do something.

Further examples of different meaning

Sammy won't eat dog biscuits. – Why don't you **try mixing** them in with his meat?	Most budgie owners **try to teach** their birds to talk.
The **gerund** after ***try*** expresses a new method of doing something.	The **infinitive** after ***try*** expresses an attempt.
Now that we've got that dog, it **means planning** our holidays much more carefully. *(Das bedeutet, dass wir … müssen.)*	I **meant to take** the dog for a walk but I didn't have time. *(Ich hatte vor, …)*
The **gerund** after ***mean*** expresses a consequence.	The **infinitive** after ***mean*** expresses an intention.

Present participle and infinitive after verbs of perception

We could **hear** the cats **fighting** and **screaming** all night.	We **saw** the cat **stop** suddenly and then **jump** on the mouse.
The **present participle** after **verbs of perception** describes an **action in progress**.	The **infinitive** after **verbs of perception** describes a **completed action**. The construction is mainly used to describe short actions or a series of actions.

1 The boxing match

Complete the sentences, using infinitives, gerunds or participles.

"What? Where are you going?" Tony asked. "But that means ___ a hell	spend
of a lot of money, just to watch two men ___ each other up."	beat
Tony's my best friend, but I didn't care. For months now I had been looking	
forward to ___ Butcher Jason ___ Tiger Robinson.	see · fight
"I remember somebody once ___ that he would live to see Jason ___	say · become
world champion," I said.	
"OK, have a nice time," Tony said.	
Before the fight began, I watched the two boxers ___ at each other,	stare
trying ___ tough and ___ each other. Then I heard the gong ___.	look · frighten · sound
For a long time I sat and watched the two boxers ___ round each other	dance
as if they were trying ___ each other. But suddenly I saw Tiger ___ a left	avoid · throw
hook and saw his red glove ___ Jason's chin. The referee stopped the fight	hit
___ Tiger to his corner. Then he started ___. I watched Butcher ___ on	send · count · hold
to the ropes. Then, all at once, I noticed his eyes ___ all funny and his	go
head ___ forward; a moment later I heard him ___ to the floor.	drop · crash
All the spectators were on their feet and started ___. I heard someone	yell
next to me ___ something I couldn't understand, but it didn't sound nice.	shout
"Get your ass off that floor, you fat slug," I yelled.	
I can't remember ___ language like that before, ever. Then I felt someone	use
___ me on the shoulder, hard. I turned round and saw this big guy ___	tap · stand
directly behind me.	
"You stop ___ my brother," he yelled at me.	insult
"I'm sorry, I didn't mean ___ you," I said, trying ___ cool.	annoy · look
But he went on ___, getting wilder all the time. Then I saw him ___ his	shout · raise
fists. It was not until I noticed the snake's head tattooed on his right biceps	
that I really regretted my decision ___ to the boxing match.	go

16 **to yell** to shout loudly • 18 **ass** (AE) slang word for the part of your body that you sit on • 18 **slug** *Nacktschnecke* • 20 **to tap** to hit lightly (with the fingers) • 22 **to insult sb** to annoy sb by speaking rudely • 25 **fist** closed hand (as a sign of threat) • 25 **biceps** ['baiseps]

"No skill? You try to cut an eye open, left-handed, wearing eight-ounce gloves."

2 School's over: What now?

Translate into English, using gerunds and infinitives wherever possible.

a „Ich freue mich darauf, endlich Geld zu verdienen.“
b „Nach der Schule will ich Architektur studieren. Ich träume schon davon, mein eigenes Haus zu entwerfen.“
c „Ich habe schon daran gedacht, für ein paar Monate nach Amerika zu gehen und dort zu arbeiten.“
d „Ich möchte ganz gern für ein Reisebüro arbeiten. Aber andererseits hätte ich kein Interesse daran, den ganzen Tag im Büro zu sitzen.“
e „Ich finde, man sollte etwas wirklich Lohnendes (something really worthwhile) machen, anstatt immer nur ans Geld zu denken.“
f „Meine Eltern wollten schon immer, dass ich im Familienbetrieb mitarbeite. Ich weiß nicht, wie ich nein sagen kann, ohne sie zu enttäuschen. Ich habe Angst, ihnen die Wahrheit zu sagen – aber andererseits hat es keinen Zweck, etwas anzufangen, das mich überhaupt nicht interessiert.“

3 Danger, mountains!

Complete the sentences, using gerunds, participles or infinitives. Choose from the given verbs.

A Every year there are reports of people ____ while ____ in the Scottish mountains. The Scottish hills are not very high, so this often makes tourists ____ they are harmless. People that are used to ____ in the Alps, may suddenly find themselves ____ in fog on much lower hills. Many people fail ____ appropriate precautions before ____.

be killed • set off • strand • take • think • walk • walk

B You often see people ____ completely unsuitable clothes. Sometimes visitors try ____ mountains without ____ the dangers of the weather. Sandals and T-shirts are not suitable ____ hikers from sudden rain, fog or even snow in summer. Hikers should remember ____ the weather forecast and they mustn't forget ____ a map or a compass with them.

check • climb • protect • realize • take • wear

C The real problem is how ____ people aware of mountain conditions. Information offices all over the country warn the millions of annual visitors ____ aware of the dangers. But the Scottish authorities are against ____ more signposts and they are also against more clearly ____ paths because they don't want unspoilt hills ____, and they are afraid of even more people ____ that the hills are more harmless than they really are. Experienced hill walkers are also against ____ things ____ easier on the mountains.

be • be spoilt • believe • make • make • mark • put up • seem

5 **to fail to do sth** not to do what is expected • 5 **appropriate** correct and suitable • 5 **precaution** an action taken to avoid possible danger • 18 **to be aware of** to know of, to realize

ADVANCED EXERCISES

This chapter contains no *Advanced Rules*.
However, the exercises here offer further opportunities to explore how the use of gerunds, infinitives and participles differs.

1 The problem of ghost nets

Choose the correct non-finite forms to complete this newspaper article.

A While environmentalists and politicians argue about how ___ the world's ___ fish stocks, there should be at least one reform everyone can agree on: '___ waste'. A good place ___ is the phenomenon ___ as 'ghost nets'. A recently ___ study of deep-sea ___ in the North Atlantic concluded that more than 780 miles of industrial fishing net is lost or discarded in that ocean every year.

Gerunds: eliminating · fishing
Infinitives: to start · to protect
Participles: declining · known · published

B Instead of just ___ to the bottom and ___, these synthetic nets end up ___ 'fences' across the sea bed. ___ practically indestructible for a century or more, they continue ___ millions of tonnes of fish year after year, without ___ anyone. It's hard ___ about the scale of the waste without ___ ill. ___ these ghost nets will be difficult.

Gerunds: benefiting · disintegrating · feeling · forming · removing · sinking
Infinitives: to snare · to be · to think
Participles: made

C They are not easy ___, and once ___, their removal requires long-distance boats, ___ divers with the right equipment for ___ the nets, and lots of time. But surely it will be worth ___. With fish stocks ___ and the world population ___, we can hardly afford ___ fish ___ on the seabed.

Gerunds: cutting · doing
Infinitives: to let · to locate · rot
Participles: collapsing · found · increasing · trained

2 **stocks** *Bestände* • 7 **to discard** to get rid of sth no longer needed • **to disintegrate** to break up into small bits • **to snare** to catch (and kill) • 13 **scale** *Ausmaß*

The use of the infinitive when referring to actions in the future

I'm planning **to study** Maths.
Do you want **to go** to University?
I'd love **to do** a gap year in India!
You need good A-Level results **to get** into Oxford or Cambridge.
The careers officer has given me this brochure **to look** at.
I'm wondering whether **to drop** Physics.

The infinitive (with *to*) often refers to the future, i.e. to an action that has not yet taken place. (e.g. after *want, would like, expect, decide, hope, it's best / important / a good idea*, etc.)

2 A meeting with Edith Piaf

In October 1960, the French composer Charles Dumont was down to his last franc, worried about not having enough to pay the rent, and almost in despair. He had made an appointment to see Edith Piaf, hoping to sell her one of his songs. But when he and his lyricist arrived at her flat, the *chanteuse* – who had by then retired – refused even to come out of her bedroom. The meeting, they were told, was cancelled. Then, just as they were about to leave, she agreed to listen to just one song. Angry at being treated so callously, Dumont went to the piano to play her his latest composition: *Non, je ne regrette rien*. At the end, Piaf gave her verdict: "That song will conquer the world."

And so, of course, it did. Piaf used the song to make a spectacular comeback, three years before her death. And the royalties from it have given Dumont a good living for over half a century. Although he has written many other songs, that one was the only one to become world famous. And he is indeed proud of having written it. "How many people," he says, "can say they helped to create something legendary, something magical, something I hope will live for ever?"

Adapted from *The Week*

2 **rent** *Miete* • 4 **lyricist** sb who writes the words for songs • 7 **to be about to** to be going to • 8 **callous** unkind, cruel, without feeling for other people • 10 **verdict** *here*: opinion • 12 **royalties** payments to a writer/composer depending on how many books, songs etc. are sold

Look carefully at the note on the previous page. Then use infinitives or gerunds to help you complete these sentences, according to what you discover from the text.

a Charles Dumont was feeling desperate about ______.
b When he and his lyricist went to Edith Piaf's apartment, they expected ______ and hoped ______.
c But Piaf wasn't interested ______ because she had already stopped ______, so she didn't even want ______.
d At the last moment, however, she changed her mind and decided ______.
e Furious, Dumont sat down at the piano ______ and waited for Piaf ______.
f She loved the new song and, of course, it helped her ______.
g It became her greatest hit, and the royalties from it enabled Dumont ______.
h Even today, so many years later, people all over the world still enjoy ______.

3 Brave New World

At the end of Aldous Huxley's famous utopian novel 'Brave New World', Mustapha Mond, one of the World Controllers, explains to the Savage, who was brought up amid primitive customs on a 'reservation' in New Mexico, about the civilization of Brave New World.

"My dear young friend," said Mustapha Mond, "civilization has absolutely no need of nobility or heroism. These things are symptoms of political inefficiency. In a properly organized society like ours, nobody has any opportunities for being noble or heroic. Conditions have got to be thoroughly unstable before the occasion can arise. Where there are wars, where there are divided allegiances, where there are temptations to be resisted, objects of love to be fought for or defended – there, obviously nobility and heroism have some sense. But there aren't any wars nowadays. The greatest care is taken to prevent you from loving anyone too much. There is no such thing as a divided allegiance; you're so conditioned that you can't help doing what you ought to do. And what you ought to do is on the whole so pleasant, so many of the natural impulses are allowed free play that there really aren't any temptations to resist. And if ever, by some unlucky chance, anything unpleasant should somehow happen, why, there's always soma to give you a holiday from the facts. And there's always soma to calm your anger, to reconcile you to your enemies, to make you patient and long-suffering. In the past you could only accomplish these things by making a great effort and after years of hard moral training. Now, you swallow two or three half-gramme tablets, and there you are. Anybody can be virtuous now. You can carry at least half of your morality about in a bottle. Christianity without tears – that's what soma is."

From *Brave New World* by Aldous Huxley

---

2 **nobility** admirable behaviour or attitude • 2 **inefficiency** working or performing in a badly organized way • 4 **thoroughly** completely • 4 **unstable** not firm, likely to change or fail • 4 **occasion** opportunity, reason for doing sth • 5 **allegiance** [ə'li:dʒəns] support for a group, person or belief • 5 **temptation** attraction to sth forbidden • 5 **to resist** to fight successfully against • 7 **to prevent** to stop • 8 **conditioned** influenced by training • 8 **you can't help doing sth** it is impossible for you not to do sth • 12 **to calm** to make quiet, to soften • 12 **to reconcile** to make friendly again after a quarrel • 13 **long-suffering** patiently bearing problems or bad treatment • 13 **to accomplish** to achieve, to manage • 14 **to swallow** to eat without chewing • 15 **virtuous** ['vɜ:tʃʊəs] well behaved and morally correct

3.1 **Explain in a few sentences why being 'noble' or 'heroic' is not important in the 'ideal' society described by Mustapha Mond.**
Do you think it might ever be possible to create a society of this kind?

3.2 **What role does *soma* play in Brave New World? Use non-finite constructions, where appropriate, to help explain in what way *soma* can be seen as 'Christianity without tears'.**

4 Traveling through the dark

Traveling through the dark I found a deer
dead on the edge of the Wilson road.
It is usually best to roll them into the canyon:
that road is narrow: to swerve might make more dead.

By the glow of the tail-light I stumbled back of the car
and stood by the heap, a doe, a recent killing;
she had stiffened already, almost cold.
I dragged her off; she was large in the belly.

My fingers touching her side brought me the reason –
her side was warm; her fawn lay there waiting,
alive, still, never to be born.
Beside that mountain road I hesitated.

The car aimed ahead its lowering parking lights;
under the hood purred the steady engine.
I stood in the glare of the warm exhaust turning red;
around our group I could hear the wilderness listen.

I thought hard for us all – my only swerving –
then pushed her over the edge into the river.

From *Stories That Could Be True: New And Collected Poems*
by William Stafford

---

4 **to swerve** to turn suddenly to one side • 5 **glow** a soft light • 5 **to stumble** to put one's foot down awkwardly and almost fall • 6 **heap** *here*: a heavy lifeless mass • 6 **doe** female deer • 7 **to stiffen** to become hard • 8 **to drag** to pull along the ground • 8 **belly** lower part of the body • 10 **fawn** very young deer • 13 **lowering** [aʊ] dark and dangerous-looking • 14 **hood** AE part of the car that covers the engine • 14 **to purr** to make a noise like a pleased cat • 14 **steady** [e] moving in a regular and reliable way • 15 **glare** bright light • 15 **exhaust** Auspuff

4.1
a Why is it "usually best to roll" dead animals off the road?
b What does the speaker discover by touching the doe?
c What does "her fawn lay there waiting" and "never to be born" mean?
d What does the speaker mean when he says he "could hear the wilderness listen"?
e What is meant by "my only swerving"?

4.2
a Look carefully at the description of the deer, and compare it with the description of the car. What contrast do you see?
b The speaker seems to find it difficult to make a decision. What is the dilemma he finds himself in? How does he resolve it?
c What could the title of the poem mean? Think of various possibilities.

15 Verbs and their Objects

CHECK-UP

1 Tastes differ

Put in the objects with or without *to* and choose the best word order.

PAUL Can you lend (some money · me) for this new CD? It's Beethoven's Ninth, conducted by Simon Rattle. I showed (it · you) when we were in here yesterday.

PETE I can't remember you saying (anything · me) about it. Perhaps you showed (it · Mike) and not me. Anyway, I owe (some money · you) for the theatre tickets last week, so that's OK.

PAUL Right. We're quits then. This is a great recording! Perhaps I could lend (it · you) some time. I …

PETE Oh, Paul! You're always trying to teach (something about music · me) – I'm fed up with it. Either you're giving (a lesson on Bach · me) or trying to sell (a ticket · me) for a concert by your third-rate school orchestra. No thanks! I prefer jazz, you know that. I've explained (it all · you) hundreds of times.

PAUL OK, OK. Sorry. Hand (that jazz CD over there · me). Let's listen to it together.

2 At work

Put in the objects in the best order – with or without *to* or *for*.

a *Mrs Brown, managing director of 'Pharmaco':* I'll tell (more about my plans · you) after lunch, Mrs MacLaren. It'll only take (a few minutes · us). Those people from Johnson and White'll be here in a moment. Make (some coffee · them) when they arrive, please, and bring (a cup of tea · me) as usual. Perhaps you could get (a few biscuits · us), too.

b *Sergeant White, police officer:* Ordinary-looking? Now, it would save (a lot of time · us) if you could describe (the woman · us) in detail, sir. You were quite right to report (all this · the police), of course, but our chances of solving crimes are always greater if people can give (an exact description of the person in question · us). Perhaps if I ask (a few questions · you), your memory may improve. Right then …

c *Mr Green, salesperson:* May I suggest (something · you), madam? Buy (the more expensive model · your husband). You won't regret it. Of course, it'll cost (a few pounds more · you), but it'll be well worth it in the long run.

"Why wait till Father's Day? Give it to him now."

BASIC RULES AND EXERCISES

1 Type *give* sb sth / *give* sth to sb

Mike *showed* the customs officer **his passport.**	The basic word order is *indirect object* + **direct object**.
We *showed* **our tickets** *to the woman at the British Airways counter.*	The order is reversed and *to* is used when ▸ the *indirect object* is much longer than the **direct object**.
Please *hand* **your boarding-card** *to the flight attendant (not to me).*	▸ the *indirect object* is stressed.
What's in this bag? – Presents. I'm *giving* **them** *to friends.*	▸ the **direct object** is a personal pronoun (usually *it* or *them*).

Verbs of this type:
bring, give, hand, lend, offer, owe, promise, pass, sell, send, show, teach, tell, write

2 Type *explain* sth *to sb*

The TV presenter *explained* **the rules of the game** *to the viewers.*	The basic word order is **direct object** + *indirect object.*
We didn't see the end of the film, but Stella *described to us* **all the interesting scenes we'd missed.**	The word order can be reversed if the **direct object** is especially stressed, or very long.

Verbs of this type:
announce, describe, dictate, explain, introduce, mention, report, say, suggest

▸ **see Chapter 9 for the use of these verbs in the passive**

Type: *buy* sb sth / *buy* sth for sb They *bought him* **a motor-bike** when he was 18. They *bought* **a motor-bike** *for him* when he was 18.	The word order is either *indirect object* + **direct object**, or **direct object** + *indirect object* with *for*. Verbs of this type: *buy, fetch, get, make, order*
Type *ask* sb sth The bike cost *his parents* **a lot of money**.	The word order is always *indirect object* + **direct object** (*to* and *for* are never used!). Verbs of this type: *ask (a question), cost (time/money), take (time), save (time/money)*

A limerick
There was a señora of Spain,
Who couldn't go out in the rain,
For she'd lent her umbrella
To Queen Isabella,
Who never returned it again.

Another limerick
There was an old man of Calcutta,
Who had an unfortunate stutter.
"Please pass me," he said,
"The b-b-b-bread,
And the b-b-b-b-b-b-butter."

„George has passed on his inter in ornithology to the kids."*

* **ornithology** study of birds

1 Bits and pieces

Use the following bits and pieces to make sentences with two objects.
Example: *The children bought themselves ice-creams / bought ice-creams for themselves.*

children ✓	*announce*	ice-creams ✓	*council*
farmer	*describe*	large area of land	*traffic warden*
film director	*hand*	part in the new film	*themselves* ✓
tourist	*buy* ✓	way to the station	*waiting reporters*
demonstrators	*report*	leaflets	*impatient passengers*
loudspeaker	*promise*	news that the flight was delayed	*police*
neighbours	*ask*	burglary	*young film star*
explorers	*sell*	details of the journey	*crowds in the street*

2 The do-it-yourself cottage

There are quite a number of other verbs with two objects that are *not* included in the lists on the previous page. Here are some common ones that are used in this exercise:

Type *give*: leave (*hinterlassen*) **Type *explain*:** mean **Type *buy*:** find, book

Put in the objects in the most suitable word order – with or without *to* or *for*.

When Tom Turner's uncle died, he left (quite a sum of money · Tom). This unexpected legacy gave (an idea · him). Why not buy (an old cottage · his family) in the Yorkshire Dales? Holidays in the country had always meant (a lot · him and his wife). Tom gave (a lot of thought · the question) before announcing (his decision · his family), who especially liked the idea of renovating the cottage themselves. He also mentioned (his idea · their friends), and some of them offered (their help and advice · him). Soon Tom found (a dream cottage · his family) – in the little Yorkshire village of Masham. A friend who was an architect drew the plans for the alterations, and the council gave (planning permission · them). Tom booked (rooms in the local inn · everybody), and the little group of friends travelled to Masham to help, at the same time promising (a little holiday · themselves). A local builder sent (building materials · Tom and his helpers), and local workmen gave (help · them) with jobs they could not do themselves. It took (a long time · them) to finish the work – but all in all it had not cost (very much · the Turners). And it had been a wonderful summer, the first of many: the Turners offered (free use of the cottage · their friends) – whenever they felt like a holiday in the Yorkshire Dales.

2 **legacy** ['legəsɪ] money etc. that you receive after sb has died • 15 **builder** *Bauunternehmer*

3 How much to tip?

Esther is one of twelve bright American college girls who have won a free month in New York as a prize in a fashion magazine's writing competition.

When I first arrived at the Amazon, a man in a bellhop's uniform carried my suitcase up in the elevator and unlocked my room for me. Of course I rushed immediately to the window and looked out to see what the view was. After a while I was aware of this bellhop turning on the hot and cold taps in my washbowl and saying "This is the hot and this is the cold" and switching on the radio and telling me the names of all the New York stations and I began to get uneasy, so I said firmly, "Thank you for bringing up my suitcase."

"Thank you thank you thank you. Ha!" he said in a very nasty tone, and before I could wheel round to see what had come over him he was gone, shutting the door behind him with a rude slam.

Later, when I told Doreen about his curious behaviour, she said, "You ninny, he wanted his tip." I asked how much I should have given and she said a quarter at least and thirty-five cents if the suitcase was too heavy. Now I could have carried that suitcase to my room perfectly well by myself, only the bellhop seemed so eager to do it that I let him.

I thought that sort of service came along with what you paid for your hotel room.

I hate handing over money to people for doing what I could just as easily do myself.

Doreen said ten per cent was what you should tip a person, but I somehow never had the right change and I'd have felt awfully silly giving somebody half a dollar and saying, "Fifteen cents of this is a tip for you, please give me thirty-five cents back."

The first time I took a taxi in New York I tipped the driver ten cents. The fare was a dollar, so I thought ten cents was exactly right and gave the driver my dime with a smile. But he only held it in the palm of his hand and stared and stared at it, and when I stepped out of the cab, hoping I had not handed him a Canadian dime by mistake, he started yelling, "Lady I gotta live like you and everybody else," in a loud voice which scared me so much I broke into a run …

From *The Bell Jar* by Sylvia Plath

---

to tip to give a tip *(Trinkgeld)* • 1 **Amazon** hotel in New York • 2 **bellhop** a hotel porter • 16 **ninny** silly person • 17 **quarter** 25 cent piece • 19 **eager** keen • 29 **fare** price of the journey • 30 **dime** 10 cent piece • 30 **palm** [pɑ:m] inner part of the hand • 31 **cab** taxi • 32 **to yell** to shout

3.1 **Pick out the examples of verbs with two objects (lines 1-11; 20-34). Which 'type' are they?**

3.2 **The bellhop carried Esther's luggage for her. Say what else he did for her, showed / told her.
Then explain why he got so angry.**

3.3 **Describe the incident with the taxi-driver in a sentence or two, and explain the 'misunderstanding'.**

3.4 **A good hotel offers all kinds of service to its guests. Think of as many as you can.**

receptionist • porter • waiter (waitress) • barman (barmaid) • chambermaid • …
order • show • bring • make • get • fetch • carry • give • reserve • …
early-morning call • meals • taxi • room key • theatre tickets • bed • menu • drinks • room • luggage • …

Example: *The receptionist will order a taxi for you / order you a taxi if you need one.*

3.5 **What do you think of the problem of 'tipping'?
In what situation (if at all) is it 'correct' to give / leave someone a tip?**

4 At the tourist information centre

Translate these sentences into English.

a Könnten Sie mir bitte ein Hotelzimmer reservieren?
b Der Weg zum alten Schloss ist ziemlich kompliziert. Leider kann ich's Ihnen nicht gut beschreiben. Am besten gebe ich Ihnen einen Stadtplan.
c Die Stadtrundfahrt ist wirklich ein Erlebnis. Wir empfehlen sie allen unseren Gästen.
d Ich verstehe nicht ganz, was Sie meinen. Könnten Sie es mir noch mal erklären?
e Ich kann Ihnen billige Karten für Freitag anbieten. Wenn Sie sie an der Theaterkasse kaufen, kosten sie Sie erheblich mehr.

"I'm going to give you something for your depression – it's an airline ticket to the Bahamas!"

ADVANCED RULES AND EXERCISES

Verbs with a direct object and object complement	
Type 1: object + object complement with *as*	
Not all young people *regard* **further education** *as the key to success.*	Verbs of this type: *acknowledge, choose, look upon, recognize, regard, think of*
Type 2: object + object complement without *as*	
Tom talked to the careers officer, and *found* **her advice** *a great help.*	Verbs of this type: *appoint, call, crown, declare, elect, find, make, think*

Practical experience *is regarded as a big advantage.* Mr Fox *was made managing director.*	The verbs above (Types 1 and 2) are often used in the passive.
Many young workers *find* **an eight-hour day** *very long.*	The complement is often a noun, but some verbs (e.g. *call, declare, find, make, regard, think*) can also be followed by an adjective.
Most people *consider* **a friendly atmosphere** *(as) an important factor at work.*	The verb *consider* can be used with or without *as*.

"I'm going to call it football."

1 Innocent or guilty?

Use suitable complements (adjectives or nouns) to complete the sentences.

There was a moment of silence, then the judge pronounced the accused man ___. Not everyone in the courtroom considered the verdict ___. In fact, a large number of people thought it ___. Loud shouts of protest filled the court as some declared the witnesses ___, and others called the judge ___. Sitting alone at the back of the courtroom, the man's wife thought the judge's decision ___. She had always found her husband ___, and personally regarded him ___. So the verdict, which she looked upon ___, had naturally made her ___.

2 **verdict** (in a court of law) decision whether a prisoner is guilty or not guilty • 3 **witness** (in a court of law) person who appears in court and says what they know about the case

2 Marks of a man?

Girls regularly outperform boys at school. Statistics have been telling us this for years. We now know the reason why efforts to tackle boys' underachievement have so far failed: boys regard avoiding schoolwork and 'acting tough' as marks of a man.

A survey of more than 320 boys found that they still look upon being good at sport as a sign of being a 'real man', while working hard is looked upon as 'unmasculine'. Boys who are dominant and swear a lot are considered 'cool' by their classmates, even though these characteristics tend to lead to poor academic results.

The survey looked at pupils aged 11 to 14 from 12 London secondary schools. State school boys explained to researchers that challenging authority was recognized as a key to popularity among pupils, whereas hard work was regarded as 'soft'. Independent school pupils said they found academic success important, but still thought it necessary to appear 'manly' in order to win status among their friends.

Many of the boys, however, once they felt comfortable with the researchers, admitted that their 'macho act' often gave them feelings of isolation – and sometimes made them afraid to express themselves.

The leader of the project, a professor of psychology, said schools must teach boys more flexible attitudes.

Asked about their fathers, the boys were critical, although most teenagers said they had a good relationship with them. Fathers were seen as emotionally unavailable, bad listeners, and only able to offer them very basic advice. As a result, most of the boys chose their mother as the one to confide in.

Adapted from *The Independent*

---

marks characteristics • 1 **to outperform** to do better than • 5 **to tackle** to deal with, to try to overcome • 5 **underachievement** doing less well than expected • 23 **independent school** private school • 33 **unavailable (of people)** very difficult to reach or talk to • 35 **to confide in** to talk to (e.g. about personal problems)

2.1 Work in groups to pick out the verbs with two objects and those with an object complement.

2.2 Use verbs with two objects – or with an object complement – to answer these questions:

a Why do boys in Britain tend to underachieve at school?
b Do the boys generally feel happy with these attitudes?
c How do most boys see their parents?

☆ **2.3 Discuss the boys' attitudes. Do you consider them 'normal' for that age group? Do you think such attitudes tend to change as teenagers get older? (If so, what might the reasons be?)**

In conversational English, the construction with object and object complement is often avoided when an opinion is stated, and a that-clause is used instead.

Examples:
Formal: I regard your decision as wise.
We do not think it important …
Informal: I think your decision is wise.
We don't think it's important …

The alternative construction with to be is also very common in formal English:
I consider racism to be one of the greatest problems we face today.
Until recently, a good education was thought to be a guarantee of a good job.

3 Historical facts

Can you get the facts right? Complete the sentences with suitable complements. Sometimes there will be a number of different possibilities.

a In June 1953, Elizabeth II was crowned ____.
b Nelson Mandela was the first non-white to be elected ____.
c After the Civil War, slaves were officially made ____, but not all Americans considered them ____.
d The Declaration of Independence is acknowledged ____.
e Eventually, after years of fighting the colonists, Britain had to recognize the United States ____.
f Before women got the vote in Britain in 1918, politics was looked upon ____.
g During the Industrial Revolution, employing children to work in factories was thought of ____.
It was a long time before child labour was finally made ____ in Britain.
h In the days of the Cold War, most Americans regarded the Soviet Union ____.

6 Relative Clauses

CHECK-UP

1 The grotesque world of competitive eating

Fill in *who, which* or *whose*. Say where *that* could be used instead, and where the relative pronoun could be left out.

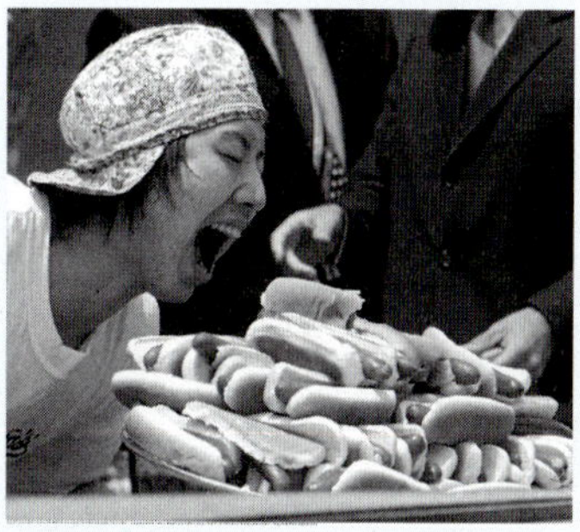

Future historians _____ want to write about American society today will be certain to mention the 'madness' _____ is so typical of our lifestyle. One of the first things _____ they will think of will surely be the grotesque phenomenon _____ is commonly described as 'competitive eating'. Eating contests, _____ started off as harmless fun at fairs, have now developed into a full-scale industry. 'Major League Eating', _____ was founded some years ago, now organizes over 80 contests a year, in _____ prize money totalling nearly $ 600,000 can be won! This organization, _____ 'Hot Dog Eating Contest' on TV is said to be watched by well over a million US households, is now famous.

As the money _____ you can win increases, so the feats _____ people perform become more outlandish. The incredible new record _____ was set in 2009 was 68 hot dogs in 10 minutes! (It is surely hard to imagine anyone _____ stomach could possibly find room for so many hot dogs: in 1999, the record number was 'only' 25!) As long as big prizes are offered, there will always be people _____ are prepared to take part in these grotesque contests, _____, of course, can only be bad for their health. And anyway, how can we congratulate them on the horrific amounts _____ they stuff themselves with – when, in other parts of the mad world _____ we live in, there are people _____ are starving?

Adapted from *The Week*

5 **fair** Jahrmarkt • 11 **feat** impressive achievement because it is so difficult to manage • 16 **to stuff oneself (with food)** to eat too much

2 Definitions

Use contact clauses with prepositions to make definitions of the following words.

Example: sleeping bag → *A sleeping bag is a bag you can sleep in.*

- **a** washing-machine
- **b** information desk
- **c** golf ball
- **d** bottle opener
- **e** cycle path
- **f** tennis net
- **g** address book
- **h** toothbrush
- **i** cricket field
- **j** teacup

BASIC RULES AND EXERCISES

Defining relative clauses (information necessary for the understanding of the sentence; no commas used)	Non-defining relative clauses (additional information; commas used)
There aren't many children ***who / that* don't like sweets.** It's unhealthy to eat food ***which / that* contains too much salt.** Weight problems often affect people ***whose* alcohol intake is high.**	My sister's children, ***who* are six and three**, both eat a lot of sugary foods. Frozen food is better than canned food, ***which* contains fewer vitamins.** We recommend the White Cross Café, ***whose* cream teas are a local speciality.**

The relative pronoun ***who*** is used for **persons, *which*** for **things.**
In defining relative clauses, ***that*** is very often used to replace ***who*** or ***which***.
Whose, the genitive form (expressing possession, etc.), can be used with **persons** and **things**.

In non-defining relative clauses, *that* cannot be used, and the relative pronoun can never be left out.

Contact clauses
(clauses without relative pronouns)

Is this the coffee (*which / that*) **you brought back from Germany**?
The friends (*who / that*) **I've invited to lunch** are both vegetarians.

The relative pronoun can be left out if it is the **object of a defining clause.**
'Contact clauses' are especially common in spoken English.

To me, without whom this book would never have been written.

Prepositions in defining relative clauses

A lot of the boxes (*which / that*) **food is packed *in*** could be recycled.
The woman (*who / that*) **we buy our eggs *from*** keeps only about twenty hens.

In defining relative clauses, the **preposition** usually **comes after the verb** (+ object). The relative pronoun is often left out.

The success of home-made bread can depend on the kind of oven ***in which* it is baked.**
In **formal style**, the preposition is usually put before the relative pronoun.
(In this case, ***that*** cannot be used.)

They were served by a waiter ***whom* they recognized from their previous holiday.**
Whom is sometimes used as the object in formal (usually written) English.

1 From wealth to poverty

This is the beginning of Beauty and the Beast, a traditional English fairy tale.

Once upon a time, in a far-off country, there lived a merchant who had been so lucky in all his undertakings that he was enormously rich. As he had, however, six sons and six daughters, he found that his money was not too much to let them all have everything they fancied, as they were accustomed to do. But one day a most unexpected misfortune befell them. Their house caught fire and was burnt to the ground, with all the splendid furniture, the books, pictures, gold, silver, and precious goods it contained, and this was only the beginning of their troubles. Their father, who had until this moment prospered in all ways, suddenly lost every ship he had upon the sea, either by dint of pirates, shipwreck, or fire. Then he heard that his clerks in distant countries, whom he trusted entirely, had proved unfaithful; and at last from great wealth he fell into the direst poverty. All that he had left was a little house in a desolate place at least a hundred leagues from the town in which he had lived, and to this he was forced to retreat with his children, who were in despair at the idea of leading such a different life. They soon found that their former friends showed no intention of offering them any help. So nothing was left for them but to take their departure to the cottage, which stood in the midst of a dark forest.

From *Blue Fairy Book*, collected by Andrew Lang

---

1 **merchant** trader (doing business with foreign countries) • 3 **not too much** just enough • 3 **to fancy** to like and want to have • 3 **to be accustomed to** to be used to • 4 **to befall sb** to happen to sb • 7 **to prosper** to be successful • 7 **by dint of** through • 8 **to trust** to believe and depend on • 9 **unfaithful** false • 9 **dire** extreme, terrible • 10 **desolate** ['desələt] lonely • 10 **league** about 3 miles • 11 **to retreat** to draw back, to retire • 11 **despair** the state of having given up hope

1.1 a **Work in groups to find the relative clauses in the text. Which are defining, and which non-defining?**
b **Comment on all the relative pronouns used in the text and replace them with different ones where possible.**
c **Pick out the contact clauses. Could any of the other relative clauses be rewritten as contact clauses?**

1.2 Rephrase the story with the help of relative clauses, using contact clauses where possible:

At the beginning, the merchant is so rich that he can buy anything ……, and his children have every luxury ……. But one day his luck is changed by a fire ……. This is not the only unfortunate thing ……. He also loses the ships ……, and the people …… are unfaithful to him. So he and his family have to leave the house …… and move to a little cottage ……. The friends …… are not prepared to help, so there is nothing else …….

1.3 Use relative clauses to define the following words from the text:

a undertakings (1)
b misfortune (4)
c precious goods (5)
d pirates (8)
e wealth (9)

1.4 Relative clauses are often used to give a short description of something. Think of suitable ones to describe interesting books or stories you have read recently, or good films you have seen.

Examples: *I saw an old film called 'Titanic' on TV a few days ago. It's a true story about a passenger ship that hits an iceberg and sinks.*
I read 'Animal Farm' recently. The story's about some farm animals that organize a revolution and drive out the farmer they have always had to work for.

2 The cure

The following text is incomplete. To improve it, and to make the meaning clear, add the extra information given below, in the form of relative clauses. The asterisks (*) will show you where.

The story:

Thomas, the country vet, turned in at the gate of the farm. A tall, thin boy* looked out of a dark building for a moment. He was helping an older man* with a cow*. The boy had his arm over the cow's neck, and his other hand was twisting up the cow's head. His father poured a red mixture* into the cow's mouth.

The man said good day to Thomas*. Thomas asked after the cow.

The farmer said it had the hoosh*.

"I've given her a red drink," added the farmer, and showed Thomas an empty bottle*. The cow showed no immediate bad effects. With a fine, careless confidence Thomas offered to cure the cow at once with his own medicine*. The farmer produced the things* from some dirty bottles on a shelf. They made the mixture, and the boy went to the house. He returned with a teaspoon*. Thomas* was surprised when the cow sank to the ground. The two men * looked from Thomas to the animal with great admiration. But Thomas was afraid the cow might die. He quickly calculated the value of the animal*.

Suddenly the cow got up and coughed energetically several times, and began to eat.

"It always works," Thomas told the two men*. "Do it daily for a few days and you'll find it will kill the worms." The cow was cured within a short time.

11 **confidence** *here*: fearless attitude • 13 **shelf** (wooden) board to put things on • 17 **value** what sth is worth

The additional information:

The boy was about 17.
The man was obviously the boy's father.
They were about to treat the cow.
The mixture smelled of aniseed.
Thomas returned the greeting.
The hoosh is a disease caused by long worms in a cow's throat.
The farmer had put the bottle on the shelf beside him.
Thomas's medicine was a mixture of linseed oil and turpentine.
Thomas needed the things for his mixture.
Thomas poured the mixture into the cow's nose with the teaspoon.
Thomas had no idea what the effect would be.
The two men were very pleased with the cow's strong reaction.
Thomas thought the value of the animal was about twenty pounds.
The two men were looking at Thomas as if he were a magician.

25 **aniseed** Anis • 29 **linseed** Leinsamen

3 The body in the library

This is a summary of the beginning of Agatha Christie's famous novel 'The Body in the Library'.

The story starts in Colonel Bantry's house. The house is in the village of Gossington. The Bantrys wake up one morning and find a body lying in their library. It's an unknown blonde girl in a white evening dress. She was killed with a belt from the dress, at some time between ten and midnight. At once, Mrs Bantry sends for her friend Miss Marple. Miss Marple comes from the village of St Mary Mead. Of course, the police arrive, too, with Inspector Slack in charge. Their first suspect is Basil Blake. The police go to his house. Basil Blake was seen with a mysterious blonde girl the weekend before. But this girl – Dinah Lee – is later found living with Blake. The police discover that the dead girl worked at the Majestic Hotel in Danemouth. So the police talk to Josie Turner. The dead girl (Ruby) worked with her. Ruby had danced an exhibition dance at 10.30 pm and should have danced another at midnight. But she didn't appear at midnight. She was last seen dancing with a young man called Bartlett, at about 11. However, the police are more interested in Colonel Bantry. They talk to him next …

4 **to send for sb** to ask for sb to come • 5 **suspect** ['--] a person you think may be responsible for a crime • 9 **exhibition** *here*: special show (given by professionals)

3.1 Answer the questions, using contact clauses with prepositions.

a What role does Gossington play in the story? → *It's the village the Bantrys live in.*
b What's special about the library? → *It's the room …*
c Why is the belt important? → *It's the thing …*
d What is important about the period ten to midnight? → *It's the time …*
e What's interesting about St Mary Mead?
f Who is Basil Blake?
g Who is the mysterious blonde girl?
h What is her relationship with Blake?
i What is the Majestic in Danemouth?
j Who is Josie Turner?
k What is the importance of 10.30 p.m.?
l Who is Bartlett?

3.2 In which of your answers could you use clauses with *where* or *when* instead of contact clauses?

4 A puzzle

4.1 Look at the box on the right and answer the question.

4.2 How long did it take you to get the answer? (Do you think there might be a significant difference between people that get the answer quickly and people that don't?)

4.3 What other jobs would this puzzle 'work' with?

A lawyer from Birmingham had a brother who went to sea …
The man that went to sea had no brother.
What relation was the lawyer to him?

Answer: The lawyer was a woman. And thus the sister of the man that went to sea.

ADVANCED RULES AND EXERCISES

More types of relative clauses	
The power of the Royal Family today is very limited, ***which* is a good thing.**	The relative pronoun ***which*** can also refer to a whole sentence. In this case, the relative clause usually expresses a comment. (Never use ***what*** here!)
Henry VIII had six wives, ***two of whom* were beheaded.** His palace of Hampton Court had about 1,000 rooms, ***all of which* were in regular use.** Today thousands of visitors come to see Hampton Court, ***part of which* is open to the public.**	Relative clauses beginning with ***… of whom / … of which*** refer to part of something or part of a group. They are normally used only in formal English.
10 Downing Street automatically becomes the home of ***whoever* is elected Prime Minister.** Some people criticize ***whatever* the Government plans to do.** There won't be any overnight improvements, ***whichever* party wins the election.**	***Whoever***, ***whatever*** and ***whichever*** are generalizing relative pronouns, meaning 'anyone / anything that …,' 'the person / thing that …' / 'it doesn't matter who / what / which …'.

Success in war was ***what* people expected of their king in the Middle Ages.**
What is used to mean *the thing that … / something that …* (German: *'was …'/'das, was …'*).

1 Records

Join the correct pairs of sentences, using relative clauses.

1 The world's first advertised radio programme was in 1906.
2 John Baird sold his first televisions in 1930.
3 The budget for the film *Titanic* was 200 million dollars.
4 The longest film ever made (*The Cure for Insomnia*) lasts 85 hours.
5 *Avatar*, described in 2010 as the most technically sophisticated film in history, got 9 Oscar nominations.
6 Michael Jackson's best-selling album is *Thriller*.
7 Agatha Christie's play *The Mousetrap* has been playing in London since 1952.

a None of the nominations was for an actor.
b 3 million dollars were spent on film stunts.
c Handel's *Largo* was played during the programme.
d By 2010 its global sales are said to have reached over 100 million.
e The cost of the televisions was 27 pounds each.
f This is longer than any other theatre production.
g Its first complete performance was in Chicago between 31st January and 3rd February 1987.

insomnia sleeplessness

2 A question of style

Britain before the Romans

About the year 5000 BC, the waters of what we now call the English Channel and the North Sea joined together, and Britain became an island.

The human population of the new island at that time was a few hundreds, who lived by hunting with the tools they had laboriously chipped from the softer stones about them. But at the very time that this separation of Britain from the Continent was taking place, a revolution was occurring thousands of miles away in the Near East which was to change for ever the life of man. He was learning not merely to hunt and kill for his food, but to keep the animals who provided it in captivity. He was learning, too, to gather the seeds of the grasses he found he could eat and scatter them about him to grow into the food he desired. He was learning, in short, to be a farmer.

Men with this new knowledge did not cross the still widening waters between Europe and Britain until about 2300 BC. And when they came they had to keep to the chalky and sandy soils where with their clumsy tools they could turn the ground over for their seeds to grow. So the area they settled on was very limited.

These first settlers were men to whom the sea was a natural barrier. They crossed it only if they had to, if they needed fresh space in which to live; and they crossed it where it was narrowest. But there were others for whom it held fewer terrors, men living along the coasts of Spain or Brittany. When they crossed, it was where the English Channel was wider. The settlements of these people can be distinguished today by their remarkable burial places, whose roof is a great stone.

It was about the year 900 BC that a large westward movement of races on the European continent, a movement at whose causes we can only guess, produced another invasion of Britain, by a people who are the first to have left this island something more than material remains. These were the Celts, and they spoke a language of which the native tongues of Ireland, Wales and the highlands of Scotland are the direct descendants.

From *A History of England* by J. Thorn, R. Lockyer & D. Smith

---

4 **laborious** [ləˈbɔːrɪəs] needing a lot of effort • 4 **to chip** to cut or break off (stone, etc.) • 7 **to keep in captivity** to keep (animals) so that they cannot run away • 8 **seed** part of a plant from which a new one grows • 8 **to scatter** to throw in all directions • 9 **to desire** to want to have • 11 **chalky** made of chalk, a soft white rock • 12 **clumsy** *here*: not finely made • 16 **Brittany** region in the north-west of France (Bretagne) • 18 **to distinguish** *here*: to recognize • 21 **remains** what is left behind, ruins • 22 **tongue** *here*: language

A much married man

"There are men who don't like being married. I can't understand them. I like being a married man. It's no difficulty to me to do the little things that women like and that some men can't be bothered with. As I was saying just now, it's attention a woman wants. I never went out of the house without giving my wife a kiss and I never came in without giving her another. And it was very seldom I came in without bringing her some chocolates or a few flowers. I never grudged the expense."

"After all, it was her money you were spending," I interposed.

"And what if it was? It's not the money that you've paid for a present that signifies, it's the spirit you give it in. That's what counts with women. No, I'm not one to boast, but I will say this of myself, I am a good husband."

From *The Round Dozen* by W. Somerset Maugham

---

2 **I can't be bothered with it** it's too much trouble for me • 5 **not to grudge** not to mind • 6 **to interpose** to 'break into' the conversation • 7 **to signify** *here*: to be of importance, to matter • 8 **to boast** to show off, to talk 'big'

Note on the two texts (on page 137)

The first text is taken from a history book. The second is from a short story in which the narrator meets Mortimer Ellis, a bigamist, who has been in prison for five years. He explains that he has had eleven wives, all of whom he left after taking charge of their money.

---

bigamist ['bɪgəmɪst] sb who has more than one wife (or husband)

2.1 Work in groups to make a list of the relative clauses in both texts. In what ways are most of the relative clauses in the second text typical of spoken English? (Look at the choice of relative pronouns and the position of prepositions. Are defining or non-defining clauses used?)

2.2 Pick out the relative clauses in the first text that you think are typical of a more formal (written) style. How could they be expressed more informally, but without changing the meaning?

2.3 Replace these constructions from the first text by relative clauses:

a the still widening waters between Europe and Britain (10)
b space in which to live (15)
c men living along the coasts of Spain and Britanny (16)

2.4 Add relative clauses with *which* to make comments on these statements.

a About 7000 years ago, the North Sea joined the waters of the English Channel.
b The first people that crossed over to Britain had a certain fear of the sea.
c Mortimer Ellis considers himself a good husband.

☆ **2.5 At the time when 'The Round Dozen' was written, the 'ideal' of a 'good husband' and a 'good wife' was rather different from what it seems to be today. Talk about this, using relative clauses where appropriate.**

Examples: *In those days, the husband was generally the one who earned all the money, while the wife was the one ...*
Most men wanted a wife who ...
Women that ... were unusual.
Women were expected to do what(ever) ...
Housework was a job that ...

17 The Use of Adjectives and Adverbs

CHECK-UP

1 Man's best friend?

Adjective or adverb? Decide which form is correct.

It is ___ known that the British have a ___ love of pets – ___ of dogs. There are ___ millions of dog-owners in Britain, a ___ ___ number of whom keep more than one. But ___ there are hundreds of thousands of stray dogs wandering the streets, and many hundreds of unwanted pet dogs have to be destroyed ___ by the RSPCA and others. Many people do not think ___ enough before buying a dog, and ___ abandon the ___ animal when the work of looking after it ___ gets too much. Others abandon their dogs because the pet's behaviour has become ___ and ___ to control. ___ this is often the owner's fault. The habit of 'spoiling' pets has ___ altered the ___ instincts of dogs, ___ those of ___ breeds. A dog which is allowed to do ___ as it likes, ___ begins to feel ___, and to see itself as the ___ leader of the family. Not ___, such dogs soon start to act ___ ___ on the street, too. When treated ___, however, dogs can have an ___ ___ effect on their owners' lives. Having a dog ___ reduces ___ everyday illnesses by 50 %. This may be because people who buy dogs ___ take five times more ___ exercise than they did before.

good · deep · particular
literal · surprising · large
unfortunate

daily
careful · final
unfortunate · proper
aggressive
hard · actual
dangerous · natural · particular
aggressive · exact · quick
dominant · real · surprising
unusual · aggressive
proper · amazing · positive
actual · common
general
regular

2 **literal** *buchstäblich* • 4 **stray** (of pets) homeless • 5 **RSPCA** Royal Society for the Prevention of Cruelty to Animals • 6 **to abandon** to leave (permanently) • 10 **to spoil** *verwöhnen* • 11 **breed** particular type of dog

2 Their problem – our problem?

2.1 Complete the sentences with adjectives, followed by the prop-words *person* or *people* where necessary.

A ___ without any disabilities is often unaware of the problems facing the ___. It is not unusual for ___ in wheelchairs to have fewer job opportunities simply because they cannot use public transport to get to work. ___ often feel shut off from society, and the mentally ___ are frequently refused jobs because employers wrongly think they are unable to do them. It is easy to forget the difficulties the ___ have in life, although a ___ generally receives more sympathy than ___, whose problems are less obvious.

healthy
disabled · disabled
deaf
challenged

blind · blind
deaf

2.2 Give the English equivalents of ...

a viele Behinderte; **b** die Reichen und die Armen; **c** zwei Schlafzimmer: ein kleines und ein großes; **d** Jugendliche; **e** ein Blinder; **f** eine schwarze Katze und zwei weiße; **g** der Kleine; **h** die Tote

BASIC RULES AND EXERCISES

Adjectives	Adjectives can be used
Television plays an **important** *role* in our society.	**attributively**, i.e. before nouns
These DVDs *are* **expensive**! Don't switch off – this programme *is getting* **interesting** now. There's a film on tonight that *sounds* quite **good**.	**predicatively**, i.e. after verbs expressing ▸ a state (e.g. *be, seem, remain*) ▸ a changing state (e.g. *get, become*) ▸ the way something appears to the senses (e.g. *look, feel, sound, taste*)

Adverbs	Adverbs can be used to modify
The play *started* **dramatically.**	▸ verbs
The first act was **terribly** *funny*.	▸ adjectives
The plot had been thought out **extremely** *well*.	▸ adverbs
Luckily, *we managed to get very good seats*.	▸ whole sentences

Adjectives with 'prop-words'	
There's something wrong with *our TV*. We may have to get **a new one**. John always looks through the week's *programmes*, and marks **the interesting ones**.	The 'prop-word' *one* is used after adjectives to describe nouns that would otherwise have to be repeated.
The old man next door has his TV on very loud. Several **disabled people** took part in the film.	Other 'prop-words' (e.g. *man, woman, person, people*) are used after adjectives to describe ▸ people seen as individuals ▸ a limited group of people

Adjectives used as nouns	
The deaf are able to enjoy quite a lot of television programmes. TV personalities can seem like real friends to **the old** and **the lonely**.	*The* + adjective is used to describe people seen as a complete group (e.g. *the deaf, the lonely, the very young*)

"It's not fair. The rich get richer, the poor get poorer, but the comfortably well-off just stay comfortably well-off."

1 Americans and their automobiles

The daily chaos on American roads costs the US economy many millions of dollars a year. Naturally, this not only includes the direct costs, such as high gasoline consumption in traffic jams, but also the indirect costs that are inevitably caused, such as lost hours at work and additional pollution.

The automobile is firmly rooted in American life. Most American workers commute daily to their jobs in private cars, and a large number of American families own two or more cars. Many people feel that the landscape of the United States has been adversely affected by the automobile; stores, restaurants and whole towns are usually planned to accommodate large numbers of cars. Even in a densely populated urban area, a grocery store can look absurdly small in comparison with the huge parking lot designed for its customers.

Some Americans feel extremely critical of the traditional attitude towards the automobile as a symbol of freedom and democracy. In a recent poll, 67% of 25- to 34-year-olds said they would definitely prefer to drive less. Some people have tried living without their cars – at least temporarily. But for many, this is hardly possible. Cycling to work, for example, may sound attractive, but the idea of bike lanes has not yet been generally accepted in the US. And public transport? The Americans have adapted terribly slowly to the idea of providing a proper system of public transport, but actually there are few places in the States that are absolutely inaccessible to some combination of transport by bus, taxi, train, subway or plane. However, the idea that the automobile may become socially and economically obsolete some time in the future seems rather remote.

---

3 **inevitable** [-'----] unavoidable • 6 **adverse** *here:* negative • 8 **dense** thick • 12 **temporary** ['temprərɪ] lasting for a limited time • 16 **inaccessible** out of reach • 18 **obsolete** *here:* no longer needed • 18 **remote** *here*: unlikely

1.1 **Work in groups to find the adverbs in the text, and say which are used to modify a) verbs, b) adjectives (including participles used as adjectives), c) other adverbs, d) whole sentences.**

1.2 **Then find all the adjectives that are used predicatively, and say what type of verb (according to the Basic Rules) each one follows.**

1.3 **Name the adjectives that belong to the same word families as these nouns:**

a chaos (1); b economy (1); c symbol (10); d freedom (11); e future (18).

Then use them to write short statements about cars (or other present-day problems).

1.4 **Decide which of the adverbs in lines 10-18 could be left out. Compare the two versions and point out in what way the use of adverbs affects the style and contents.**

1.5 **Use adjectives or adverbs to complete these sentences suitably.**

a These days traffic jams are nothing … .
b Lots of Americans drive their cars to work … .
c The freeways, highways, drive-ins and parking lots in the US have changed the countryside … .
d One day cars may become …, but right now this doesn't seem … .

2 The status-climber

In his book 'The Human Zoo', Desmond Morris takes a look at the society the 'human animal' has created over the centuries. One of the features of this society is the struggle for dominance. The person who is unable to achieve genuine dominance in society often tries to create the impression of higher status …

The really serious status-climber tends to concentrate on areas where cheap fakes are out of the question. If he can afford a small motor car, he buys a medium-sized one; if he can afford a medium-sized one, he buys a large one; if he can afford a single large one, he buys a second car as a runabout; if large cars become too common, he buys a small, but wildly expensive foreign sports car; if large rear-lights become the fashion, he buys the latest model with even bigger ones, 'to let people behind know he is in front,' as the advertisers so succinctly express it. The one thing he does not do is to buy a row of life-sized, cardboard models of Rolls-Royces and display them outside his garage. There are no fake diamonds in the world of the status-climbing fanatic.

Motor cars are a single example, and an important one because they are so public, but the ardent status-struggler cannot stop here …

From *The Human Zoo* by Desmond Morris

---

1 **fake** an imitation of the 'real' thing • 3 **runabout** small extra car • 6 **succinctly** clearly and in a few words • 7 **to display** to put up for everyone to see • 9 **ardent** full of enthusiasm or 'fire'

2.1 Explain in two or three sentences how a 'status-climber' tries to create the impression of social dominance.

2.2 Use adjectives with prop-words to help complete these ideas:

a Fake diamonds are made to look just like … .
b Our neighbours have got two cars – … and … .
c I'd like to buy a motorbike, but I can't afford … .
d The black shoes don't fit, but I like … .
e If you enjoy detective stories, I can recommend … .
f Which of these jeans do you prefer – … or …?

"That's Marcus in his prime – proud, arrogant and top of the heap, yet tenderness itself with his loved ones. I forget who the man is."

ADVANCED RULES AND EXERCISES

Adjectives used to express abstract ideas

'The Oasis' is the perfect hotel for all lovers of **the exotic** and **the luxurious**.
The amazing thing *about the voyage* was that none of us got seasick.

- *The* + adjective can be used to express an abstract idea (e.g. *the exotic, the unexpected, the impossible, the obvious*)
- The 'prop-word' *thing* is used after the adjective if the abstract idea is limited to a certain case.

1 Chain of violence

Fill in the adjectives with suitable 'prop-words' where necessary.

a	Today it is generally recognized that to hit a child, especially a very ……, is wrong.	young
b	The …… about hitting children is that they are usually powerless to defend themselves.	terrible
c	Although there are laws in most countries to protect adults from attack, the …… is that only very few countries have introduced …… to protect children.	sad · similar
d	But the …… is that most people who were beaten themselves as …… genuinely believe it did them no harm.	surprising · small
e	Not surprisingly, these people are generally the …… that later in life use violence on their own children.	same
f	Even …… are often blind to the damage that is done in this way.	intelligent
g	The …… are just as likely to beat their children as …… with little schooling.	educated · simple
h	The …… is not only to protect the …… from violence, but also to treat them as …… instead of just another part of an adult's 'belongings'.	important · young proper
i	All this may seem like stating the ……; but to expect a big change in parents' attitudes would probably be to expect the …….	obvious impossible

2 Similar adverbs – different meanings

Choose the correct adverb. Then translate the sentences into German.

a You've changed so much, I …… recognized you!
b I haven't had much time …… – I've been working so …….
c You did …… well in that quiz – you got most of the answers …….
d John's been sent off the field. – Quite …… in my opinion. After all, he really wasn't playing …….
e It's still …… early – but that's good. We don't want to risk arriving …….
f Those flowers look lovely. You've arranged them so …….

fair · fairly
hard · hardly
late · lately
pretty · prettily
right · rightly

3 The dragon

It was porch-sitting night, so Bob and I moved out to the swing. Bob liked the swing, and sometimes he rocked it so hard that I felt seasick. We could see the city from the porch. At night, the lights made it look beautiful. The oil refineries looked like castles from a children's book. Some even breathed fire, as if dragons were inside.

Bob wasn't looking at the view. Things like that didn't interest him. He was talking about his relatives. He could be so boring. I didn't really hate him. He couldn't help it if he was boring and stupid.

My mother and Bob's mother were friends. That gave Bob a reason to come to see me every night. My mother liked Bob a lot. So I had to sit on the swing getting seasick. I watched the dragon in a refinery breathing fire. Bob was talking about his cousin Jimmy, who played bridge. Bob had a habit of repeating himself. I was glad when he came to the end. "Do you play bridge, Kay?"
"No," I said. I tried to make sure we had very little in common.
"How about going to the movies Saturday night?" he asked.
"I'm going to be busy then. Sorry."
"What are you doing?"
"I have some important poetry to write."
"You've been busy a lot lately, Kay."
I almost said, "Did you ever wonder why?" But I didn't.
Bob sighed. "I'm worried. It's April, and I haven't heard from a single college."
"Everything will work out," I said.
"You can say that because you're smart. College will be a breeze for you. But I want to be a lawyer, and it will be tough."
"You worry too much." I felt strange saying this. I felt law school would be tough for Bob. But I didn't want to be cruel.
He touched my shoulder. "You really don't like me, do you, Kay?"
"Bob, that's not a nice thing to say!" Suddenly, I felt guilty.
"But it's true. I'm not as stupid as you think."
"Have I ever said I didn't like you?" It bothered me that Bob might see through me.
"You didn't have to say it. I know."
"Bob, you know I think you're a great guy."
"I'm not a great guy. We both know I'm not. You think I'm stupid because you're smart. You think you're too good for me. I used to be happy here. Now I come because my mother makes me. You think I come here because I love you or something. Well, it isn't that. Not at all."
I felt wounded. I never thought Bob would see the truth.
"Kay, I'm going and I'm not coming back."

1 **porch** (AE) veranda • 2 **swing** *Schaukel* • 11 **he couldn't help it** it wasn't his fault • 26 **a breeze** *here*: easy • 33 **to bother** to worry

Suddenly, I was speaking. "Well, leave then! You are boring and dull. I only sit here because our mothers are friends."

I expected his eyes to look hurt. But they flashed with excitement. "I think that is the first time you've ever told me the truth. You're a phony, Kay. And that's worse than being stupid." He touched my shoulder again, gently. "I could like you, Kay, I really could. But the truth isn't important to you."

He smiled. To my horror, my eyes were filling with tears. The orange flame of the refinery blurred.

"Well, I'd better be going," Bob said. "I'm going to miss this swing."

I heard his car drive away. I got up and wiped my eyes on my sleeve. I went inside. My parents were watching television.

"Where did Bob go?" my mother asked.

"He … he had some poetry to write."

I stumbled into my room. From my bed, I watched the dragon's orange-and-red flame – until the colors melted and were washed away.

Cynthia Forder wrote 'The Dragon' when she was a senior in high school in Torrance, California. It received an award in the 1974 Scholastic Writing Awards Contest.

---

40 **(a) phony** (someone) pretending to be what he/she is not • 42 **to blur** to become unclear • 44 **sleeve** arm of shirt etc. • 48 **to stumble** to walk unsteadily, almost falling

3.1 Fill in suitable adjectives and adverbs to complete this summary of the story:

Kay finds Bob's talk about his relatives _____, but she is too _____ to say so. She _____ doesn't want to go to the movies with him, so she _____ thinks of an excuse, which is so _____ that Bob _____ sees through it. Bob tells her he feels _____ about his future, but Kay doesn't want to take this remark _____, because she is _____ of showing him what she _____ thinks of him – that he is _____, and that his future _____ won't be _____. Again, Bob _____ realizes what she is _____ thinking, and he _____ decides to tell her the _____ truth. It is the first time Bob and Kay have _____ been _____ with each other, and as Kay discovers to her _____ surprise, the truth hurts.

3.2 Look at the text carefully and say how Kay feels when …

a Bob rocks the swing;
b he talks about his relatives;
c he guesses that she doesn't like him;
d he tells her he only goes there to please his mother;
e he says he is leaving and not coming back;
f she is on her own again.

3.3 What sort of a person do you think Kay is? Think of adjectives that might describe her. And what about Bob? In what way is he different? Then use adverbs to describe how Kay reacts when …

a Bob talks about college;
b he says he is not coming back.

18 Adjectives and Adverbs: Comparative and Superlative Forms

CHECK-UP

Could it be drugs?

Choose between adjectives and adverbs, using the comparative or superlative form.

a Lots of teenagers are offered drugs, but not every offer is accepted.	
In fact, ___ people say "No". But parents should remember that young	many
people who are fed up or worried may be ___ to try drugs than those	likely
that are happy at home.	
It's ___ to tell when someone is using drugs occasionally than when	difficult
they are ___ users. But here are some of the ___ warning signs that	regular · common
may help you to recognize the beginning of a problem ___. Drugs may	easy
be the cause if your child	
• acts ___, or changes from one mood to another ___ than usual,	aggressive · sudden
• begins to show ___ interest in hobbies, sports – or even food,	little
• seems to have ___ contacts with friends than before,	few
• gets tired ___ – or suffers from sleeplessness ___,	quick · often
• starts to do ___ at school.	bad
b The ___ signs would, of course, be if you noticed money disappearing,	alarming
or unusual tablets, etc. in the house.	
The ___ a drug problem is recognized, the ___. But even then,	soon · good
the ___ question for parents is how to react.	important
When Helen, 17, broke with her boyfriend, it was the ___ thing she	depressing
had ever experienced. She tried some tranquillizers she found in the	
family medicine cupboard, and they made her feel ___. A few	good
weeks ___, her parents discovered this, had the ___ row with Helen,	late · terrible
and locked up the rest of the tablets.	
c This might have worked ___, but Helen had already gone too far to	early
want to turn back. A school friend offered her something ___, which	strong
they both thought was ___ to be heroin. ___ still, Helen took up with	likely · late
a new boyfriend, ___ than herself, and ___ – in fact, a regular drug	old · experienced
user. When Helen's parents got to know, they turned to the family	
doctor for help.	

Based on a leaflet published by the *British health service*

19 **tranquillizer** ['træŋkwɪlaɪzə] tablet that helps to make you feel calmer and less worried • 21 **row** [raʊ] an angry scene between two or more people

BASIC RULES AND EXERCISES

1 Comparative and superlative forms

Adjectives	
	-er, -est with
This road has been made **wider**.	▸ adjectives of one syllable (exception: past participles used as adjectives)
It's **simplest** to park here. There would have been an accident if the road had been **narrower**. Automatic cars are **easier** to drive.	▸ adjectives of two syllables ending in *-le, -ow, -y*
	more, most with
That girl at the travel agent's couldn't have been **more helpful**.	▸ most other adjectives of two syllables
I find flying the **most comfortable** form of travelling.	▸ all adjectives of three or more syllables

Adverbs	
The InterCity leaves **later**, but it travels **faster**, so it gets to London **sooner**.	***-er, -est*** with adverbs of one syllable
	more, most with
We can get to the airport **most quickly** by underground.	▸ adverbs formed by adding *-ly*
Do you usually go into town by bus? – No, I **more often** walk.	▸ other adverbs of more than one syllable

We had **better** weather in Scotland than in Ireland, but the traffic was **worse**.
Of all the trips we've had, I enjoyed the hike over the moors **best**.
Some common adjectives and adverbs have irregular comparative and superlative forms:

good/well: better, best	***many: more, most***	***little*** **(= not much):** ***less, least***
bad/badly: worse, worst	***much: more, most***	***little*** (= small): ***smaller, smallest***

2 Making comparisons with adjectives and adverbs

I'll take this suitcase. It's **bigger than** the leather bag. Let's go by Underground. The trains run **more regularly than** buses.	■ > □	comparative + than
The train fare was**n't as expensive as** I'd expected/ was **less expensive than** I'd expected.	□ < ■	not as … as/less … than
There may be heavy traffic on the M25, so we'll leave for the airport **as early as** we can.	■ = □	as … as

1 Some good, some bad, all different

In Alan Ayckbourn's short play 'A Talk in the Park', four people are sitting apart from each other on four park benches, when Arthur enters and goes up to Beryl, a young girl on one of the benches. He sits down and tries to start a conversation, but Beryl refuses to be drawn into it. In spite of this, Arthur begins to talk to her about himself …

ARTHUR: … I'm a very fulfilled person. I have, for example, one of the biggest collections of cigarette cards of anyone alive or dead that I know of. And you don't get that by sitting on your behind all day. But I'll let you into a secret. Do you know what it is that's the most valuable thing there is you can hope to collect? People. I'm a collector of people. I look at them, I observe them, I hear them talk, I listen to their manner of speaking and I think, hallo, here's another one. Different. Different again. Because I'll let you into a secret. They are like fingerprints. They are never quite the same. And I've met a number in my lifetime. Quite a number. Some good, some bad, all different. But the best of them, and I'm saying this to you quite frankly and openly, the best of them are women. They are superior people. They are better people. They are cleaner people. They are kinder-hearted people. If I had a choice, I'd be a woman. Now that makes you laugh, I expect, but it's the truth. When I choose to have a conversation, I can tell you it's with a woman every time. Because a woman is one of nature's listeners. Most men I wouldn't give the time of day to. Now, I expect that shocks you but it's the truth. Trouble is, I don't get to meet as many women as I'd like to. My particular line of work does not bring me into contact with them as much as I would wish. Which is a pity.

From *A Talk in the Park* by Alan Ayckbourn

---

2 **cigarette card** small card (with a picture of sb or sth of interest) included in a cigarette packet • 9 **superior** of a better 'type' or quality • 13 **Trouble is** … The only problem is …

1.1 Why does Arthur 'collect 'people? What sort of people does he like best, and why?

1.2 Look at Arthur's statements about women, and try to imagine what experiences may have formed his opinion. Use comparatives and superlatives where you can. (Think of his family, people he has known at school/at work, friends, TV personalities he knows or films he has seen.)

Examples: *Perhaps Arthur's mother was kinder to him / treated him more kindly than his father.*
It's possible that he had a brother who didn't play with him as much as his sister.

☆ 1.3 Arthur has very fixed ideas – but he is not alone. Lots of people have strange ideas about others. Look at the following sentences (some of them may sound familiar to you). Then give your opinion on them, using comparative or superlative forms where appropriate.

a It's more important for a woman to be good-looking than it is for a man.
b Women are better at looking after children than men because they are naturally more patient and understanding.
c All the most famous artists and musicians are men.
d The Germans work harder than other Europeans, but the French are the best cooks.

2 Human aggression

That man is an aggressive creature will hardly be disputed. With the exception of certain rodents, no other vertebrate habitually destroys members of his own species. No other animal takes positive pleasure in the exercise of cruelty upon another of his own kind. We generally describe the most repulsive examples of man's cruelty as brutal or bestial, implying by these adjectives that such behaviour is characteristic of less highly developed animals than ourselves. In truth, however, the extremes of 'brutal' behaviour are confined to man; and there is no parallel in nature to our savage treatment of each other. The sombre fact is that we are the cruellest and most ruthless species that has ever walked the earth.

From *Human Aggression* by Anthony Storr

1 **dispute** to call into question • 1 **rodents** rats, mice, etc. • 2 **vertebrate** ['vɜːtɪbreɪt] animal with a backbone • 2 **species** ['spiːʃiːz] Art • 4 **repulsive** sickeningly horrible • 6 **confined** limited • 7 **sombre** ['sɒmbə] dark, serious • 7 **ruthless** determined to achieve one's own goals without caring about others

2.1 Note down the positive, comparative and superlative forms of adjectives and adverbs in the text. Then choose from them to complete this summary sensibly:

The adjectives '______' and '______' are ______ supposed to describe behaviour that is ______ of animals, but in fact the ______ creatures of this earth do not show such ______ behaviour towards each other as we do. Man is the ______ and ______ creature in the world. This can ______ be doubted.

2.2 Give opposites of:

most repulsive (3-4); less highly developed (5); cruellest (7).

2.3 Compare the following, using adjectives and adverbs in various forms.

a man – animals
b horses – cattle
c rats – mice ✓
d pets – wild animals
e cats – dogs
f people – robots
g primitive weapons – modern weapons

clean • cruel • useful • fast • aggressive • dangerous • friendly • natural • frightening • …

Examples: *Most people find rats more frightening than mice because they are more dangerous. Rats act more aggressively than mice.*

"We've decided that it's healthier to eat a vegetarian."

ADVANCED RULES AND EXERCISES

The weather got **colder and colder.**	For a steady increase (German: *immer* + comparative): ▸ comparative + *and* + comparative (with adjectives / adverbs that take *-er, -est,* and irregular forms with one syllable)
As the snow fell **more and more thickly**, driving conditions became **worse and worse.**	▸ *more and more* + adjective / adverb (in all other cases).
The longer we waited for our flight to be called, **the more impatient** we began to feel.	*the ... the ...* (each with the comparative) is the equivalent of German *je ... desto ...*

1 Buy, buy, buy

The most powerful, the loudest and the most persistent command in our society is the command to buy, to consume. The voice of advertising urges us to buy, buy, buy, and it never lets up.

Advertising intended for an audience that can afford what it offers also works (with perhaps even greater effectiveness) on those who cannot afford it; it inflames the desires of the poor without offering them any satisfaction at all. A continuous display of better living is paraded before them. Rich people know that not every day is filled with sports and glamour; they even know that the person who has everything might not even want all these things. The poor have no way of knowing this: television advertising is far more effective with the unsophisticated. Is there any wonder that we have riots? Television might rightly be called a riot box; it raises a fury of dissatisfaction. But even the well-paid, highly motivated executive, after a demanding day, may feel troubled emotions if he views a TV scene of surfers. The screen tells him to work harder so he can vacation in California. But perhaps he senses, in some way, that the harder he works, the less likely it is that he ever will surf: in fact, real surfers don't work at all ...

The one thing that we can be sure of is that the aim of advertising is to create dissatisfaction.

From *The Greening of America* by Charles Reich

1 **persistent** going on without stopping, persuasive • 3 **to urge** to try to persuade • 3 **to let up** to stop • 6 **to inflame** to excite • 7 **display** show • 9 **glamour** ['glæmə] here: beauty and social success • 11 **unsophisticated** naturally simple • 11 **riot** outbreak of violence, rebellion • 12 **fury** anger, rage; *here:* violent feeling • 13 **executive** [ɪg'zekjʊtɪv] (powerful) person in the business world

1.1 Use constructions containing comparisons / comparatives to explain the meaning of:

a it inflames the desires of the poor (6);
b not every day is filled with sports and glamour (8-9)
c it raises a fury of dissatisfaction (12).

1.2 What are the reasons why advertising works more effectively on the poor than it does on the rich?

1.3 "The harder he works, the less likely it is that he ever will surf." (15) Try to explain the logic of the author's argument.

1.4 Complete the following sentences with your own ideas:

a The more material possessions you have, …
b The better educated a person is, …
c Now that more and more people all over the world have access to television, …

1.5 Which do you think affects your own buying habits more strongly – the voice of advertising, or 'peer pressure' (the influence of people of your own age and status)? Explain why.

2 Advertising techniques

Have you ever thought how advertising 'works'? Think of your own experience of advertising techniques, and complete with suitable comparisons.

Example: *Products described by words with pleasant associations, like 'golden' or 'soft', are most likely to sell well/have a stronger effect on potential buyers.*

a New 'scientific discoveries' are used in adverts in order to …
b With the help of photographic tricks, products can …
c The more often the advertiser repeats the name of the product, …

3 Bloodthirstier times?

Well-chosen adjectives and adverbs can improve your style and make a text more interesting. Work in groups to complete the text, using positive, comparative or superlative forms of suitable adjectives or adverbs. Sometimes there will be a number of different possibilities.

Example: In this *modern/civilized/enlightened/advanced/progressive* age of ours …

In this ___ age of ours, we tend to think that people living in ___ centuries were ___ than people today. In the early Middle Ages, there were no law courts, and people were often ___ punished by the Sheriff, even for ___ crimes like stealing firewood or hunting deer. In those ___ days, a person could be put to death for committing a crime no ___ than stealing a loaf of bread.

In the 17th century, when there was still no police force in Britain, the streets of London were much ___ than they are today, and people behaved altogether ___ than they ___ do now. The ___ of all the Londoners were the watermen, who rowed passengers across the Thames. They were so ___ that they prevented the building of bridges over the Thames, as they feared these developments would mean ___ and ___ passengers for them – and ___ and ___ money. The 17th century was probably one of the ___ times in history; ___ crowds came to watch the ___ public executions, and it is ___ to imagine a ___ sight than the heads of the executed prisoners put up on spikes on London Bridge.

Travelling was ___ and ___ than it is today, because of the ___ condition of the roads, and because of highwaymen. By the 18th century, however, roads had become far ___, and, of course, the ___ coaches were able to travel, the ___ it became for robbers to attack. But there were still a few highwaymen, the ___ of them all being Dick Turpin, who was ___ caught and hanged in 1739.

Today, of course, the legal system works ___ than in those days, there is a ___ organized police force, and punishments are ___. But it is ___ whether people ___ behave ___ towards each other than they used to.

11 **spike** a stick with a sharp point at one end • 16 **highwayman** person (usually on horseback) who used to rob travellers

19 The Position of Adverbs and Adverbials

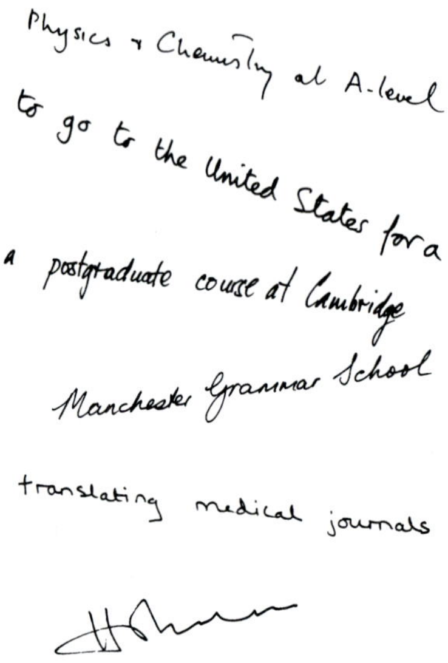

CHECK-UP

1 Your character in your handwriting?

Put in the adverbs / adverbials in the most suitable position.

a According to graphologists, your hand is connected with your brain. (closely)
b When you write, it is difficult to hide your personality. (extremely)
c When applying for a job, people are asked to write their application by hand. (often)
d Here are some simple signs to look out for. (quite)
e If you are in a hurry (always), you forget to dot your 'i's. (probably) Or you don't cross your 't's. (properly)
f An energetic person will press the paper. (hard)
g An aggressive person will form his or her letters. (sharply)
h People whose writing leans to the right are enthusiastic people. (usually)
i Those whose writing slopes backwards could be interpreted as rather cold. (possibly)
j When you write a letter, you sign your name. (at the bottom) Can people read it? (hardly) If so, it means that you are a self-important person. (certainly) Or does it?
k The 'science' of graphology has its limits. (obviously) There are lots of other ways of getting to know people! (fortunately)

---

i **to slope** to lean to one side

2 A trip to London

Put the pieces together to form sentences. Think carefully about the best word order.

a we went | last April | for a couple of days | to London
b at King's Cross Station | we arrived | in the afternoon | at 2 o'clock
c by Underground | then | to our hotel | we went on
d the weather | all the time | luckily | was really good
e to the Tower of London | by boat | on the first afternoon | we went
f we saw | the next morning | at Buckingham Palace | the Changing of the Guard
g at the shops | then | in the Oxford Street area | we looked | for a while
h time | after that | very quickly | began to go | not surprisingly
i 'The Mousetrap' | that evening | we went to see | in the West End | at St. Martin's Theatre
j home | the next day | we had to go | unfortunately | again

BASIC RULES AND EXERCISES

Adverbs of manner	
I *read* **slowly**. I *enjoyed that book* **immensely**. Oliver *speaks French* **well**.	**end position:** ▸ after the verb if it has no object ▸ after verb + object – for emphasis
He **quickly** *paid* for the newspaper. You*'ll* **easily** *have* time to buy a magazine before the train comes in.	**mid position** (before the main verb): if the adverb is used descriptively (not for emphasis)
Adverbs of indefinite time and frequency	
Gill **often** *plays* the piano after tea. Brown's *is* **usually** the best place for CDs. I *should* **never** *have bought* that cheap guitar.	**mid position:** ▸ before the main verb, but after the verb *be* ▸ after the first auxiliary
Sometimes we have the radio on at breakfast time. Have you finished that computer game **already**? That was quick!	**front or end position** is possible in some cases (usually for emphasis)
Adverbs and adverbials of definite time and place	
We saw 'Julius Caesar' **yesterday**.	**end position** (in most cases)
Today we want to practise those songs again. **Up here** the acoustics are much better.	**front position** (usually for emphasis)
Adverbs and adverbials of comment	
Unfortunately, it's impossible to get tickets for 'The Phantom of the Opera' tonight.	**front position** (in most cases)
'The Lion King' is worth seeing too, **of course**.	**end position** (as an 'after-thought')
You'll **probably** get good seats.	**mid-position** (usual with *probably*, *certainly*, etc.)

Marion played *beautifully at the concert last night.*
The circus *begins at 3 o'clock on Saturday afternoon.*

When several adverbs are used together at the end of a sentence, the usual word order is MANNER – PLACE – TIME.
The more exact time comes before the more general.

"Once upon a time – well, yesterday, actually ..."

1 Going to college

Improve these sentences with the adverbs given, being careful to put them in the most suitable place. Sometimes more than one position is possible.

> Adverbs are often used to make what you want to say livelier – or more exact.

- a A lot of American students choose to do a four-year college or university program. (after high school)
- b Strictly speaking, a college is different from a university in that it takes undergraduates. (only)
- c A university has an undergraduate college of arts and sciences, a graduate section, and a program for adults. (normally)
- d But universities are also called 'colleges'. (very often)
- e You have to be in the top bracket of your high school class to have a chance of getting into a college or university. (nowadays)
- f The 'Ivy League' colleges (including the universities of Harvard and Yale) are famous. (extremely)
- g It is difficult to get a place at one of these. (not surprisingly)
- h The guidance counsellor (a member of the high school staff) is trained to advise students about their college careers. (specially)
- i As there are so many different kinds of college, each student must consider the alternatives. (carefully)
- j For an intellectually gifted person, a college specializing in academics would be the right choice. (certainly)
- k But for someone athletic, a college emphasizing sports offers more. (probably)
- l Nearly all students work to help finance their studies. (during the summer vacation)
- m Some have regular part-time jobs. (even)
- n Most colleges are not difficult to get into. (terribly)
- o But quite a number of people flunk out before they finish their studies. (unfortunately)

---

b **undergraduate** [ˌɑndɐˈgraedʒʊˌt] student (before taking a degree) • c **graduate** *here*: sb studying for a higher degree (M.A., PhD, etc.) • e **bracket** *here*: section, group • o **to flunk out** (AE) to fail (an exam)

2 Frozen Britain

Adverbs and adverbials can sometimes be so important to a sentence that the meaning is not complete without them. Turn the information below into a lively text, by adding the given adverbs and adverbials in suitable places.

- a People love talking about the weather. ← usually • in Britain • here
- b Westerly winds keep Britain warm. ← from the Atlantic • normally • in the winter
- c So everyone expects the winter months to be mild. ← naturally • pleasantly
- d But the cold weather brought Britain to a halt. ← last year • for several weeks • incredibly • suddenly
- e Motorists were trapped. ← on the A3 • in their cars • overnight
- f Two pensioners were found dead. ← even • in Northampton • in their freezing homes
- g And snow and ice have surprised us. ← this winter • yet again • all over the country
- h A third of all schools were closed. ← this week • in Scotland • because of the snow
- i But things were worse. ← in the past • often • considerably • actually
- j The Thames was frozen solid, and a Frost Fair took place. ← for two months • for example • in 1684 • on the river • even
- k The British population endured freezing weather. ← bravely • in 1947 • for three months • in the days before modern central heating
- l So we shouldn't complain. ← really • too bitterly • perhaps

ADVANCED RULES AND EXERCISES

Never in my life have I laughed so much! **Little** did we know what would happen later that evening. **Not only** were they late, but they didn't even apologize.	Certain negative or restrictive adverbials (e.g. *never, hardly, no sooner, not only, little*) can be put at the beginning of a sentence or clause for special emphasis. This causes **inversion** (a reversal of the usual word order). Inversion can also be used with *so* and *such (+ adjective/adverb).*

1 What a honeymoon!

They had booked a skiing holiday to start their married life together. But it is hard to imagine a worse honeymoon, so unlucky were the two newlyweds, John and Paula B. from Worthing, West Sussex. Little did they realize, when their taxi was late to take them to Gatwick Airport, that their troubles were only just beginning. No sooner had they arrived at the check-in desk, than they were told there was a delay because the captain of their aircraft had called in sick. Taking it philosophically, they settled down to a long wait in the airport lounge, and eventually their flight was called.
The flight went well, and they landed safely in Toulouse, France. Confident that their troubles were finally at an end, they boarded the coach taking them on the five-hour transfer to Andorra. Not only did their coach break down shortly after leaving Toulouse, but its replacement crashed en-route!
In the end they arrived at their hotel. But worse was yet to come. Scarcely had their skiing holiday begun when John B. had a bad fall and broke his arm. No more skiing for him! And only a few days later, the unfortunate couple received an unexpected call from home to inform them that burglars had raided their flat while they were away. So great was the shock that Paula B. burst into tears when she heard the news.

Based on an article in *The Weekly Telegraph*

3 **newlyweds** a couple who have just got married • 12 **confident** feeling certain • 14 **en-route** on the journey • 18 **to raid** to break into, usually in order to steal things or look through them

1.1 **Replace all the examples of inversion in the text by sentences with normal word order.**

1.2 **Work in groups to translate all the sentences containing inversion into German.**

2 Different styles

A The Murder Hunt

Mrs Oliver has organised a 'murder hunt' as a party game. In this scene she and Hercule Poirot, her guest, are checking on the 'clues'.

"Let's go and see how that Marlene child is getting on. I don't really trust that girl, you know. No sense of responsibility. I wouldn't put it past her to sneak away quietly instead of being a corpse, and go and have tea."

They proceeded amicably along the woodland path and Poirot commented on the geography of the property. A short steep slope led down to the door of the boathouse. Mrs Oliver took a key from a pocket concealed amongst her purple folds and unlocked the door.

"We've just come to cheer you up, Marlene," she said brightly as she entered.

She felt slightly remorseful at her unjust suspicions of Marlene's loyalty, for Marlene, artistically arranged as 'the body', was playing her part nobly, sprawled on the floor by the window. She lay quite motionless. The wind blowing gently through the open window rustled a pile of comics spread out on the table.

"It's alright," said Mrs Oliver impatiently. "It's only me and M. Poirot. Nobody's got any distance with the clues yet."

Poirot was frowning. Very gently he pushed Mrs Oliver aside and bent over the girl on the floor. A suppressed exclamation came from his lips.

From *Dead Man's Folly* by Agatha Christie

---

clues hints that help detectives to solve a crime • 2 **I wouldn't put it past her to do it** I wouldn't be surprised if she did it • 2 **to sneak away** to go off secretly, without being seen • 2 **corpse** dead body • 4 **amicable** friendly • 5 **property** buildings and the land belonging to them • 6 **folds** *here*: (loosely fitting) clothes • 8 **remorseful** sorry • 9 **sprawled** lying with legs and arms spread out • 12 **not any distance** not very far • 14 **to frown** to show anger or worry by moving the eyebrows together • 15 **suppressed** *unterdrückt*

B The Killers

The door of Henry's lunch-room opened and two men came in. They sat down at the counter.

"What's yours?" George asked them.

"I don't know," one of the men said. "I don't know what I want to eat."

Outside it was getting dark. The street light came on outside the window. The two men at the counter read the menu. From the other end of the counter Nick Adams watched them. He had been talking to George when they came in.

"I'll take ham and eggs," the man called Al said. He wore a derby hat and a black overcoat buttoned across the chest. His face was small and white and he had tight lips. He wore a silk muffler and gloves.

"Give me bacon and eggs," said the other man. He was about the same size as Al. Their faces were different, but they were dressed like twins. Both wore overcoats too tight for them. They sat leaning forward, their elbows on the counter.

From *The Killers*, a short story by Ernest Hemingway

---

7 **derby hat** (AE) *Melone* • 8 **muffler** old-fashioned word for scarf

2.1 **Compare the use of adjectives and adverbs in the two texts, referring especially to lines 8-11 (Text A) and lines 4-6 (Text B). What do you discover?**

2.2 **Discuss in groups and compare Agatha Christie's style with Hemingway's. These adjectives may help you:**

atmospheric • clear • colourful • complex • concise • conventional • descriptive • dry • emotional • impersonal • matter-of-fact • mysterious • simple • straightforward

Then say which style impressed you more, and why.

2.3 **Go through the first part of the Hemingway text again, and say where adverbs/adverbials could have been put in (give examples!). How would these changes affect the style?**

3 'The King'

Work in groups to translate the text into English. Think carefully about where to put the adverbs/adverbials. These words will be useful:

unexpectedly (1) • heart failure (1) • to wend one's way (2) • above all (3) • mansion (3) • to be acknowledged as (6) • to take steps towards (7) • singing contest (8) • undoubtedly (10) • to be seen as (11) • to be recognized as (11) • with sales of (11-12) • disc (12) • bestselling solo artist (12)

Im Alter von 42 Jahren starb Elvis Presley überraschend an Herzversagen. Seit seinem Tod 1977 pilgern jährlich tausende von Fans nach Memphis, Tennessee. Alle wollen in erster Linie die Villa ‚Graceland' besichtigen, wo Elvis lebte, und im Garten der Villa besuchen sie natürlich auch das Grab des Superstars. Etwa 600,000 Menschen kommen jedes Jahr nach Graceland, das seit 2006 als ‚National Historic Landmark' ausgewiesen ist.

Elvis machte [schon] mit 10 Jahren die ersten Schritte auf dem Weg zu einer musikalischen Karriere, als er in einem Gesangswettbewerb in seiner Heimatstadt Tupelo, Mississippi, fünf Dollar gewann. Er wurde 1956 zum großen Star und dominierte ohne jeden Zweifel bis 1963 die Rockmusik. Während Michael Jackson als erfolgreichster Entertainer aller Zeiten angesehen wird, gilt Elvis mit weit über einer Milliarde verkauften Tonträgern als weltweit erfolgreichster Solo-Künstler.

20 The Definite and the Indefinite Article

CHECK-UP

1 Talking about university, students and careers

Use the definite or indefinite article to fill in the gaps where necessary.

Mary Williams (17, still at school): I plan to go to ___ university when I leave ___ school. I'll probably study ___ English because I love ___ English literature. At ___ moment I'm very interested in ___ poetry of T. S. Eliot. Actually, what I'm looking forward to most is ___ freedom of ___ university life.

Professor Richards (Oxford University): ___ quite ___ large number of ___ candidates who have applied for ___ place at Oxford this year are from ___ European Union. ___ most of ___ foreign students come to Britain because ___ courses they can take here are shorter – and less crowded – than at ___ home. All ___ students I've talked to especially like our traditional system of ___ close contact with tutors.

John Whitely (19, first-year music student): My father is ___ clergyman and my mother is ___ social worker. They always hoped I might study ___ theology and become ___ priest – or at least do something to help ___ society. As ___ child, when I still used to go to ___ church regularly, I thought ___ missionary work mightn't be ___ such ___ bad idea. But when I started ___ secondary school, I began to get interested in ___ music. That was when ___ life really got going for me. By ___ time I was 15, I knew I had to take up ___ music as ___ career. So here I am! Luckily my parents have given me ___ full support. They realize I'm not doing all this as ___ act of ___ protest or ___ rebellion against ___ upbringing I had.

2 Taken down from the bookshelf

Translate these book titles into English, being careful with your use of definite and indefinite articles.

a Krieg und Frieden
b Das tägliche Leben im alten (ancient) Rom
c Das Leben Napoleons
d Die chinesische Küche (cooking)
e Die Geschichte der Vereinigten Staaten
f Als ich König war
g Ein halbes Pfund Reis
h Alle Vögel am Himmel
i Die Schule als Brücke zum Erfolg?
j Mein Vater war Indianer

BASIC RULES AND EXERCISES

The use of the definite article

Without *the*	With *the*
Life is full of ups and downs.	Not much is known about **the life of Shakespeare.**
Technology is an important part of **modern life.**	**The life we lead** today is very complicated, partly because of **the technology we have developed.**
Cold water can taste delicious.	Let's bathe here. **The water** looks so clear.
No article is used before abstract nouns (e.g. *life, society, happiness*) and uncountable nouns (e.g. *water, paper*) when referring to things generally, even if an adjective is used (e.g. *modern life*).	**The definite article** is used only when these nouns are defined more closely (e.g. with an *of*-phrase or a relative clause), or – with uncountable nouns – when a particular case or example is meant.
I missed **school** for two weeks when I was in **hospital**. We sometimes go to **church** by **car**.	That's **the hospital** over there. It's next to **the school**. You can park **the car** behind **the church**.
No article is used before institutions when referring to their function (e.g. *school* = lessons), and before means of transport (with *by*).	**The definite article** is used when referring to a particular institution (usually the building itself) or a particular vehicle.

The use of the indefinite article

With *a*	Without *a*
My mother is **a dentist**. Who wants to be **a millionaire**? Judy's grandfather was **a Frenchman**. Her mother is **a Catholic**. She lived in France **as a child**.	I wonder who will be **Prime Minister** next year at this time. John F. Kennedy became **President** (of the USA) when he was only 43. My father was **captain** of the golf club last year.
The indefinite article is used when referring to a person as a member of a certain group (e.g. a profession, nationality, religion), and after *as*.	**No article** is used when referring to functions and titles that can only be given to one person at one particular time.

I'll be ready in **half an** hour.
We've been waiting for **such a** long time!
We were up **half the** night.
All the guests stayed till late.

The article comes **after** *half, such, all, quite, both*, etc., **not before.**

Most children love ice cream.

No article before *most (die meisten).*

"Typical! You make it all the way to the front door and then summer's over."

1 The price of happiness

"Dear Albert! Farewell, I have found love."

Last week Andrew Oswald, Professor of Economics at Warwick University, unveiled the results of his research into the relationship between money and happiness. "Most people assume that more money makes you happier. In fact, it is the assumption on which all economic theory is based. Now we think we have proved it," he said.

Mick Maplesden, a lottery winner who won £4 million, says, "Has life improved for me since the win? Are you kidding? Of course it has!" But another lottery winner provided a reminder last week that money does not automatically guarantee a better life: Phil Kitchen drank himself to death just 18 months after collecting £1.8 million. Since he won the money, Mr Kitchen had consumed an average of two bottles of whisky a day.

Professor Oswald's study had a database of 9,000 people, several hundred of whom had received windfalls ranging from a few thousand pounds to half a million. People were asked to say how happy they felt on a scale of 1 to 4, and were also asked questions about the stress they felt they were under. Finally, they gave details about their income and the money they had received in the past two years.

Oswald found that people with bigger bank balances usually felt happier and less stressed than those with smaller ones. He was even able to say how much money it would take to raise someone from the bottom of the 'happiness scale' up to the top. That sum, for an average person, is £1 million.

Barbara Wragg, a nurse, and her husband Ray, a supervisor on building sites, won £7.6 million on the lottery two years ago. "We were a happy family before this happened," Barbara says, "and now the happiness we feel is even greater! But we didn't need such a large sum for it to happen. No one does."

To prove that they mean it, Mr and Mrs Wragg have already given £5.5 million to charity. "With a million pounds each – which is quite a large sum! – we have enough to be very happy," says Mrs Wragg.

Some lottery winners change their lives radically, others choose not to. Either way, money provides autonomy and independence. "People who feel they control their own worlds are generally much happier," Professor Oswald says. "What's important is not *things*, but control over your life. And, of course, the control you feel you have over your life depends on the money you have."

Adapted from *The Sunday Telegraph*

---

2 **to unveil** [ʌn'veil] *here:* to make known • 3 **to assume** to suppose • 7 **Are you kidding?** Are you joking? • 14 **windfall** money you receive unexpectedly • 19 **bank balance** the amount of money in your bank account • 24 **supervisor** sb who makes sure work is done correctly • 30 **charity** organization(s) collecting money to give to people in need, etc.

1.1 Answer the questions, using nouns with or without articles wherever possible.

a Who is Andrew Oswald? What was the subject of his research?
b What was the connection between Phil Kitchen's death and his lottery win?
c What details did the people taking part in the study have to give about themselves?
d What has the sum of £1 million to do with happiness?
e What were Mr and Mrs Wragg's jobs when they won the lottery? How has their win affected them? Why have they given so much of it away?
f What, according to Prof. Oswald, are the great advantages of having plenty of money?

1.2 Work in groups to find all the examples of *a/an* and *the* in the text. Where would the use of the article be different in German?

1.3 What do you think one needs in life in order to achieve happiness? Write a list of what you feel would probably be especially important. (How high would 'money' rank on your list?)

2 I'll put the kettle on

Complete the text, where necessary, with the definite and indefinite article.

___ ritual of 'having ___ tea' in ___ afternoon has been ___ popular source of ___ enjoyment in England for more than ___ century and ___ half. To enjoy ___ tea at its best, use ___ china teapot. First warm ___ pot with ___ hot water, then throw ___ water away. Put ___ teaspoonful of ___ tea in ___ pot for each person, pour ___ plenty of ___ boiling water on, and leave ___ tea to brew for 3 to 5 minutes before serving. ___ most people in Britain take ___ milk, and sometimes ___ sugar, too, in their tea. ___ hot water is served separately, to add to ___ tea if it gets too strong.

But ___ tea is more than just ___ drink! Classically, '___ afternoon tea' is ___ three-course meal, starting with ___ little sandwiches made with ___ thinly cut bread, followed by ___ scones with ___ jam and ___ cream, and ending with ___ piece of ___ cake!

'___ tea time' is traditionally at four. But of course, ___ afternoon isn't ___ only time for ___ cup of ___ tea. It is also popular as ___ refreshing 'pick-me-up' throughout ___ day, often quickly made with ___ tea-bag and drunk from ___ mug. Although ___ coffee is also drunk ___ lot in England, it still isn't ___ such ___ popular drink as ___ tea. Worldwide, ___ tea is in ___ fact drunk by ___ more people and in ___ greater quantities than any other beverage except ___ water.

---

4 **china** *Porzellan* • 9 **to brew** *ziehen* • 14 **course** *here*: *Gang* • 15 **scone** [skɒn] *brötchenartiges Gebäck* • 18 **pick-me-up** *Muntermacher* • 21 **beverage** ['bevrɪdʒ] a hot or cold drink

ADVANCED EXERCISES

This chapter contains no *Advanced Rules*. However, the exercises here offer further opportunities for practising the use of articles.

1 The Queen of Crime

Write a short text about the life of Agatha Christie. These words may be useful:

detective story writer (1) • of all time (1) • hospital dispenser (5) • detective novels (8) • suicide (11) • blackmail (11) • masterpiece (12) • detective fiction (12) • to recognize as (12)

Agatha Christie, die berühmteste Kriminalautorin aller Zeiten, wurde 1890 in Torquay (Devon) geboren. Sie ging nie zur Schule, denn ihre Eltern ließen sie zu Hause erziehen. Als junge Frau ging sie nach Paris, wo sie Musik studierte mit dem Ziel, Sängerin zu werden. 1914 heiratete sie, und als der erste Weltkrieg ausbrach, arbeitete sie als Krankenhausapothekerin in Torquay. Ihre genauen Kenntnisse über Gifte, die sie später in ihren Romanen zeigte, stammten aus der Zeit in diesem Krankenhaus.

Während dieser Zeit fing sie an, Kriminalromane zu lesen; diese Geschichten machten einen so großen Eindruck auf sie, dass sie beschloss, selbst ihr Glück als Autorin zu versuchen. ‚The Mysterious Affair at Styles', der erste von über 60 Kriminalromanen, erschien 1920. ‚The Murder of Roger Ackroyd', ein Roman, der von Mord, Selbstmord und Erpressung handelt, wurde 1926 herausgegeben und wird als Meisterwerk der Kriminalliteratur angesehen.

Agatha Christie, die ‚Königin des Verbrechens', starb 1976. Ihre Bücher leben jedoch weiter und sind in mehr als hundert Sprachen übersetzt worden. Kein Wunder, dass die Namen ‚Hercule Poirot' und ‚Miss Marple' für die meisten Leute heute mindestens so viel bedeuten wie ‚Sherlock Holmes'.

2 The joy of life …

Abstract themes are often the subject of poetry. Choose one of the themes from the box, think about what the theme means to you and write a short poem. (It doesn't have to rhyme.) Or, if you prefer, a short text. Before you begin, look at the example below.

space • time • travel • electricity • evolution • light • speed • joy • change • technology • beauty • sadness • happiness • loneliness • love • …

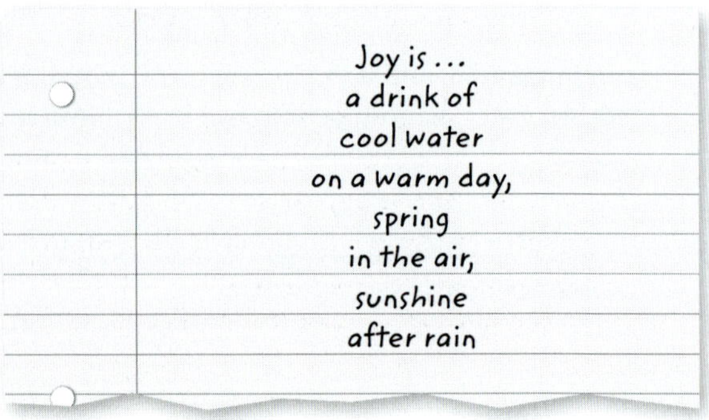

21 Indefinite Pronouns and Determiners

CHECK-UP

Everybody needs a break

Complete the text with suitable pronouns or determiners.

all • any • each • every • everyone • everyone • none • some

A ___ goes on holiday. Kings, presidents and dictators – ___ of them is too grand to take a holiday somewhere. Just like ___ else, they ___ need ___ time off work. There is only one exception to this: Her Majesty the Queen does not take ___ holidays. Rather, she resides, at set times ___ year, at ___ of her various homes – Sandringham, for example, in the winter, Balmoral in the summer.

all • anybody • each • everyone • few • most • no

B ___ people now think of holidays as necessary. ___ who doubted the need of regular holidays ___ year would be regarded as not quite right in the head. Until the 1950s, ___ people in Britain had more than two weeks' paid holiday a year. By 2010 ___ workers were entitled to 28 days. ___ politician would suggest a reduction in people's holidays – ___ would be against it.

3 **to be entitled to sth** to have the right to sth

a few • a little • all • everyone • little • most • something

C The modern idea of a holiday developed in the 1920s with the German invention of sunbathing. People now thought of a holiday as ___ completely different from their usual everyday life and work. The modern holiday depends on the idea that for ___ people work is of ___ interest because it is often boring and mechanical, so that what ___ needs is ___ relaxation and a break from the daily routine. The best holiday is one which helps us ___ to forget about our normal lives for ___ weeks.

all • all • a little • many • much • nobody • nothing • nothing • some • something

D The complete opposite of working is doing absolutely ___ in ___ perfectly natural surroundings. For ___ people the purest expression of this idea is to lie on a beach, sunbathing. Sunbathing is one of the strangest of ___ human inventions. On the one hand it is an example of perfect sloth – of doing ___ at all. On the other, it is a passive way of doing ___. ___ medical evidence speaks against spending too ___ time in the sun. But, of course, ___ can deny that ___ sunshine can do us a world of good – whether on holiday or not!

4 **sloth** [sləʊθ] laziness • 4 **evidence** knowledge of facts

BASIC RULES AND EXERCISES

some	*any*
My uncle usually gives me **some** *money* for my birthday. Could I have **some** *20p coins* for this machine, please?	I'm afraid there aren't **any** *postcards* for less than 50p. I haven't got **any** *small change*. Have you got **any**?
Some and its compounds (***someone, somebody, something***) are used in affirmative statements. In questions, *some* is used when the speaker expects a positive reply. (These questions are in fact offers or requests.)	***Any*** and its compounds (***anyone, anybody, anything***) are used in negative statements. In genuine questions (when either *yes* or *no* is expected as an answer) ***any*** is used.

no and *none*
Most people have **no** *idea* how to invest their money. How much *money* did you save last month? – **None.** **None** *of my friends* have started earning yet.
No (*kein*) can only be used before a noun. ***None*** can be used to avoid repeating the noun. It is also used before an *of*-phrase. (the compounds of ***no*** are ***no one, nobody*** and ***nothing***).

much, a little (= some), *little* (= not much)	*many, a few* (= some), *few* (= not many)
Have you had **much** *experience* in this field? Of course, it takes **a little** *time* to adjust to a new job. (*ein bisschen / einige Zeit*) At the moment John shows very **little** *interest* in his work. (*sehr wenig Interesse*)	Mrs Russell has worked with us for **many** *years*. We've only had the new machine for **a few** *months*. (*seit ein paar Monaten*) I'm afraid we have only very **few** *jobs* to offer at the moment. (*sehr wenige offene Stellen*)
Much, a little and ***little*** are used with uncountable singular nouns.	***Many, a few*** and ***few*** are used with countable plural nouns.

I haven't got **much** *money* left.
– Well, you've spent rather **a lot** *(of money)* on unnecessary things.

Much is mainly used in questions and negative statements.
In affirmative statements *a lot of, lots of* and *plenty of* are preferred.

every, each and *any* for German *jeder*

I play golf **every** *week*.	***Every*** can only be used before a noun (German: *jede(r/s) ohne Ausnahme*).
Each *hole* / **Each** *of the holes* on our course is different in some way.	***Each*** can be used before a noun or an *of*-phrase.
These *golf balls* aren't very expensive. They're only £1.80 **each**.	It can also be used alone to refer to something already mentioned. ***Each*** describes persons or things seen individually (*jede(r/s) einzelne*).
Any *time* you feel like a game just give me a ring.	***Any*** can mean 'practically every', 'it doesn't matter which' (*jeder(r/s) x-beliebige*).

Everybody enjoys playing on our course. (*jeder ohne Ausnahme*) Anyone can learn how to play. No matter how old they are. (*jeder x-beliebige*)	The compounds of ***every*** and ***any*** (***everyone***, ***anything***, etc.) are used similarly.

all and *all the*

I think **all** *golfers* are fanatics.	***All*** without the article means 'everyone/everything in general'.
All the *players* that I know have got golf on the brain.	***All*** with the article means 'everyone/every thing from a limited number or amount'.

both, neither, either

Both *my parents* / *My parents* **both** used to play.	***Both*** means 'one and the other'.
Neither (*of them*) was very good, but they enjoyed a round on a Sunday afternoon.	***Neither*** means 'not one and not the other'.
Shall I use a 6 or 7 iron from here? – I think **either** would do.	***Either*** means 'one or the other, it doesn't matter which'.

Do you see **the two** *men* on the 16th green? They **both** look pretty hopeless. (*Sie … beide*)	***Both*** is never used after *the*. For German *die beiden/die zwei*, ***the two*** must be used.

"Everybody has an off day occasionally, Bill!"

1 I wondered why I was here at all

Complete the text with *any, every, no, some* or their compounds.

In America there are many different religious beliefs and religious groups. Here a 'Jesus Freak' talks about an emotional crisis in his life.

The people I came into contact with ___ day were bumming me out so much I wanted to scream. ___ cared about ___. ___ had ___ meaning for their lives, and it scared me because I was the same way. One day I was home in my room. I had ___ to do, didn't want to see ___. ___ was zero. I was just waiting for ___ to bring me a key and unlock me out of my misery. I walked over to my window and looked up into the sky and thought, "Why are people so evil? Why am I so burnt out? Why is there always a hassle in my head? Why do I hate?"
I wondered why I was even in the world in the first place. I didn't have ___ answers. I just wanted Jesus to take over. I said, "Jesus, forgive me. I don't know what to say to you. I don't know ___, but I know you're listening. I'm just tired of the hassling in my head." After that, my head stopped churning, and I felt calm for the first time. I had a smile on my face. I never used to smile much, but from that day on I've had a smile on my face and my mind's been calm! Before, I couldn't talk to people, but now I can talk to ___ – old ladies, kids, ___.

Adapted from *Truth*, the Jesus People's newspaper

---

1 **to bum sb out** (slang) to get on sb's nerves • 3 **zero** *here:* at the lowest possible level • 4 **misery** great unhappiness • 5 **evil** bad • 6 **hassle** confusion • 8 **to take over** to take control • 10 **to churn** to turn round and round

2 Rangers – few spectators and little enthusiasm

The following sentences are taken from a newspaper article, written in formal style. Change the style by replacing *(a) little* and *(a) few* by expressions that sound less formal.

Example: There is little enthusiasm for Rangers' matches just now.
→ *There isn't much enthusiasm … / There is hardly any enthusiasm …*

a There seems to be little hope of Rangers finishing at the top of the league this season.
b So far they have won fewer home games than in previous seasons.
c The club has a few good players, but so far they have scored very few goals.
d Few towns have such an attractive stadium, but very few people want to spend money on second-rate football.
e The club must have a little money left from selling Alan Bates, but so far the management has given little thought to investing in new players.
f Peter Thomson, the ever-optimistic coach, says, "All that is needed now is a little patience."

Especially in conversation, avoid *few* and *little*. *Not many, not much, hardly any* are less formal. *A bit of* (informal) is often used instead of *a little*.

3 UK statistics of the year

Statistics and diagrams can provide interesting information but when we talk about them, the exact figures and percentages are often less important than the general tendencies or trends they reveal. Talk or write about the information below – but without mentioning the exact figures.

Example: *I am surprised to hear that there are such a lot of different types of British cheese. I'd always thought there were hardly any!*

so much/many	such a large number of ...
so few ...	such a small amount of ...
such a lot of ...	quite a lot of ...
hardly any ...	more than half of ...
very few ...	less than a quarter of ...
not very many ...	an awful lot of/a vast amount of ...
masses of ...	an incredible amount of ...

Food
700 varieties of cheese are made in Britain
600 varieties are made in France

The British eat 10,000,000,000 bags of crisps a year (more than the rest of Western Europe put together)

Mobiles
Mobile phones are owned by
50% of five- to nine-year-olds
75% of seven- to 15-year-olds

Music
60% of Brits say they like classical music
a third have never actually played a classical CD
10% have never heard of Mozart

Education
Of English 16- to 19-year-olds
21% are unable to do simple arithmetic
16% are practically unable to read or write

Ambition
When children were asked to name their highest goal
20% of girls said: "fame"
25% of boys said "to get rich"

Pay
Top managers working for the 100 biggest UK companies earn nearly 80 times the average full-time worker's wage

Couples
25% of couples sleep in separate beds
8% of British men can't name their partner's natural hair colour
25% of men say they would dump their partner if they found someone better

Waste
Food items that are thrown away every day in the UK:
5,500 whole chickens and nearly half a million ready meals

Also thrown away every day:

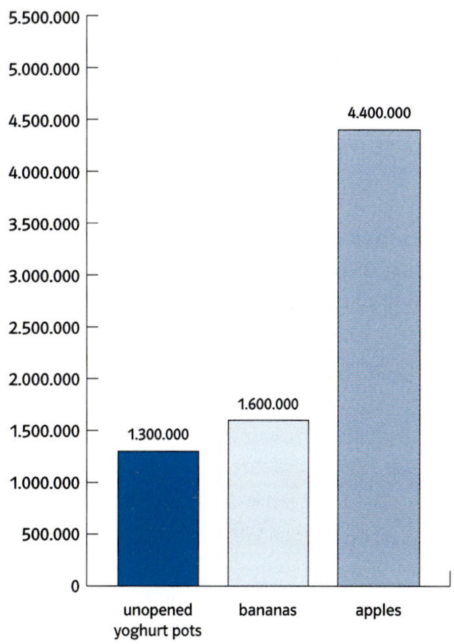

ADVANCED RULES AND EXERCISES

Everyone always tries to do **their** best. There's **somebody** on the phone for you. – Tell **them** to call again later.	Although *somebody, anybody, everybody, nobody* are singular forms, they are usually accompanied by the plural forms *they, them, their* and *themselves*. In this way misunderstandings and inappropriate masculine forms are avoided.

1 Is everyone enjoying themselves?

Complete the sentences with *they*, *them*, *their* or *themselves*.

a Everybody had a chance to express ...... opinion.
b If anyone disagrees, ... can say so.
c Nobody wants to do all the work ....
d Surely, someone will help us if we ask ....
e Why does no one dare to say what ...... really think?
f Everybody enjoyed ...... at the party.
g There's somebody at the door. Tell ...... to come in.
h Can anybody lend me ...... mobile?

Whose fault was it? Anybody's?
There is a true story about four people named Everybody, Somebody, Anybody *and* Nobody*:*
There was an important job to be done, and Everybody was sure Somebody would do it. Anybody could have done it, but Nobody did it. Somebody got angry, because it was Everybody's job. Everybody thought Anybody could do it, but Nobody realized that Everybody was too lazy to do it. It ended up with Everybody blaming Somebody because Nobody had done what Anybody could easily have done.

2 Famous words

A lot of well-known quotations are written in quite formal language. In order to appreciate the full meaning of the quotations here, you may find it helpful to refer back to the Basic Rules.

a For many are called, but few are chosen. (Holy Bible, St. Matthew)
Who do you think are the 'many' and the 'few'? Who calls and chooses them?

b You can fool all the people some of the time, and some of the people all the time, but you cannot fool all the people all of the time.
(Abraham Lincoln, 1809-1865)
Try to explain what Lincoln could have meant.

c When everyone is somebody, Then no one's anybody.
(Sir William Schwenck Gilbert, 1836-1911)
Explain the meaning of this quotation.

d Anybody can make history. Only a great man can write it.
(Oscar Wilde, 1854-1900)
Why did Oscar Wilde use *anybody* rather than *everybody*?

e Never in the field of human conflict was so much owed by so many to so few.
(Winston Churchill, 1874-1965)
Winston Churchill spoke these words after 'The Battle of Britain' in 1940. Can you explain who the 'few' were that did 'so much'? And who were the 'many'?

f We shall bear any burden, support any friend, oppose any foe to assure the survival and success of liberty.
(John F. Kennedy, 1917-1963)
to bear to accept bravely • **foe** opponent, enemy • **to assure** to make certain
How is *any* used in this quotation? Translate Kennedy's words into German.

22 Reflexive and Reciprocal Pronouns

CHECK-UP

1 What's the problem?

Put in the correct verb forms from the list below, deciding where reflexive pronouns are necessary.

apologize • behave • change • cut • defend • feel (2x) • hurt • lie down • move (2x) • quarrel • relax • tell • wonder • worry

A "Kate and I ___ again last night. Now I ___ what to do to put things right."
"Why not ring up and ___ ? That would probably make you both ___ much better."

sich streiten · sich überlegen · sich entschuldigen · sich fühlen

B "What's all that blood?"
"Oh, I've ___ with the bread knife. Don't ___ . I haven't ___ badly."
"You look a bit pale, though. Perhaps you should ___ for a few moments and ___ ."

sich schneiden · sich Sorgen machen · sich verletzen · sich hinlegen · sich entspannen

C "John keeps criticising me for ___ too slowly on the tennis court." – "How do you generally react?"
"By ___ , of course."
"Well, don't. Another time, just quietly ___ not to ___ that way. Then say to John, 'You're right, I do ___ slowly.' You'll ___ less aggressive that way – and maybe John will ___ after a while."

sich bewegen · sich verteidigen · sich sagen · sich verhalten · sich bewegen · sich fühlen · sich ändern

2 Help each other – don't just think of yourselves!

Use reflexive or reciprocal pronouns to complete these sentences

Examples: – *Cooperative people are people that help each other/one another.*
– *Selfish people usually think only of themselves.*

a In an ideal society, people wouldn't try to take advantage of … .
b Modest people do not make a habit of praising … .
c When their eggs are hatched, most parent birds help … to look after the young ones until they are old enough to feed … .
d At Christmas time we all give … presents; but most of us buy the sort of presents we would choose for … .
e Quite a lot of people talk to … when they're alone.
f Good friends can always depend on … .

"Yeah, I'm a rhinoceros, so what? Jesus! Why do people always have to categorise each other?"

b **modest** *bescheiden*

BASIC RULES AND EXERCISES

Reflexive pronouns

Marion fell down the stairs yesterday.
Luckily she **didn't hurt** ***herself***.

A reflexive pronoun is used if the object of a sentence is the same person or thing as the subject.

By the time John was five, he had learnt to **wash** and **dress** ***(himself)*** without help.

After some verbs, the reflexive pronoun can be left out, e.g. *wash* (o.s.), *dress* (o.s.), *hide* (o.s.), *prepare* (o.s.).

Verbs that are not reflexive in English

Sally **lies down** for a while after lunch if she **feels** tired.

Many verbs, unlike their German equivalents, are not reflexive in English.

Some common examples of verbs that are not reflexive in English

to apologize	*sich entschuldigen*	to open	*sich öffnen*
to change	*sich (ver)ändern*	to quarrel	*sich streiten*
to hurry	*sich beeilen*	to remember	*sich erinnern*
to feel	*sich fühlen*	to sit down	*sich setzen*
to move	*sich bewegen*	to wonder	*sich fragen, sich überlegen*

Reciprocal pronouns

Judy and Tim often fight – but they **like** ***each other*** a lot really.

The reciprocal pronoun *each other / one another* is used to express an exchange between persons or things.

Compare:
The children **bought** ***themselves*** big ice creams. = Each child bought one for himself/herself.
Tom and Susie **bought** ***each other*** presents. = Each bought a present for the other.

Do it *yourself*!
Reflexive pronouns can also be used for emphasis.

1 The graduation party

Rebecca Davitch is a professional party organizer. One day she has a phone call from Mrs Border, whose daughter's graduation party is booked for that very evening. But her daughter has failed chemistry and hasn't graduated! Mrs Border wants to cancel the party, but the preparations have already gone so far that Rebecca tries to persuade her to change her mind …

"Well, isn't it fortunate," Rebecca told Mrs Border, "that you've already set up this party. It sends a message, don't you think?"

"Message?"

"When your daughter must be feeling so disheartened, so discouraged with herself. But here's this wonderful party to show her how much you love her."

"Oh, Mrs Davitch, I can't imagine –"

"And a message to your friends, as well. A sort of statement."

"My friends! I don't know how I'll face them. They're all going to feel so sorry for me. Behind my back they'll be telling each other –"

"Mrs Border, have you ever stopped to consider what a marvelous purpose a party serves? Think about it! At a moment when you and your daughter would normally not be speaking, when you know she must feel ashamed in front of the world at large and the world is surely wondering what to say to you, why everyone's thrown together in a gigantic celebration. Everyone's forced to hug, and kiss, and announce to everyone else that what matters is you all love each other. It's like that scientific discovery they made a few years back; remember? They discovered that if you fake a smile, your smile muscles somehow trigger some reaction in the brain and you'll start feeling the way you pretended to feel, happy and relaxed. Remember?"

"Well …"

"Imagine if you hadn't had the foresight to schedule this party! Because we've been booked for months and months ahead, this time of year. You'd call and say, 'Do you have an evening this week when we could throw a little fete for our daughter? She's experiencing such, um … low – self-esteem yes, that's the term: 'self-esteem' – and we want to show her we love her.' I would have to say, 'Sorry, Mrs Border –' "

"And it's true it's going to be hard to cancel our guests," Mrs Border said. "I'd be forced to make all these complicated excuses."

"Oh! It would be so difficult," Rebecca told her.

Mrs Border said, "I guess we do have to remember what's important here."

"Absolutely," Rebecca said. "Oh, one thing I'd meant to call you about: when shall I expect Binstock to bring the flowers?"

"Well, they promised them for three o'clock, but now I don't know if –"

"Three is fine," Rebecca said smoothly. "I'll make sure to be here. See you this evening, Mrs Border."

"Well … so … well, yes, I suppose," Mrs Border said. Rebecca hung up and sank into a chair.

From *Back When We Were Grownups* by Anne Tyler

---

graduation [ˌgrædʒʊ'eɪʃn] (AE) the successful completion of high school studies • **to cancel** to stop (an arrangement from taking place) • 4 **disheartened** disappointed, discouraged • 12 **at large** *here:* as a whole, generally • 13 **to hug** to put one's arms around (each other) • 15 **to fake sth** to make sth false appear genuine or real • 16 **to trigger** to set in motion • 19 **to schedule** ['skedʒu:l] (AE) to plan • 31 **to hang up** to end a telephone conversation

1.1 What is wrong? Correct the following statements, according to what you have understood of Rebecca's arguments.

a Mrs Border's daughter is probably feeling quite O.K. about herself, even though she hasn't graduated.
b Having a party now will give everyone a chance to express their feelings, whatever they may be.
c It's unfortunate that the evening was booked so far in advance, as the daughter's feelings of self-doubt may be reinforced by having a party now.

1.2 Translate lines 6-17 into German. Note which verbs are reflexive only in German.

1.3 The following words and expressions with *self* are very common in English. Explain what they mean. (You may need a dictionary for some of them.)
Example: self-esteem → *Self-esteem is a good opinion of oneself. → If you have self-esteem, it means that you feel good about yourself.*

a self-centred
b self-control
c self-defence
d self-help book
e self-pity
f self-portrait
g self-service restaurant
h self-sufficient

Do you know any other examples?

☆ **1.4 What do you think of Rebecca's arguments? What effect is the party likely to have?**

2 The tale of Hansel and Gretel

Translate the text into English. These words will be useful:

to comfort (5) • to lose one's way (6) • gingerbread house (7) • witch (8) • to lock up (9) • oven (11) • to hug (12)

Erinnerst du dich noch an das Märchen von Hänsel und Gretel? Die Eltern sind arm und entschließen sich dazu, die Kinder in den Wald zu führen und dort zu verlassen. Als die Kinder merken, dass sie allein sind, versuchen sie sich erst zu trösten.

Aber sie verirren sich im Wald. Als sie an das Knusperhäuschen kommen, freuen sie sich. Die Tür öffnet sich aber, und eine alte Hexe kommt heraus. Die Hexe sperrt Hänsel in einen Käfig ein, und Gretel überlegt sich, wie sie sich und ihren Bruder retten kann. Als Gretel die Hexe in den heißen Backofen gestoßen und Hänsel befreit hat, umarmen sich die beiden Kinder. Im Hexenhaus befindet sich eine Kiste mit Goldmünzen. Die Kinder nehmen sich den Schatz und machen sich glücklich auf den Heimweg.

"Eat it yourself!"

ADVANCED EXERCISES

This chapter contains no *Advanced Rules*. However, the exercises here offer further opportunities for practice.

1 Ernest and the two girls

Ernest is a lonely, middle-aged man, who has never got over the shellshock he suffered during the First World War. One morning, when he is sitting by himself in a café, two sisters, the elder girl about 12 years old, come in and sit down at his table, each with a cup of tea. As he listens to their conversation, his feeling of loneliness deepens …

The two girls sat before him wholly engrossed in themselves, still debating whether they should buy a cake, or whether they should ride home on a bus.

"But it'll be cold," reasoned the elder, "walking home."

"No, it won't," the other said, but with no conviction in her words. The sound of their voices told him how lonely he was, each word feeding him with so much more loneliness that he felt utterly unhappy and empty.

Time went slowly: the minute-hand of the clock seemed as if it were nailed immovably at one angle. The two girls looked at each other and did not notice him: he withdrew into himself and felt the emptiness of the world and wondered how he would spend all the days that seemed to stretch vacantly, like goods on a broken-down conveyor belt, before him. He tried to remember things that had happened and felt panic when he discovered a thirty-year vacuum. All he could see behind was a grey mist and all he could see before him was the same unpredictable fog that would hide nothing. He wanted to walk out of the café and find some activity so that he would henceforth be able to mark off the passage of his empty days, but he had no will to move. He heard someone crying so shook himself free of such thoughts and saw the younger girl with hands to her eyes, weeping. "What's the matter?" he asked tenderly, leaning across the table.

The elder girl replied for her, saying sternly:

"Nothing. She's acting daft."

"But she must be crying for some reason. What is it?" Ernest persisted quietly, bending closer still towards her. "Tell me what's wrong." Then he remembered something. The girls' conversation came to him through an intricate process of recollection. "I'll get you something to eat," he ventured. "Can I?"

---

shellshock mental disorder caused by shells (Granaten) going off • 1 **engrossed in** totally concentrating on • 5 **conviction** firm belief • 10 **to withdraw** to retire or go back • 12 **vacant** ['veɪkənt] empty • 12 **conveyor belt** moving band of an assembly line • 15 **mist** fog • 17 **henceforth** from now on • 20 **to weep** to cry • 21 **tender** gentle, soft • 22 **stern** strict • 23 **daft** informal word for 'silly' • 25 **to persist** to keep on (asking) • 27 **intricate** complex • 27 **recollection** remembering • 28 **to venture** to dare (to say)

She unscrewed clenched fingers from her eyes and looked up, while the elder girl glared at him resentfully and said: “We don’t want anything. We’re going now.”

“No, don’t go,” he cried. “You just sit down and see what I’m going to get for you.” He stood up and walked to the counter, leaving them whispering to each other.

He came back with a plate of pastries and two cups of tea, which he set before the girls, who looked on in silence. The younger was smiling now. Her round eager eyes were fascinated, yet followed each movement of his hands with some apprehension. Though still hostile the elder girl was gradually subdued by the confidently working actions of his hands, by caressing words and the kindness that showed in his face. He was wholly absorbed in doing good and, at the same time, fighting the feeling of loneliness that he still remembered, but only as a nightmare is remembered.

The two children fell under his spell, began to eat cakes and sip the tea. They glanced at each other, and then at Ernest as he sat before them smoking a cigarette. The café was still almost empty, and the few people eating were so absorbed in themselves, or were in so much of a hurry to eat their food and get out that they took little notice of the small company in the corner. Now that the atmosphere between himself and the two girls had grown more friendly, Ernest began to talk to them …

From *Uncle Ernest* by Alan Sillitoe

---

29 **clenched** tightly closed • 30 **to glare at** to look at angrily • 30 **resentful** angry and bitter • 35 **pastry** ['peɪstrɪ] kind of cake; *Plundergebäck* • 37 **eager** enthusiastic • 38 **apprehension** fear and doubt • 38 **hostile** unfriendly • 39 **to subdue** [səb'dju] to quieten and soften • 39 **confident** sure, self-assured • 40 **caressing** [-'--] kind and caring • 43 **nightmare** bad dream • 44 **spell** magical influence

1.1 Use reflexive or reciprocal pronouns in your answers to these questions:

a Why don’t the two girls notice Ernest at first?
b How does Ernest react when he hears one of them crying?
c How do the girls behave when Ernest gets up to fetch them something to eat?
d Why does nobody else notice what is going on at their table?

1.2 Look closely at lines 8-21, and find the equivalents of:

a sich erinnern
b sich bewegen
c sich anschauen
d sich beugen
e sich ereignen
f sich fragen
g sich erstrecken
h sich zurückziehen
i sich losreißen

1.3 Note the author’s use of reflexive and reciprocal pronouns. In what way do they help to underline the difference between Ernest’s situation and that of the two girls?

2 The only perfection

Andre Agassi, one of the most gifted tennis players of all time, writes in 'Open', his autobiography, about the ups and downs of his career, and his search for happiness. The sudden decision to support a friend financially in order to help him with his children's college education, turns out to be an experience Agassi will never forget.

Frankie's bottom lip trembles. Andre, he says, I can't believe you'd do that for me.

The look on his face is a complete shock. I didn't understand the meaning and value of education, the hardship and stress it causes most parents and children. I've never thought of education like that. School was always a place I managed to escape, not a thing to be treasured. Setting aside the stock was merely something I did because Frankie specifically mentioned college and I wanted to help. When I saw what it meant to him, however, I was the one who got educated.

Helping Frankie provides more satisfaction and makes me feel more connected and alive and *myself* than anything else that happens in 1996. I tell myself: Remember this. Hold on to this. This is the only perfection there is, the perfection of helping others. This is the only thing we can do that has any lasting value or meaning. This is why we're here. To make each other feel safe.

From *Open* by Andre Agassi

---

7 **stock** *here*: *Aktien* • 7 **merely** only

2.1 Comment on Agassi's experience. In what way does it 'educate' him? Can you symphathize with his feelings? Or do they surprise you? (Apart from his many Grand Slam victories, Agassi won the Olympic Gold Medal in 1996.)

2.2 Explain in German what Agassi means when he talks about the 'only perfection'. (lines 10-15)

Key to the Check-up Exercises

1 Present Tense – Simple and Progressive Aspects

1 The law of attraction?

It is 12.30 on a fine June day, and the sun **is shining** as Tom **comes** out of his office, **walks** down Queen's Street and **goes** into the park. On a bench near the duck pond he **sees** someone he **knows**.

TOM Hello, Amy! What **are** you **doing** here?
AMY Oh, hi, Tom! I **am sitting** here for a while, enjoying the sun. I **often come** here during the lunch hour, usually with a book!
TOM Well, I **hope** I **am not interrupting** you! What **are** you **reading**?
AMY An absolutely fascinating book! It **belongs** to Emily. I **am just getting** to the end of the first chapter. It's called 'The Strangest Thing', and it's about the law of attraction. Emily **says** a lot of people **are talking** about that these days.
TOM The law of attraction? What **does** that **mean**?
AMY Well, as far as I **understand** it, it **seems** to mean that you **attract** things into your life through your thoughts and feelings. Like a magnet! That's why people who **expect** bad luck **usually get** it, but happy feelings **bring** more happiness into your life!
TOM What? But that **sounds** absurd. You **don't believe** that, surely?
AMY Well I **am beginning** to wonder! – Hey, look, Emily **is coming**! How weird! Normally I **never see** her here.
TOM Strange. Well, as my mother **always says**: Talk of the devil and the devil **appears**.
AMY Quiet, Tom! Hi, Emily! Come and join us. We **are just discussing** the ideas in that book you lent me.

2 The new postman

One day, a new postman **comes** to a house and **walks** in through the gate. To his horror, a big, angry-looking dog **is barking** on the front doorstep.
"Don't worry," **says** the lady of the house. "He **is just making** a noise. He **always does** that when anyone **comes** to the door. And anyway, you **know** the old proverb: 'A barking dog **never bites**.'"
"Yes," **says** the postman. "I **know** the old proverb, and you **know** the old proverb. The only trouble is: **does** the dog **know** the old proverb?"

2 Past Tense – Simple and Progressive Aspects

1 The Hollerday Hill fire

About 18 months ago, I **had** a most unusual experience. At the time, I **lived (was living, *if considered temporary*)** in a house on the cliffs between the two Devon villages of Lynton and Lynmouth. I **used** the

railway station at Taunton quite regularly to go to London, and I always **enjoyed** the drive back across Exmoor and along the coast to Lynton.
At about nine o'clock one winter evening, while I **was returning** from Taunton in my car, I **drove** round a bend in the road and suddenly **saw** that the whole of the sky above the hill in front of me **was** bright orange and red with flames. I **was** about five miles from Lynton, and I **knew** that must be where the flames **were coming** from. Wanting to get home as soon as possible, I **increased** my speed and, while I **was driving**, I **tried** to keep my eye on the flames. Sometimes I **lost** sight of them when the road **twisted** and **turned**. But even from several miles away, it **seemed** clear that a major fire **was spreading** rapidly through the village.
Even though I **was driving** quickly now, it **took** me several minutes to cross the moors to the top of Countisbury Hill, where there is a good view down to the two villages. When I **reached** the top of the hill, I **expected** to see at least ten or twenty houses on fire. Strangely, from this position I **saw** nothing at all. There **was** no fire to be seen, and none of the houses below **was/were burning**. Everything **looked** just as quiet and peaceful as ever.
Next morning, when I **went** into the village to collect my newspaper, I **asked** the newsagent about it, and he **told** me there had been no fire in the village at all the previous night.
"Where **did** you **see** the flames?" he **asked**.
"They **seemed** to be coming from some houses on the hill behind the village."
"Ah. Hollerday Hill," he **said**, and **nodded** wisely. "The big house on Hollerday Hill. It **burnt/burned** right down to the ground."
"But I **thought** you **said** there hadn't been any fire last night!"
Suddenly I **noticed** that the old man **was looking** at me rather strangely. "You misunderstand me," he **explained**. "The Hollerday Hill fire **happened** over fifty years ago."

3 Present Perfect – Simple and Progressive

1 Dear Annie

Fed up *Sun Sep 19th, 20:35 GMT*
Ever since my parents split up last year, I **have been living** with my mother. Everything was great at first, but now she **has found** a new boyfriend, and I can only say our home life **has changed** for the worse. They **have been going** out together for about six weeks, and now he **has started** coming round here regularly for meals. Mum **has stopped** helping me with my homework, and since school started again last week, she **has been sending** me to bed early so they can spend time alone together. I **have had** enough of it! At least he **hasn't moved** in yet, but who knows what they're planning? **I've tried** to talk to Mum several times about how I feel, but so far nothing **has helped**. She says she **has been** without a partner long enough so I just have to adapt. For a while now I **have been wondering** whether to go back to my dad. What do you think?

Unhappy parent *Sun Sep 19th, 20:30 GMT*
Help! Ever since our son, aged 13, got his new computer, he **has been sitting** up in his room, playing games, and he **has been neglecting** his homework. What worries me most, though, is that he **has stopped** going to basketball practice. In fact, apart from going to school, he **has not been** outside the house for days. The only positive aspect of all this is that he **has stopped** watching TV.

Pig-in-the-middle *Sun Sep 19th, 20:29 GMT*
My problem is my two best friends. They **have never liked** each other, and recently the situation **has been** worse than ever. Whenever the three of us do things together, they start arguing. For months now I **have been trying** to think of a way of solving the problem, but nothing I **have thought** of so far **has worked**. Since their last big quarrel, I **have been meeting** them separately, which I thought might be the best solution, but they both **have reacted** to this badly – each of them **has been blaming** me all the time for liking the other one better. What should I do?

2 At the station

a She has been waiting for 20 minutes.
b They have eaten their hamburgers.
c He has lost his ticket / money / purse / ...
d It has been standing there / at the platform for 15 minutes / a quarter of an hour.
e She has not bought anything / any other magazine.
f He has just said good-bye to his girlfriend. / ...

4 Past Tense and Present Perfect Contrasted

1 It's common knowledge

a When did the Normans conquer England? → They conquered England in 1066.
b Since when has the present British government been in power? → *appropriate answer here*
c How many times has Britain been invaded since the Norman conquest? → It has never been invaded since then.
d Where did the potato plant come from originally? → It came from America.
e Where did the World Cup take place in 2010? → It took place in South Africa.
f How long has the present British monarch been on the throne? → *appropriate answer here*
g Who first climbed Mount Everest? → Sir Edmund Hillary and Tenzing Norgay first climbed Mount Everest in 1953.
h In which century did the USA become independent of Britain? → It became independent in the 18th century.
i Which American president was shot after the Civil War? → President Abraham Lincoln was shot after the Civil War.
j How many countries have become members of the EU so far? → *appropriate answer here*
k In what year did the Berlin Wall fall? → It fell in 1989.
l What city has been chosen for the next Summer Olympics? → *appropriate answer here*

2 Good to see you!

A

MARK There you are at last! I **have been waiting** for absolutely ages.
NINA Sorry! – When **did** you **get** here?

MARK	At least quarter of an hour ago. I **have been standing** about in the rain all this time, and as you can see, I haven't got an umbrella. Look how wet I **have got**. Why **didn't** you **leave** home earlier?
NINA	Serena **called** just as I **was putting** my coat on. She **kept** me on the phone till nearly half past. You know what she's like. Anyway, I'm sorry I **didn't get** here at the time we **arranged**, Mark.
B	
AUTHOR	Nice to see you. Er – **have** you **read** the book yet?
FRIEND	Which book? Oh, you mean the one you **gave** me a month or so ago. Your first novel. Ah yes, well, I **started** reading it last week, but I'm rather a slow reader really, so I **haven't finished** it yet. So far, I **have liked** it very much, though.
AUTHOR	How far **have** you **got**?
FRIEND	Oh, not very far yet, I'm afraid. – But tell me now, **have** you **started** work on another book yet? Last time we **met** you **said** you might write another.
AUTHOR	Well, actually, I **have been collecting** ideas most of the time since then, so I **have been** very busy. One of my best ideas **came** to me while I **was bathing** the dog in the kitchen sink last weekend. I –
FRIEND	Sorry – I must rush. Tell me about it another time, OK?

5 Forms of the future

1 Messages on the family fridge

a Hi Dad, Pete Richards rang.
He says he **will come / is going to come** round when he finishes work.
(That **will** probably **be** at about six, he thinks.)
Jack

b Sam! I expect I **will be** back late this evening – I **am going to stay on** at the office all afternoon. Could you take some steaks out of the freezer for supper? Don't worry about vegetables – we **will have** ***(spontaneous decision)*** / **are going to have** ***(plan made before)*** a tomato salad, that's quick.
Love, Jenny

c MUM! Sue Barton rang up about your trip to London with her. As she can't get tickets for "Romeo and Juliet", she **is going to book** seats for a musical. **Will** that **be** OK? (You **will have to** ring her when you get back.)
Tina

d Hi Tina – Freddy and I **are going to sail** out to the island this evening. Want to come with us? Ring me (at Freddy's!) if so. (There **will be** room in the boat for Foxie, too, if you want to bring her along.) We **are going to take** a picnic.
Jack

e Jack!! Thanks for your note. I **am going to spend** the evening at Moira's. She **is going to show** me her photos of Austria (as planned – or didn't I tell you?). Enjoy your picnic. Perhaps I **will come** next time!
Tina

2 It's all arranged

TED	David and I **are going** skiing for a week after Christmas. Like to come too?
JOHN	**Are** you **going** to the Alps?
TED	No – the Cairngorms. It **will be** great! We **are setting off** on Boxing Day. The train to Edinburgh **leaves** in the morning. We **change** trains at Edinburgh, and we **arrive** at Aviemore in the early evening. Our ski course **starts** at ten the next morning. Look – I **will show** you the catalogue.
JOHN	Hmm. What **will** you **do** if there **isn't** any snow – like last year?
TED	There **will be** plenty of snow, you just wait. According to the long-range forecast, we **will have** a really hard winter this year. Temperatures **will reach** all-time lows!
JOHN	Well, as long as you believe it. Anyway, I can't come with you. My French penfriend **will be** here when you **go**. He **is spending** Christmas and New Year with us.

6 Sequence of Tenses

1 In town

a "When Dick Randall **came** out of the cinema last Thursday evening, he couldn't remember which street he **had parked** his car in."
b "I wanted to walk back along the river, but when I got to the bridge, I **discovered** that they **had closed** the public footpath."
c "The play starts at 7.30. If we **leave** here at half past six, we **will have** plenty of time. I expect we **will arrive** at the theatre shortly after seven."
d "There were so many people waiting for the Underground at Waterloo, it **looked** as if we **wouldn't get** onto the train at all!"
e "You ought to try the King George. I **have had** lunch there several times recently. They **serve** excellent pub food."
f "Sorry we're late. We **got** to the station in good time, but the train **was** late."

2 Jenny's A-level results

a She knows what will await her when she and her parents get home. Her A-level results. A little white envelope or a postcard from the school will be on the mat with all the other post that came while they were away.
b No, all through the holiday she has been trying to forget about it.
c She'll take the envelope up to her room, then she'll lock the door and read the results on her own.
d (She knows that) her parents are expecting her to do well, but (she also knows that) her biology teacher wasn't very impressed with her efforts before the exams.
e (The worst thing is that) (she knows that) she didn't do as much revision as some of her friends.
f If her marks aren't good enough, she won't get into University – which has always been her dream.

7 Conditional Sentences

1 Sunday trip to the seaside

MOTHER	Let's go to the seaside tomorrow. If the weather **is** nice, we **will have** a great time, I'm sure!
FATHER	OK. But if I **were/was** you, I **would check** the forecast first.
DAUGHTER	Well, I'm afraid I **won't be able** to get up all that early if I **go** to Dan's party tonight.
MOTHER	You and your parties. If you **didn't go** to so many parties, you **would do** a lot better at school, you know.
DAUGHTER	Oh, Mum! If you **didn't complain** all the time, I **would feel** much more like trying!
SON	I'm sick of hearing about school. – What about Whitby then? If you **give** me the map now, Dad, **I'll work** out the best route.
12.30 next day:	
MOTHER	If we **had left** earlier, we **wouldn't have got** stuck in that awful traffic jam back there.
SON	Well, we **would have been able** to start in time if 'Sleeping Beauty' **hadn't spent** so long in the bathroom.
DAUGHTER	That's not true! Anyway, we **wouldn't have got** into that stupid traffic jam at all if we **had listened** to the traffic news on the radio like I suggested.
FATHER	Now then, now then. If Junior here **hadn't forgotten** his bathing trunks, we **wouldn't have needed** to go back, and we **wouldn't have wasted** that half hour to begin with.
MOTHER	And who forgot to fill the tank up yesterday?
FATHER	Well, let's not worry about whose fault it all was. We've still got a nice day – hm – afternoon – on the beach to look forward to. If this rain **stops**, we **will have** a great time, I'm sure!

2 In the news today

a If the drivers hadn't been surprised by the fog, **they would have been able to slow down in time.**
b Driving conditions wouldn't have **been so difficult if the road hadn't been icy.**
c If the lorry **hadn't broken down shortly before, one of the lanes wouldn't have been blocked.**
d There would be fewer accidents if **drivers took enough notice of weather conditions.**
e Drastic fines will be the only answer if **people don't learn to be more responsible behind the wheel.**

8 Indirect Speech

1 An interview

That evening, Sue talks to her friend Jessica about the interview.
"What happened?" Jessica asks.
"Well, Mrs Beale told me to **sit down**, and then she asked me why **I had applied for this kind of work** and so I told her **(that) I liked the idea of helping other people,** and **(that) I thought I'd enjoy the work**. Then she asked **whether/if I had ever worked with elderly people before**, and of course I said **(that) I hadn't**, but that **I didn't think I'd have any problems**. She also wanted to know **where I live/lived**, and asked **whether/if I would be able to start work at 7.30 most mornings**. I told her **(that) I'd easily be**

able to manage it by then as **I live/lived quite near**. Then she asked me **whether/if I could cook**, so I said **(that) I often helped to get meals ready at home**, but that **I hadn't often cooked a whole meal by myself**. She told me **not to worry** about that, and explained that **I wouldn't have to cook whole meals without help**, but that **she did need / she needed someone with a bit of experience in the kitchen**. She also told me **(that) I would have to do jobs like vacuum-cleaning, washing, setting tables and so on**."
"When will you know if you've got the job?" Jessica asks.
"Well, Mrs Beale said **(that) a young man was coming to see her in the afternoon**, so **naturally she couldn't make a decision until she'd talked to him, too**. She told me **to call tomorrow morning** to find out."

9 The Passive Voice

1 Police kicked and beaten in quiet area of Canterbury

Two policemen **were attacked** as they tried to break up a fight in a quiet area of Canterbury in the early hours of Sunday. The trouble **was/had been started** by two rival gangs. Within seconds the peace and quiet of Surrey Road **was/had been shattered** by the noise of breaking glass and shouting. Police officers Sean Murphy and Bob Wilcox arrived at the scene only after considerable damage **was /had been done**. When they tried to make arrests, they **were beaten** and **kicked**. Hospital treatment **was not required**, however, and they were able to remain on duty.
They **were helped** by more police officers who arrived before any further damage **was/had been done**. So far, seven people **have been arrested**. They **will be heard** in court next month. Further investigations **are** still **being carried out**, and witnesses **are asked** to pass on any information that might help the police.

2 The by-pass

The plan for the new road had been passed by the county council two years ago.
... but now the council has been informed (by the Department of Transport) that the project cannot be financed for at least five years.
"The by-pass is needed now,"...
"The existing road through the village is used by enormous numbers of cars on their way to the East Coast.
People living on Botesdale High Street are badly affected by the constant noise of traffic.
Over the past six years nine people have been killed or seriously injured by lorries driving at high speed.
Botesdale is no longer considered a safe place for children, who are especially at risk;
not surprisingly, property is being sold here at an alarming rate.
Our village community must be saved before it is too late."
At the end of the meeting, a course of action was decided on.
People were asked to sign a petition, which will be sent to the Department of Transport before the end of the month.

10 Modal Auxiliaries

1 Summer time

A "Let's go down to the beach now. It **may not** be so sunny later, you never know."
"O.K. Wait – I **can't** find my sunscreen."
"You **can** use mine. – Hey, whose are those flippers over there?"
"John's. But we **can't** take them. He **won't** let *anyone* borrow his things."
"Hmm. This snorkel here **will** be his, too, I suppose?"
"Yes. Oh come on! Swimming **can** be just as much fun *without* all this equipment."
"OK. You **may** be right."

B "How much further do you plan to go? We **must** have walked miles along this beach by now!"
"All right. We **needn't** go any further. Let's put our things down and go in the water here."
"Have you seen that sign? 'No swimming beyond this point.' We **mustn't** swim over there, then."
"I wonder why. It **may/must** be because of the river mouth. There **must** be some reason."
"I'll have a swim later. **May** I borrow your camera to take a photo of those birds?"
"OK, but you **mustn't** wade out to those rocks with it! I know what you're like."
"You **needn't** worry. I won't go near the water – even if you're drowning!"

2 Life in the days of Queen Victoria

In the 19th century many poor people (including children) **had to** work long hours in factories and down coal mines. There were no trade unions, so they **weren't able to** protest against the terrible conditions. Middle-class families **didn't have to** suffer in this way, but even their 'comfortable' way of life would seem strange now. The Victorian father was 'head of the house' and everyone **had to** treat him with great respect. At meal times the children **weren't allowed to** talk unless they were spoken to by a grown-up. Their mother, often with ten or more children, **had to** work hard to organize the household. Even with servants to help, she **wasn't able to** relax for long.
On Sundays the maid **was allowed to** get up an hour later than usual and **was able to** relax a little during the day. But nobody **was allowed to** play games or read books (except the Bible or religious books). Everyone **had to** go to church.
Until 1870 very few working-class children **were able to** read or write. When Parliament finally decided that now all children **had to** go to school from age 5 to 13, many parents were angry, arguing that if their children **had to** go to school, they **wouldn't be able to** earn money, so their families would be poorer than ever!

11 The Infinitive

1 The dinner party

The guests were expected **to arrive** at eight o'clock. The Fergusons didn't want them **to be** late as they had arranged for some delicious Chinese food **to be delivered** by that time. And, of course, they didn't

want it **to get** cold. The first **to arrive** was Major Winterbottom. It was, of course, easy for him **to be** on time as he was the Fergusons' next-door neighbour. He said he would love **to help** in the kitchen, but Mrs Ferguson made him **sit** down and invited him **to have** a drink.
At 8.30 the Chinese takeaway rang up **to say** that their driver had no idea where **to deliver** the food, and that he would like **to be informed** of the exact address. A few minutes later they heard a car **stop** in their drive. But it was only someone that had used their drive **to turn** in. Then they heard the telephone **ring** again. It was the MacAlisters, announcing that their babysitter had let them down. They were wondering whether **to come** or not, as they didn't want **to leave** the children at home on their own. At nine the Chinese takeaway rang **to let** them **know** that it was now impossible for them **to come** because their driver had somehow managed **to run** into one of the trees on the High Street, so they wanted **to know** if the Fergusons wouldn't like **to collect** the food themselves. While the Fergusons were discussing what **to do**, the phone rang again.
It was Sue Jones, saying that she and Mike had been delighted **to be invited** to their party next Friday. But what time exactly were the Fergusons expecting them **to come**?

2 Christopher Columbus

a ... the only sailor to explore...
b ... the first explorer to think that west was the direction to take/to be taken.
c ... the only person to believe the earth was round.
d ... it was impossible for any ship to (be able to) make ...
e ... decided to travel west and expected to get to India ...
f ... A lot of money was needed (for him) (to be able) to buy and equip the ships ...
g ... the distance to be covered.
h ... they had hoped to find land ... told him to turn back.
i He promised to give up the search ...
j ... was relieved to see the joy in his men's faces.

12 Gerunds

1 At the doctor's

a "Twenty cigarettes a day, Mr Miller?! I think it would be better if you stopped **smoking** altogether.
b And you should also avoid **eating** too much meat."
c "But I'm not keen **on eating** nothing but salads and vegetables. And I always look forward **to having** a drink when I come home from work."
d "Well, well. How **about having/eating** muesli for breakfast now and then instead **of eating/having** egg and bacon every morning?
e And I'm afraid you're a bit overweight. Have you ever thought **of losing** weight? How **about taking** some exercise?"
f "But I've always hated **running** around in a tracksuit or **swimming** in some crowded pool."
g "Well, if you go on like this you might be in danger **of having** a heart attack."
h "Hm, perhaps I'll give up **going** to work in the car. I might get used **to riding/using** my old bike again. Oh, and another thing, doctor. I don't seem to get enough rest at night. I have difficulty **(in) sleeping/ falling asleep/getting to sleep**.
i "What **about going** for a nice walk before you go to bed? That may help.
j And carry on **taking** those red pills. They'll also help you to relax. See you again on Wednesday then, Mr Miller."

2 The successful politician

The successful politician ...
- a ... has no/doesn't have any difficulty (in) remembering people's names.
- b ... doesn't worry about/is not afraid of speaking in public.
- c ... looks forward to becoming a government minister after the next elections.
- d ...is (very) good at shaking hands and kissing babies/hand-shaking and baby- kissing.
- e ... avoids disagreeing with her or his party bosses.
- f ... enjoys appearing in TV discussions or chat shows.
- g ... never gets/doesn't get tired of praising her or his party's achievements.
- h ...is not afraid of answering/doesn't worry about having to answer awkward questions.
- i ...is (very) good at acting.

13 Participles

1 Proverbs

- a A **barking** dog never bites.
- b A penny **saved** is a penny **earned**.
- c A **rolling** stone gathers no moss.
- d Let **sleeping** dogs lie.
- e Once **bitten**, twice shy.
- f First come, first **served**.
- g First impressions are the most **lasting**.
- h There's many a good tune **played** on an old fiddle.
- i A trouble **shared** is a trouble **halved**.
- j **United** we stand, **divided** we fall.
- k If you want a thing **done** well, do it yourself.
- l Well **begun** is half **done**.

2 Finnegan's rest

- a Wanting to relax after supper, he sat down on the sofa and switched on the TV.
- b On the screen he could see two men getting into a car.
- c With heavy eyes he watched them driving slowly away.
- d The man driving the car looked very much like Franco Costellini.
- e Finnegan leaned back on the sofa, closing his eyes./Leaning back on the sofa, Finnegan closed his eyes.
- f His beer stood on the table next to him, untouched./His beer stood untouched on the table next to him.
- g He heard some soft voices talking about something he couldn't quite make out.
- h Then he noticed a third man standing in front of the bank waiting for someone.
- i Never having seen him before, Finnegan tried to concentrate on the other two.
- j Then he suddenly found himself in some dark room, lying on a bed./ Then he suddenly found himself lying on a bed in some dark room.
- k He lay there covered with some sort of blanket.
- l Not knowing where he was, he felt frightened.
- m Then he heard someone opening a door somewhere.
- n When he tried to get up/Trying to get up, he noticed someone standing in front of him.
- o Jumping up in panic, he screamed for help./He jumped up in panic, screaming for help.

14 Non-finite Verb Forms: Mixed Exercises

1 96-year-old fined for speeding

A motorist of 96 was fined £20 yesterday – for **speeding** – his first offence in 70 years of **motoring**.
Mr Dale was warned **to drive** more carefully in future but was not ordered **to take** a **driving**-test. He was caught by a radar trap, **doing** 49 mph in a 30 mph area, while **travelling** near his home in Folkestone. He refused **to give** his age to police when **stopped**, but later wrote a letter to a newspaper, **complaining** about the radar trap. He said he was 96 and was looking forward to **going** around Brands Hatch on his 100th birthday.
Police Constable William Holton, one of the men **operating** the radar trap, said: "We heard an engine **roar** and then saw him **coming** round the corner. He appeared **to be** in some hurry."

Mr Dale said: "Oh, I'm 96 all right, but I'm fit. I've no doubt that I could **pass** any test they might have asked me **to take**. I remember **driving** my first motor-bike when I was 25. More than 70 years of trouble-free **motoring** is not a bad record, and I've got no reason **to stop thinking** that I'm one of the safest drivers on the road. But I'm still annoyed about **being caught**. On that particular stretch of road **having to do** 30 mph is absurd. I take regular medical check-ups, and my heart and lungs are first class. I do **need** glasses, and I don't **hear** as well as I used to, but that won't make me **think** of **handing in** my licence, I'm still fit enough **to drive**."

2 On holiday

a Look, it's stopped **raining**. We can go back to the beach.
b What a fantastic view! Let's stop **to take** some pictures.

c We must remember **to send** Aunt Agatha a postcard from the States.
d I'll always remember **seeing** New York for the first time.

e I forgot **to pack** my shorts. How silly of me.
f I'll never forget **climbing** Ben Nevis. What an experience!

g We should try **to get** to the hotel before 8 p.m. if possible.
h My skin burns so easily! Try **using** some of my sunblock. That may help.

i The flight leaves at 8.20. That'll mean **getting up** quite early.
j I've heard so much about Australia. I really mean **to go** there soon.

15 Verbs and their Objects

1 Tastes differ

PAUL	Can you lend **me some money** … . I showed **it to you / you it** when …
PETE	I can't remember you saying **anything to me** … Perhaps you showed **it to Mike** … I owe **you some money** …
PAUL	… Perhaps I could lend **it to you / you it** some time. I …

PETE	You're always trying to teach **me something about music** ... Either you're giving **me a lesson on Bach** or trying to sell **me a ticket** for a concert ... I've explained **it all to you** hundreds of times.
PAUL	OK, OK. Sorry. Hand **me that jazz CD over there**. ...

2 At work

a *Mrs Brown, managing director of 'Pharmaco':* I'll tell **you more about my plans** after lunch, Mrs MacLaren. It'll only take **us a few minutes**. Those people from Johnson and White'll be here in a moment. Make **them some coffee / some coffee for them** when they arrive, please, and bring **me a cup of tea** as usual. Perhaps you could get **us a few biscuits / a few biscuits for us**, too.

b *Sergeant White, police officer:* Ordinary-looking? Now, it would save **us a lot of time** if you could describe **the woman to us** in detail, sir. You were quite right to report **all this to the police**, of course, but our chances of solving crimes are always greater if people can give **us an exact description of the person in question**. Perhaps if I ask **you a few questions**, your memory may improve. Right then ...

c *Mr Green, salesperson:* May I suggest **something to you**, madam? Buy **your husband the more expensive model / the more expensive model for your husband**. You won't regret it. Of course, it'll cost **you a few pounds more**, but it'll be well worth it in the long run.

16 Relative Clauses

1 The grotesque world of competitive eating

Future historians **who/that** want to write about American society today will be certain to mention the 'madness' **which/that** is so typical of our lifestyle. One of the first things **which/that/---** they will think of will surely be the grotesque phenomenon **which/that** is commonly described as 'competitive eating'. Eating contests, **which** started off as harmless fun at fairs, have now developed into a full-scale industry. 'Major League Eating', **which** was founded some years ago, now organizes over 80 contests a year, in **which** prize money totalling nearly $ 600,000 can be won! This organization, **whose** 'Hot Dog Eating Contest' on TV is said to be watched by well over a million US households, is now famous.

As the money **which/that/---** you can win increases, so the feats **which/that/---** people perform become more outlandish. The incredible new record **which/that** was set in 2009 was 68 hot dogs in 10 minutes! (It is surely hard to imagine anyone **whose** stomach could possibly find room for so many hot dogs: in 1999, the record number was 'only' 25!) As long as big prizes are offered, there will always be people **who/that** are prepared to take part in these grotesque contests, **which**, of course, can only be bad for their health. And anyway, how can we congratulate them on the horrific amounts **which/that/---** they stuff themselves with – when, in other parts of the mad world **which/that/---** we live in, there are people **who/that** are starving?

2 Definitions

a A washing-machine is a machine you wash clothes in.
b An information desk is a desk you (can) get/ ask for information at.
c A golf ball is a ball you (can) play golf with.
d A bottle opener is a thing you (can) open bottles
e A cycle path is a path you (can) cycle on.
f A tennis net is a net you hit tennis balls over.
s An address book is a book you (can) write people's) addresses in.
h A toothbrush is a brush you clean your teeth with.
i A cricket field is a field you (can) play cricket on/in.
j A tea cup is a cup you can drink tea from/out of.

17 The Use of Adjectives and Adverbs

1 Man's best friend?

It is **well** known that the British have a **deep** love of pets – **particularly** of dogs. There are **literally** millions of dog-owners in Britain, a **surprisingly large** number of whom keep more than one. But **unfortunately** there are hundreds of thousands of stray dogs wandering the streets, and many hundreds of unwanted pet dogs have to be destroyed **daily** by the RSPCA and others. Many people do not think **carefully** enough before buying a dog, and **finally** abandon the **unfortunate** animal when the work of looking after it **properly** becomes a nuisance. Others abandon their dogs because the pet's behaviour has become **aggressive** and **hard** to control. **Actually** this is often the owner's fault. The habit of 'spoiling' pets has **dangerously** altered the **natural** instincts of dogs, **particularly** those of **aggressive** breeds. A dog which is allowed to do **exactly** as it likes, **quickly** begins to feel **dominant**, and to see itself as the **real** leader of the family. Not **surprisingly**, such dogs soon start to act **unusually aggressively** on the street, too. When treated **properly**, however, dogs can have an **amazingly positive** effect on their owners' lives. Having a dog **actually** reduces **common** everyday illnesses by 50%. This may be because people who buy dogs **generally** take five times more **regular** exercise than they did before.

2 Their problem – our problem?

2.1

A **healthy person** without any disabilities is often unaware of the problems facing the **disabled**. It is not unusual for **disabled people** in wheelchairs to have fewer job opportunities simply because they cannot use public transport to get to work. **Deaf people** often feel shut off from society, and the mentally **challenged** are frequently refused jobs because employers wrongly think they are unable to do them. It is easy to forget the difficulties the **blind** have in life, although a **blind person** generally receives more sympathy than **deaf people**, whose problems are less obvious.

2.2 a many disabled people; b the rich and the poor; c two bedrooms; a small one and a large/big one; d young people; e a blind person/man; f a black cat and two white ones; g the little one/boy; h the dead woman/girl

18 Adjectives and Adverbs: Comparative and Superlative Forms

1 Could it be drugs?

a Lots of teenagers are offered drugs, but not every offer is accepted. In fact, **most** people say "No". But parents should remember that young people who are fed up or worried may be **more likely/likelier** to try drugs than those that are happy at home.
It's **more difficult** to tell when someone is using drugs occasionally than when they are **more regular** users. But here are some of the **most common/commonest** warning signs that may help you to recognize the beginning of a problem **more easily**. Drugs may be the cause if your child

- acts **more aggressively**, or changes from one mood to another **more suddenly** than usual,
- begins to show **less** interest in hobbies, sports – or even food,
- seems to have **fewer** contacts with friends than before,
- gets tired **more quickly** – or suffers from sleeplessness **more often**,
- starts to do **worse** at school.

b The **most alarming** signs would, of course, be if you noticed money disappearing, or unusual tablets, etc. in the house.
The **sooner** a drug problem is recognized, the **better**. But even then, the **most important** question for parents is how to react.
When Helen, 17, broke with her boyfriend, it was the **most depressing** thing she had ever experienced. She tried some tranquillizers she found in the family medicine cupboard, and they made her feel **better**. A few weeks **later**, her parents discovered this, had the **most terrible** row with Helen, and locked up the rest of the tablets.

c This might have worked **earlier**, but Helen had already gone too far to want to turn back. A school friend offered her something **stronger**, which they both thought was **most likely** to be heroin. **Later** still, Helen took up with a new boyfriend, **older** than herself, and **more experienced** – in fact, a regular drug user. When Helen's parents got to know, they turned to the family doctor for help.

19 The Position of Adverbs and Adverbials

1 Your character in your handwriting?

a According to graphologists, your hand is **closely** connected with your brain.
b When you write, it is **extremely** difficult to hide your personality.
c When applying for a job, people are **often** asked to write their application by hand.
d Here are some **quite** simple signs to look out for.
e If you are **always** in a hurry, you **probably** forget to dot your 'i's. Or you don't cross your 't's **properly**.
f An energetic person will press the paper **hard**.
g An aggressive person will form his or her letters **sharply**.
h People whose writing leans to the right are **usually** enthusiastic people.
i Those whose writing slopes backwards could **possibly** be interpreted as rather cold.
j When you write a letter, you sign your name **at the bottom**. Can people **hardly** read it? If so, it **certainly** means that you are a self-important person. Or does it?
k The 'science' of graphology **obviously** has its limits. **Fortunately** there are lots of other ways of getting to know people!

2 A trip to London

- a Last April we went to London for a couple of days./ We went to London for a couple of days last April.
- b We arrived at King's Cross Station at 2 o'clock in the afternoon.
- c Then we went on to our hotel by Underground.
- d Luckily the weather was really good all the time.
- e On the first afternoon we went to the Tower of London by boat. / We went to the Tower of London by boat on the first afternoon.
- f The next morning we saw the Changing of the Guard at Buckingham Palace. / We saw ... the next morning.
- g Then we looked at the shops in the Oxford Street area for a while.
- h Not surprisingly time began to go very quickly after that.
- i That evening we went to see 'The Mousetrap' at St. Martin's Theatre in the West End. / We went to see ... that evening.
- j Unfortunately we had to go home again the next day.

20 The Definite and the Indefinite Article

1 Talking about university, students and careers

Mary Williams (17, still at school): I plan to go to --- university when I leave --- school. I'll probably study --- English because I love --- English literature. At **the** moment I'm very interested in **the** poetry of T.S. Eliot. Actually, what I'm looking forward to most is **the** freedom of --- university life.

Professor Richards (Oxford University): --- Quite **a** large number of **the** candidates who have applied for **a** place at Oxford this year are from **the** European Union. --- Most of **the** foreign students come to Britain because **the** courses they can take here are shorter – and less crowded – than at --- home. All **the** students I've talked to especially like our traditional system of --- close contact with tutors.

John Whitely (19, first-year music student): My father is **a** clergyman and my mother is **a** social worker. They always hoped I might study --- theology and become **a** priest – or at least do something to help --- society. As **a** child, when I still used to go to --- church regularly, I thought --- missionary work mightn't be --- such **a** bad idea. But when I started --- secondary school, I began to get interested in --- music. That was when --- life really got going for me. By **the** time I was 15, I knew I had to take up --- music as **a** career. So here I am! Luckily my parents have given me --- full support. They realize I'm not doing all this as **an** act of --- protest or --- rebellion against **the** upbringing I had.

2 Taken down from the bookshelf

- a War and Peace
- b Daily Life in Ancient Rome
- c The Life of Napoleon
- d Chinese Cooking
- e The History of the United States
- f When I was King
- g Half a Pound of Rice
- h All the Birds in the Sky
- i School as a Bridge to Success?
- j My Father was an Indian

21 Indefinite Pronouns and Determiners

Everybody needs a break

A **Everyone** goes on holiday. Kings, presidents and dictators – **none** of them is too grand to take a holiday somewhere. Just like **everyone** else, they **all** need **some** time off work. There is only one exception to this: Her Majesty the Queen does not take **any** holidays. Rather, she resides, at set times **every** year, at **each** of her various homes – Sandringham, for example, in the winter, Balmoral in the summer.

B **Most** people now think of holidays as necessary. **Anybody** who doubted the need of regular holidays **each** year would be regarded as not quite right in the head. Until the 1950s, **few** people in Britain had more than two weeks' paid holiday a year. By 2010 **all** workers were entitled to 28 days. **No** politician would suggest a reduction in people's holidays – **everyone** would be against it.

C The modern idea of a holiday developed in the 1920s with the German invention of sunbathing. People now thought of a holiday as **something** completely different from their usual everyday life and work. The modern holiday depends on the idea that for **most** people work is of **little** interest because it is often boring and mechanical, so that what **everyone** needs is **a little** relaxation and a break from the daily routine. The best holiday is one which helps us **all** to forget about our normal lives for **a few** weeks.

D The complete opposite of working is doing absolutely **nothing** in **some** perfectly natural surroundings. For **many** people the purest expression of this idea is to lie on a beach, sunbathing. Sunbathing is one of the strangest of **all** human inventions. On the one hand it is an example of perfect sloth – of doing **nothing** at all. On the other, it is a passive way of doing **something**. **All** medical evidence speaks against spending too **much** time in the sun. But, of course, **nobody** can deny that **a little** sunshine can do us a world of good – whether on holiday or not!

22 Reflexive and Reciprocal Pronouns

1 What's the problem?

A "Kate and I **quarrelled** again last night. Now I **wonder** what to do to put things right."
"Why not ring up and **apologize**? That would probably make you both **feel** much better."

B "What's all that blood?"
"Oh, I've **cut myself** with the bread knife. Don't **worry**. I haven't **hurt myself** badly."
"You look a bit pale, though. Perhaps you should **lie down** for a few moments and **relax**."

C "John keeps criticising me for **moving** too slowly on the tennis court." – "How do you generally react?"
"By **defending myself**, of course."
"Well, don't. Another time, just quietly **tell yourself** not to **behave** that way. Then say to John, 'You're right, I do **move** slowly.' You'll **feel** less aggressive that way – and maybe John will **change** after a while."

2 Help each other – don't just think of yourselves!

a In an ideal society, people wouldn't try to take advantage of **each other / one another**.
b Modest people do not make a habit of praising **themselves**.
c When their eggs are hatched, most parent birds help **each other / one another** to look after the young ones until they are old enough to feed **themselves**.
d At Christmas time we all give **each other / one another** presents; but most of us buy the sort of presents we would choose for **ourselves**.
e Quite a lot of people talk to **themselves** when they're alone.
f Good friends can always depend on **each other / one another**.

Acknowledgements

p. 20 from The Accidental Tourist by Anne Tyler, published by Chatto and Windus. Reprinted by permission of The Random House Group Ltd. · **p. 23** adapted from Mind over Body by Vernon Coleman. Reproduced by permission of Octopus Publishing Group Ltd. · **p. 25** from Winnie the Pooh by A.A. Milne. © The Trustees of the Pooh Properties 1926. Published by Egmont UK Ltd. London and used with permission. · **p.27** from Das Brot der frühen Jahre by Heinrich Böll, © 1955, 1980, 2003 by Verlag Kiepenheuer & Witsch GmbH & Co. KG, Köln · **p. 28** from Alice's Adventures in Wonderland by Lewis Carroll · **p. 30** from The Children of the Night by Edward Arlington Robinson · **p. 33** adapted from Farmers under Siege by Lucy Pinney, The Times 27.11.1999 · **p. 38** adapted from The Prairie is alive again as buffalo roam back by Ben Fenton, The Daily Telegraph 26th May 2001 · **p. 40** from The Growing Pains of Adrian Mole by Sue Townsend, published by Methuen. Reprinted by permission of The Random House Group Ltd. · **p. 49** from The Riddle of the Sands by Erskine Childers · **p. 54** from A Concise History of Costume by James Laver. © James Laver 1969. Reprinted by kind permission of Thames & Hudson Ltd., London. · **p. 54** from Rebecca by Daphne du Maurier. Reproduced with permission of Curtis Brown Group Ltd, London on behalf of the Chichester Partnership, © Daphne Du Maurier 1938 · **p. 56** from To Build a Fire by Jack London · **p. 66** from Fifteen by Beverly Cleary. © 1956 Beverly Cleary (Harper Collins, USA) · **p. 71** from The Way Up to Heaven by Roald Dahl. Reprinted from Kiss Kiss by Roald Dahl, Penguin Books, by permission of David Higham Associates Ltd., London. · **p. 73** from The Return of Heroic Failures, © by Stephen Pile. Reprinted by permission of the author c/o Rogers, Coleridge & White Ltd, 20 Powis Mews, London, W11 1JN. · **p. 76** from A Kind of Loving by Stan Barstow © 1960 by Stan Barstow. Reproduced by permission of the author c/o Rogers, Coleridge & White Ltd., 20 Powis Mews, London W1 1 JN, UK. · **p. 78** aus: Patricia Highsmith: A Dog's Ransom. Die Originalausgabe ist 1972 bei Heinemann, London erschienen. Die amerikanische Ausgabe ist bei W.W. Norton & Company Inc., New York lieferbar. Copyright © 1993 Diogenes Verlag AG Zürich. · **p. 82** From The new Noah by Gerald Durrell. Reproduced with permission of Curtis Brown Group Ltd., London n behalf of The Estate of Gerald Durell, © 1955 The Estate of Gerald Durell · **p. 88** from How to be Green by John Button, published by Ebury Press. Reprinted by permission of The Random House Group Ltd. · **p. 96** from The Hound of the Baskervilles by Sir Arthur Conan Doyle House · **p. 100** excerpted from Another April by Jesse Stuart. Copyright Jesse Stuart and the Jesse Stuart Foundation. Used by permission of Marian Reiner on behalf to the Foundation. · **p. 104** from Summerhill by A. S. Neill, Orion Publishing Group, London. · **p. 108** from Looking at History by R.J. Unstead, A & C Black Ltd. · **p. 110** from Room at the Top by John Braine. Reprinted from Room at the Top, Random House, by permission of David Higham Associates Ltd., London · **p. 111** from I was Vermeer – The Legend of the Forger Who Swindled the Nazis by Frank Wynne, Bloomsbury Publishing. · **p. 113** The Journey of the Magi from Collected Poems 1902-1962 by T.S. Eliot. Reprinted by kind permission of Faber and Faber Ltd., London. · **p. 121** from Brave New World by Aldous Huxley. © 1932, 1946 by Aldous Huxley. Reprinted by permission of Georges Borchardt, Inc., on behalf of the Aldous Laura Huxley Trust. All rights reserved. · **p. 122** William Stafford, "Traveling through the Dark" from The Way It Is: New And Selected Poems. © 1962, 1998 by William Stafford and the Estate of William Stafford. Reprinted with the permission of Graywolf Press, Minneapolis, Minnesota, www.graywolfpress.org. · **p. 126** from The Bell Jar by Sylvia Plath. Reprinted by kind permission of Faber and Faber Ltd., London. · **p. 137** From The Round Dozen by W. Somerset Maugham. Reprinted by permission of The Royal Literary Fund. · **p. 142** From The Human Zoo by Desmond Morris, published by Jonathan Cape. Reprinted by permission of The Random House Group Ltd. · **p. 148** From A Talk in the Park by Alan Ayckbourn, © Alan Ayckbourn, 'A Talk in The Park' from 'Confusions', Methuen Drama, an imprint of A&C Black Publishers Ltd. · **p. 149** from Human Aggression by Anthony Storr, (© Anthony Storr). Reproduced by permission of PFD (www.petersfraserdunlop.com) on behalf of the Estate of Anthony Storr. · **p. 156** from Dead Man's Folly by Agatha Christie. Reprinted by permission of HarperCollins Publishers Ltd. © 1956 Agatha Christie · **p. 156** from The Killers, a short story by Ernest Hemingway. Copyright © 1927: all rights outside U.S., Hemingway Foreign Rights Trust. · **p. 160** from The price of happiness by Alasdair Palmer, © Telegraph Media Group Limited (TMG) 2002 · **p. 171** from Back when we were Grownups by Anne Tyler, published by Chatto and Windus. Reprinted by permission of The Random House Group Ltd. · **p. 173** from Uncle Ernest from The Loneliness of the Long Distance Runner by Alan Sillitoe. Reprinted by permission of HarperCollins Publishers Ltd. © 1959 Alan Sillitoe. · **p. 175** from Open: An Autobiography by Andre Agassi, © 2009 by AKA Publishing, LLC. Used by permission of Alfred A. Knopf, a division of Random House, Inc.

Bildquellennachweis

17 Punch Limited, London; **18; 21; 31; 49; 52** Sven Palmowski, Barcelona; **20** ddp images GmbH, Hamburg; **23; 122** Christa Janik, Leinfelden-Echterdingen; **24** © Watterson/Universal Uclick/Distr. Bulls; **25** Illustration from WINNIE-THE-POOH by A.A. Milne, illustrated by E. H. Shepard, © 1926 by E.P. Dutton, © renewed 1954 by A.A. Nilne. Used by permission of Dutton Children´sBooks, A Division of Penguin Young Readers Group. All rights reserved.; **26** Punch Limited, London; **28** Aus: Alice in Wonderland, London, McMillan 1911.; **32** © Watterson/Universal Uclick/Distr. Bulls; **33** © Telegraph Media Group Limited 2001; **34.1** iStockphoto (Gerri Hernández), Calgary, Alberta; **34.2** © Al Ross/The New Yorker Collection/www. cartoonbank.com; **35** Punch Limited, London; **37** Knight Features Limited (Peter Knight), London; **38** Thinkstock (Comstock), München; **39** Punch Limited, London; **42** Yahoo! Deutschland GmbH (Duke Human Rights), München; **44** Punch Limited, London; **46** Cinetext GmbH, Frankfurt; **48** © Watterson/Universal Uclick/Distr. Bulls; **50.1** shutterstock (JeremyRichards), New York, NY; **50.2** iStockphoto (Coldimages), Calgary, Alberta; **50.3** shutterstock (guentermanaus), New York, NY; **51** Thinkstock (iStockphoto), München; **56** iStockphoto (Marco Kopp), Calgary, Alberta; **58** Punch Limited, London; **61** © Paws/Universal Uclick/Distr Bulls; **62.1; 62.2** Punch Limited, London; **65** © Watterson/Universal Uclick/Distr. Bulls; **66** iStockphoto (Linda Kloosterhof), Calgary, Alberta; **68** www.cartoonstock.com (Bryant, Adey), Bath; **74** © Watterson/Universal Uclick/Distr. Bulls; **76** iStockphoto (Ryan Lane), Calgary, Alberta; **79** www.cartoonstock.com (Percival, Matt), Bath; **80** Punch Limited, London; **83** © Paws/Universal Uclick/Distr Bulls; **85** iStockphoto (Renata Osinska), Calgary, Alberta; **89** www.cartoonstock.com (Joseph Farris), Bath; **90** Punch Limited, London; **91** www.cartoonstock.com (Nick Kim), Bath; **92** Fotolia LLC (Bernard Breton), New York; **94** Punch Limited, London; **95** Punch Limited, London; **96** © The Estate of Norman Thelwell. Reproduced by permission of Momentum Licensing.; **97** McDonald's Inc., München; **99** Corbis (Christie's Images/Curtis), Düsseldorf; **100** iStockphoto (Christopher Farrugia), Calgary, Alberta; **101** www.cartoonstock.com (Roy Nixon), Bath; **102** © Telegraph Media Group Limited 2002; **104** Ullstein Bild GmbH, Berlin; **105** shutterstock (Walter G Arce), New York, NY; **106** Punch Limited, London; **107** Punch Limited, London; **108.1** A&C Black Ltd. 35 Bedford Row, London WC 1R4JH, 1975, reprinted 1983; **108.2; 108.3** Alamy Images, Abingdon, Oxon; **109** iStockphoto (Nick Free), Calgary, Alberta; **111** Picture-Alliance (Museum Boijmans Van Beuningen), Frankfurt; **112** Corbis (Michael Childers/Sygma), Düsseldorf; **113** Keller, Gerlinde, München; **117** Punch Limited, London; **118** iStockphoto (Vladimir Piskunov), Calgary, Alberta; **119** Ullstein Bild GmbH (Still Pictures), Berlin; **120** Ullstein Bild GmbH, Berlin; **121** iStockphoto (t3000), Calgary, Alberta; **123** Punch Limited, London; **124** Punch Limited, London; **125** iStockphoto (Paula Connelly), Calgary, Alberta; **126** iStockphoto (tempurasLightbulb), Calgary, Alberta; **127** www.cartoonstock.com (Lowe, Paul), Bath; **128** Punch Limited, London; **129** iStockphoto (Rich Seymour), Calgary, Alberta; **131** Corbis (Corbis-00000105366510-Preview.JPG), Düsseldorf; **132** Punch Limited, London; **134** iStockphoto (Vladimir Mucibabic), Calgary, Alberta; **135** iStockphoto (Vladislav Gurfinkel), Calgary, Alberta; **140** Punch Limited, London; **142** Punch Limited, London; **144** iStockphoto (George Clerk), Calgary, Alberta; **149** Punch Limited, London; **150** iStockphoto (Stígur Karlsson), Calgary, Alberta; **153** Punch Limited, London; **155** iStockphoto (-ilkeryuksel-), Calgary, Alberta; **157** AKG (album), Berlin; **158** © Watterson/Universal Uclick/ Distr. Bulls; **159** Solo Syndication (Jonathan Pugh), London; **160** VG Bild-Kunst, Bonn 2011 (André Francois); **161** iStockphoto (laughingmango), Calgary, Alberta; **162** Picture-Alliance (Everett Colle), Frankfurt; **165** Telegraph Group LTD, London, The Sunday Telegraph; **167.1** iStockphoto (appleuzr), Calgary, Alberta; **167.2** iStockphoto (roccomontoya), Calgary, Alberta; **167.3** iStockphoto (Dane Wirtzfeld), Calgary, Alberta; **167.4; 167.5; 167.7; 167.8** iStockphoto (browndogstudios), Calgary, Alberta; **167.9** iStockphoto (bubaone), Calgary, Alberta; **169** Punch Limited, London; **170** © Paws/Universal Uclick/Distr Bulls; **172** www.cartoonstock.com (Wilbur Dawbarn), Bath; **175** shutterstock (lev radin), New York, NY

Sollte es einmal nicht gelungen sein, den korrekten Rechteinhaber von Text oder Bild ausfindig zu machen, so werden berechtigte Ansprüche selbstverständlich im Rahmen der üblichen Regelungen abgegolten. Die Positionsangabe der Bilder erfolgt je Seite von oben nach unten, von links nach rechts.